®

S0-BSC-008

Swahili
phrase book

Berlitz Publishing Company, Inc.

Princeton   Mexico City   Dublin   Eschborn   Singapore

How best to use this phrase book

● We suggest that you start with the **Guide to pronunciation** (pp. 6-8), then go on to **Some basic expressions** (pp. 10-15). This gives you not only a minimum vocabulary, but also helps you get used to pronouncing the language. The phonetic transcription throughout the book enables you to pronounce every word correctly.

● Consult the **Contents** pages (3-5) for the section you need. In each chapter you'll find travel facts, hints and useful information. Simple phrases are followed by a list of words applicable to the situation.

● Separate, detailed contents lists are included at the beginning of the extensive **Eating out** and **Shopping guide** sections (Menus, p. 38, Shops and services, p. 97).

● If you want to find out how to say something in Swahili, your fastest look-up is via the **Dictionary** section (pp. 164-189). This not only gives you the word, but is also cross-referenced to its use in a phrase on a specific page.

● If you wish to learn more about constructing sentences, check the **Basic grammar** (pp. 159-163).

● Note the **colour margins** are indexed in Swahili and English to help both listener and speaker. And, in addition, there is also an index in Swahili for the use of your listener.

● Throughout the book, this symbol ☛ suggests phrases your listener can use to answer you. If you still can't understand, hand this phrase book to the Swahili-speaker to encourage pointing to an appropriate answer.

● Since there are regional differences in Swahili, we have provided alternatives in brackets [] in the text. If your listener cannot understand your first expression, try the alternative.

Copyright © 1995 Berlitz Publishing Company, Inc.,
400 Alexander Park, Princeton, NJ 08540, USA
9-13 Grosvenor St., London W1X 9FB UK

ISBN 2-8315-6205-8
Printed in Spain

Second revised edition - Printed June 2000

862242

Contents

4

Travelling around 65

Sightseeing 80

Relaxing 87

Making friends 92

Shopping guide 97

Acknowledgements
We are particularly grateful to Zainab Yalya and Saidi el-Gheithy for their help in the preparation of this book.

Guide to pronunciation

The Swahili language

Swahili is rapidly becoming the international language of Africa and thereby one of the important languages of the world. It is spoken primarily in Kenya, Tanzania and Uganda, but it is also heard in parts of the neighbouring countries of Burundi, Malawi, Mozambique, Rwanda, Zaire and Zambia. There are also Swahili-speaking communities in the Gulf States, Western Europe, North America and India. That means that it's spoken by almost 50 million people.

The term "Swahili" originated from the Arabic language, and was used by the Arabs to categorise the coast of East Africa. However, the city states of the East African coast have always had their own languages and cultures. Hence prior to the ascription of the term Swahili, the East African coastal people themselves described their own languages according to the city state wherein they lived. For example a person from Lamu, even today, would say he speaks "Kiamu" and his self identity would be "Mwamu".

There are several dialects of Swahili and differences in usage depending upon the region, but the leading version is that of Zanzibar City, which is the basis of standard Swahili. In this phrase book we have used standard Swahili, but have also included the most common variants, in brackets [ ], to help overcome any communication difficulties throughout East Africa.

Swahili belongs to the Bantu family of languages and is part of the group of languages spoken in central, eastern and southern Africa. However, throughout history, traders and settlers – mainly Arab and European – coming to the East and West African coasts have greatly influenced the language spoken there, as the newcomers themselves have been enriched by Swahili culture. Moreover, Swahili was originally only a spoken language and was subsequently put into a written form by foreigners who thus also influenced the tongue. The Arabs and the English, in particular, have left their imprint on present-day Swahili.

An outline of the spelling and sounds of Swahili

Although a relatively easy language to pronounce, Swahili does require some effort on the part of the learner. However, careful review of the indications given below will provide you with a solid basis for acquiring a good accent.

Originally Swahili was written in Arabic characters. When British missionaries introduced our alphabet, they managed to adopt a transliteration as phonetic as possible. You shouldn't find it too difficult to pronounce Swahili, especially if you carefully follow our explanations. As an additional aid we have included a transcription next to each phrase, but you should soon find that you can read the Swahili direct after you have mastered the rules below.

The imitated pronunciation should be read as if it were English, except for any special rules set out below. Of course, the sounds of any two languages are never exactly the same; but if you follow carefully the examples given here, you will have no difficulty in reading our transcriptions.

Letters shown in **bold** should be read with more stress (louder) than the others.

As a minimum vocabulary for your trip, we have selected a number of basic words and phrases under the title "Some Basic Expressions" (pages 10-15).

Consonants

These are pronounced as in English, but the following points should be noted:

Letter	Approximate pronunciation	Symbol	Example
f	always as in few, never as in of	f	**af**ya **af**ya
g	always as in go, never as in gin	g	**gi**za **gee**za

m	1) when it occurs as a prefix for nouns, it sounds like a separate syllable, as if it has a short **oo** sound in front of it, like the **oo** in l**oo**k	m	**mpunga**	m**poo**nga
	2) when followed by **b** or **v**, it is not a separate syllable and should be elided with the following letter; however, in words containing only one vowel, sounds like **m** 1) above	ᵐ	**mbali**	ᵐbali
			mbu	m**boo**
n	as in English, but it can come before a consonant at the beginning of a word	n	**ndogo**	**ndo**go
r	in mainland speech, this letter is confused with **l**	r	**rafiki**	ra**fee**kee
s	always as in **so**, never as in vi**s**it	s	**hesabu**	he**saboo**

Groups of consonants

dh	like **th** in **th**is	∂	**dhuru**	∂**oo**roo
gh	appears in a few words of Arabic origin and has no English equivalent. Can sound like the **ch** of Scottish lo**ch**, but immediately preceded by a faint rolling of the tongue	RH	**ghafula**	RHa**foo**la
ng	like **ng** in fi**ng**er	ng	**ngapi**	**nga**pee
ng'	like **ng** in si**ng**er. It can come at the beginning of a word; to produce this sound, divide si**ng**er into si-**ng**er and then say the second syllable on its own	ng'	**ng'a**	ng'a
ny	before a vowel, like **ni** in o**ni**on; elides with the following vowel	nʸ	**nyasa**	nʸasa
th	always like **th** in **th**in; appears only in words of Arabic origin	th	**thelathini**	thela**thee**-nee

Vowels

a	like **a** in **ah**	a	**paka**	pa**ka**
e	like **e** in **fetch**; it is a pure vowel, not a diphthong like English **ay** in **May**; at the end of a word, this same sound is represented by **eh** in our transcription to help pronunciation	e eh	**enda** **pale**	**en**da **pal**eh
i	like **ee** in **meet**	ee	**fisi**	**fee**see
o	like **o** in **ostrich**	o	**toka**	**to**ka
u	like **oo** in **soot**	oo	**rudi**	**roo**dee

Notes

1) Unstressed vowels have the same quality as when they are stressed; therefore **paka** should not be pronounced *parker*, but rather the two **a**'s should have the same pronunciation.

2) When two vowels are next to each other, each retains its own pronunciation. Thus, **bei** is pronounced something like *bay*, **tai** like *tie*, **au** like the vowel in *cow*. In such cases the vowels are, in fact, separate syllables and the words could be divided **be-i**, **ta-i**, **a-u**. Hyphens are used in our phonetic transcription to help pronunciation.

3) When two similar vowels stand next to each other, they are pronounced as one long vowel, e.g. **kaa**.

4) Syllables in Swahili always end with a vowel, so a word like **pembeni** is divided pe-mbe-ni.

5) Intonation is more even than in English, and words are not emphasized in normal speech.

Stress

Stress is always on the next to last syllable, except in one or two words borrowed from Arabic.

Some basic expressions

Yes.	**Ndiyo [Sawa].**	ndeeyo [sawa]
No.	**A-a [Hapana].**	a-a [hapana]
Please.	**Tafadhali [Kwa hisani yako].**	tafaðalee [kwa heesanee yako]
Thank you.	**Asante [Nashukuru].**	asanteh [nashookooroo]
Thank you very much.	**Asante sana [Nashukuru sana].**	asanteh sana [nashookooroo sana]
That's all right/You're welcome.	**Sawa [Si kitu].**	sawa [see keetoo]

Greetings *Hujambo? [Habari?]*

A greeting—even a simple *Habari* or *Jambo*—is an essential preface to any social contact in Swahili.

Good morning.	**Habari ya [za] asubuhi?**	habaree ya [za] asooboohee
Good afternoon.	**Habari ya mchana.**	habaree ya mchana
Good evening.	**Habari za jioni.**	habaree za jeeoonee
Good night.	**Lala salama [Usiku mwema/Ala msiki].**	lala salama [ooseekoo mwema/ala mseekee]
Good-bye.	**Kwaheri.**	kwaheree
See you later.	**Tutaonana baadaye.**	tootaonana baadayeh
Hello/Hi!	**Vipi? [Mambo!]**	veepee [mambo]
This is Mr....	**Huyu ni Bwana ...**	hooyoo nee bwana
This is Mrs./Miss ...	**Huyu ni Bibi ...**	hooyoo nee beebee
How do you do? (Pleased to meet you.)	**Hali gani? [Nimefurahi kukutana nawe.]**	halee ganee [neemefoorahee kookootana naweh]
How are you?	**Hujambo/Habari yako [zako]?**	hoojambo/habaree yako [zako]
Very well, thanks. And you?	**Sijambo, asante. Na wewe je?**	seejambo asanteh. na weweh jeh
How's life?	**Habari ya maisha?**	habaree ya maeesha
Fine.	**Nzuri [Salama].**	nzooree [salama]
I beg your pardon?	**Samahani?**	samahanee
Excuse me. (May I get past?)	**Samahani. [Naomba kupita tafadhali.]**	samahanee [naomba koopeeta tafaðalee]

Questions *Masuala*

Where?	**Wapi?**	wapee
How?	**Vipi?**	veepee
When?	**Lini?**	leenee
What?	**Nini?**	neenee
Why?	**Kwa nini?**	kwa neenee
Who?	**Nani?**	nanee
Which?	**Gani/Ipi?**	ganee/eepee
Where is...?	**Iko wapi...?**	eeko wapee
Where are...?	**Ziko wapi...?**	zeeko wapee
Where can I find/ get...?	**Wapi naweza [Ninaweza] kupata...?**	wapee naweza [neenaweza] koopata
How far?	**Umbali gani?**	oombalee ganee
How long?	**Muda gani?**	mooda ganee
How much/How many?	**Bei gani (Shilingi ngapi?)/Ngapi?**	be-ee ganee (sheeleengee ngapee)/ngapee
How much does this cost?	**Hii ni bei gani?**	hee-ee nee beee ganee
When does...open/ close?	**Wakati gani... inafunguliwa/ina-fungwa?**	wakatee ganee... eenafoongooleewa/ eenafoongwa
What do you call this/that in...?	**Hii/ile inaitwaje kwa....?**	hee-ee/eeleh eenaeetwajeh kwa
What does this/that mean?	**Hii/Ile ina maana gani?**	hee-ee/eeleh eena maana ganee

Do you speak...? *Unasema...?*

Do you speak English?	**Unasema [kizungu] Kiingereza?**	oonasema [keezoongoo] kee-eengereza
Does anyone here speak English?	**Yupo mtu hapa anayesema [Kizungu] Kiinge-reza?**	yoopo mtoo hapa anayesema [keezoongoo] kee-eengereza
I don't speak Swahili.	**Sisemi Kiswahili sana.**	seesemee keeswaheelee sana
Could you speak more slowly?	**Sema pole pole, tafadhali?**	sema poleh poleh tafaðalee
Could you repeat that?	**Sema tena tafad-hali. [Rudia, tafad-hali.]**	sema tena tafaðalee [roodeeya tafaðalee]

Could you spell it?	Vipi unaandika? [Unaandikaje?]	veepee oonaandeeka [oonaandeekajeh]
How do you pronounce this?	Vipi unatamka? [Unatamkaje?]	veepee oonatamka [oonatamkajeh]
Could you write it down, please?	Niandikie, tafadhali.	neeyandeekee-eh tafaðalee
Can you translate this for me?	Nifasirie hii, tafadhali.	neefaseeree-eh hee-ee tafaðalee
Can you translate this for us?	Tufasirie hii, tafadhali.	toofaseeree-eh hee-ee tafaðalee
Could you point to the...in the book, please?	Nioneshe...katika kitabu, tafadhali?	neeonesheh...kateeka keetaboo tafaðalee
word	neno	neno
phrase	kifungu cha maneno	keefoongoo cha maneno
sentence	sentensi [mtungo]	sentensee [mtoongo]
Just a moment.	Ngoja kidogo [Subiri kidogo].	ngoja keedogo [soobeeree keedogo]
I'll see if I can find it in this book.	Nitaangalia kama nitaiona kitabuni.	neetaangaleeya kama neetaeeona keetaboonee
I understand.	Nafahamu [Naelewa].	nafahamoo [naelewa]
I don't understand.	Sifahamu [Sielewi].	seefahamoo [see-elewee]
Do you understand?	Unafahamu? [Unaelewa?]	oonafahamoo [oonaelewa]

Can/May...? *Kupata/Kuweza...?*

Can I have...?	Nipatie...tafadhali? [Naweza kupata...?]	neepatee-eh ...tafaðalee [naweza koopata]
Can we have...?	Tupatie... tafadhali? [Tunaweza kupata...?]	toopatee-eh ... tafaðalee [toonaweza koopata]
Can you show me...?	Nioneshe... tafadhali? [Unaweza kunionesha]	neeonesheh ... tafaðalee [oonaweza kooneeonesha]
I can't.	Siwezi.	seewezee
Can you tell me...?	Niambie... tafadhali? [Unaweza kuniambia...?]	neeyambee-eh ... tafaðalee [oonaweza kooneeyambeeya]

Can you help me?	**Nisaidie ... tafadhali? [Unaweza kunisaidia?]**	neesaee**dee**-eh ... tafa∂a**lee** [oona**we**za kooneesaee**dee**ya]
Can I help you?	**Nikusaidie nini? [Naweza kukusaidia?]**	neekoosaee**dee**-eh **nee**nee [na**we**za kookoosaee**dee**ya]
Can you direct me to...?	**Nielekeze kwenda ... tafadhali. [Unaweza kunielekeza ...?]**	nee-ele**ke**zeh **kwe**nda ... tafa∂a**lee** [oona**we**za koonee-ele**ke**za]

Do you want...? *Unataka...?*

I'd like...	**Ningependa ...**	neenge**pe**nda
We'd like...	**Tungependa ...**	toonge**pe**nda
What do you want?	**Unataka nini?**	oona**ta**ka **nee**nee
Could you give me...?	**Nipatie...tafadhali? [Unaweza kunipatia ...?]**	neepa**tee**-eh ...tafa∂a**lee** [oona**we**za kooneepa**tee**ya]
Could you bring me...?	**Niletee ... tafadhali ? [Unaweza kuniletee ...?]**	neele**te**-eh ...tafa∂a**lee** [oona**we**za koonee**le**tea]
Could you show me...?	**Nioneshe ... tafadhali ? [Unaweza kunionesha ...?]**	nee-o**ne**sheh ... tafa∂a**lee** [oona**we**za koonee-o**ne**sha]
I'm looking for...	**Ninatafuta ...**	neenata**foo**ta
I'm searching for...	**Ninatafuta ...**	neenata**foo**ta
I'm hungry.	**Nina njaa. [Ninasikia njaa.]**	**nee**na njaa. [neenasee**kee**ya njaa]
I'm thirsty.	**Nina kiu. [Ninasikia kiu]**	**nee**na **kee**oo. [neenasee**kee**ya **kee**oo]
I'm tired.	**Nimechoka.**	neeme**cho**ka
I'm lost.	**Nimepotea.**	neeme**po**tea
It's important.	**Ni muhimu.**	nee moo**hee**moo
It's urgent.	**Haraka.**	ha**ra**ka

It is/There is... *Kuna [Iko]...*

It is...	**Ni ...**	nee
Is it...?	**Ni ...?**	nee
It isn't...	**Siyo [La] ...**	**see**yo [la]
Here it is.	**Hii hapa.**	**hee**-ee **ha**pa
Here they are.	**Hizi hapa.**	**hee**zee **ha**pa

There it is.	**Ile pale.**	eeleh paleh
There they are.	**Zile pale.**	zeeleh paleh
There is/There are ...	**Iko/Ziko ...**	eeko/zeeko
Is there/Are there ...?	**Kuna/Iko/Ziko ...?**	koona/eeko/zeeko
There isn't/aren't ...	**Hakuna/Haiko/ Haziko ...**	hakoona/haeeko/hazeeko
There isn't/aren't any.	**Hakuna/Haiko/ Haziko kabisa.**	hakoona/haeeko/hazeeko kabeesa

It's ... *Ni ....*

beautiful/ugly	**maridadi [nzuri]/ mbaya**	mareedadee [nzooree]/ ᵐbaya
better/worse	**bora [afadhali]/ mbaya**	bora [afaðalee]/ᵐbaya
big/small	**kubwa/ndogo**	koobwa/ndogo
cheap/expensive	**rahisi/ghali [gali]**	raheesee/ʀHalee [galee]
early/late	**mapema/chelewa**	mapema/chelewa
easy/difficult	**rahisi [nyepesi]/ ngumu**	raheesee [nʸepesee]/ ngoomoo
free (vacant)/ occupied	**hamna mtu/kuna mtu**	hamna mtoo/koona mtoo
full/empty	**imejaa/kutupu**	eemejaa/kootoopoo
good/bad	**nzuri/mbaya**	nzooree/ᵐbaya
heavy/light	**nzito/nyepesi**	nzeeto/nʸepesee
here/there	**hapa/pale**	hapa/paleh
hot/cold	**joto/baridi**	joto/bareedee
near/far	**karibu/mbali**	kareeboo/ᵐbalee
next/last	**ya pili/ya mwisho**	ya peelee/ya ᵐweesho
old/new	**ya zamani/mpya**	ya zamanee/mpya
old/young	**mzee/kijana**	mze-eh/keejana
open/shut	**fungua/funga**	foongoowa/foonga
quick/slow	**upesi [haraka]/pole pole [taratibu]**	oopesee [haraka]/poleh poleh [tarateeboo]
right/wrong	**sawa/si sawa**	sawa/see sawa

Quantities *Wingi*

a little/a lot	**kidogo/nyingi**	keedogo/nʸeengee
few/a few	**chache**	chacheh
much	**nyingi/mengi**	nʸeengee/mengee
many	**nyingi**	nʸeengee
more/less (than)	**zaidi/kasoro (kuliko)**	zaeedee/kasoro (kooleeko)
enough/too	**inatosha/vilevile**	eenatosha/veeleveeleh
some/any	**baadhi/yoyote**	baaðee/yoyoteh

A few more useful words *Maneno kidogo yafaayo kujuwa*

above	**juu**	joo-oo
after	**baadaye**	baadayeh
and	**na**	na
at	**kwa/kwenye**	kwa/**kwen**yeh
before (time)	**kabla [saa]**	**kab**la [saa]
behind	**nyuma ya**	nyooma ya
below	**chini ya**	cheenee ya
between	**baina ya**	baeena ya
but	**lakini**	lakeenee
down	**chini**	cheenee
downstairs	**chini**	cheenee
during	**wakati wa [kipindi cha]**	wakatee wa [keepeendee cha]
for	**kwa**	kwa
from	**kutoka**	kootoka
in	**ndani**	ndanee
inside	**ndani ya**	ndanee ya
near	**karibu na**	kareeboo na
never	**hapana kabisa [katu]**	hapana kabeesa [katoo]
next to	**karibu na**	kareeboo na
none	**hamna/hakuna**	hamna/hakoona
not	**si**	see
nothing	**si kitu**	see keetoo
now	**sasa**	sasa
on	**juu ya**	joo-oo ya
only	**tu**	too
or	**au [ama]**	aoo [ama]
outside	**nje**	njeh
perhaps	**labda**	labda
since	**tangu**	tangoo
soon	**sasa hivi/upesi**	sasa heevee/oopesee
then	**halafu/kisha/tena**	halafoo/keesha/tena
through	**katika**	kateeka
to	**kwa [mpaka]**	kwa [ᵐpaka]
too (also)	**pia/vilevile**	peeya/veeleveeleh
towards	**kuendea/kuelekea**	kooendea/kooelekea
under	**chini ya**	cheenee ya
until	**mpaka [hadi]**	ᵐpaka [hadee]
up	**juu**	joo-oo
upstairs	**juu [darini]**	joo-oo [dareenee]
very	**sana**	sana
with	**na**	na
without	**bila**	beela
yet	**bado**	bado

Arrival

Passport control *Uhamiaji*

If you're a British citizen you don't need a visa to enter East Africa. Citizens of the Commonwealth or of certain European countries may well not need a visa to enter Uganda or Tanzania, but check this with the embassy before travelling. All other nationalities require a visa.

Here's my passport/visa.	**Hii hapa pas poti/ viza yangu.**	hee-ee **ha**pa pas **po**tee/ **vee**za yan**goo**
I'll be staying...	**Nitakaa...**	nee**taka**-a
a few days	**siku chache**	**see**koo **cha**cheh
a week	**wiki moja [juma moja]**	**wee**kee moja [**joo**ma moja]
2 weeks	**wiki mbili [majuma mawili]**	**wee**kee ᵐ**bee**lee [ma**joo**ma ma**wee**lee]
a month	**mwezi mmoja**	**mwe**zee ᵐ**mo**ja
I don't know yet.	**Sijui bado.**	see**joo**ee **ba**do
I'm here on holiday.	**Niko hapa kwa likizo.**	**nee**ko **ha**pa kwa lee**kee**zo
I'm here on business.	**Niko hapa kwa kazi.**	**nee**ko **ha**pa kwa **ka**zee
I'm just passing through.	**Ninapita njia tu.**	neena**pee**ta **njee**ya too

If things become difficult:

I'm sorry, I don't understand.	**Samahani, sielewi. [Samahani, sifahamu]**	samaha**nee** see-ele**wee**. [samaha**nee** seefaha**moo**]
Does anyone here speak English?	**Kuna/Yuko mtu hapa anayesema Kizungu [Kiingereza]?**	**koo**na/**yoo**ko mtoo **ha**pa anaye**se**ma kee**zoo**ngoo [kee-eenge**re**za]

> **FORODHA**
> CUSTOMS

You can bring any amount of foreign currency into East Africa and take it out again, but you must declare it on arrival. The import or export of local currency, however, is not permitted.

Vitu vya kulipia ushuru	Vitu visivyolipiwa ushuru
Goods to declare	Nothing to declare

The export of ivory and other animal trophies is illegal, and any such goods will be confiscated at customs.

The chart below shows what you can bring in duty-free

	cigarettes		cigars		tobacco	liquor
Kenya Tanzania Uganda	200	or	50	or	½lb.	1 bottle 1 bottle ¼ gal.

I have nothing to declare.	**Sina kitu cha kuli-pia ushuru.**	**see**na **kee**too cha koolee**pee**ya oo**shoo**roo
I have...	**Nina...**	**nee**na
a carton of cigarettes	**boksi moja la sigara**	**bok**see **mo**ja la see**ga**ra
a bottle of whisky	**chupa moja ya wiski**	**choo**pa **mo**ja ya **wee**skee
It's for my personal use.	**Ni kwa matumizi yangu binafsi.**	nee kwa matoo**mee**zee **ya**ngoo bee**naf**see
It's a gift.	**Ni zawadi.**	nee za**wa**dee

Nipe pasipoti yako, tafadhali.	Your passport, please.
Una kitu cha kulipia ushuru?	Do you have anything to declare?
Fungua mkoba [Mfuko] huu, tafadhali.	Please open this bag.
Lazima ulipe ushuru kwa vitu hivi.	You'll have to pay duty on this.
Una mizigo zaidi?	Do you have any more luggage?

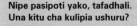

Baggage–Porter *Mizigo–Mchukuzi*

Porters are readily available to carry your luggage for a modest tip.

Porter!	**Mzee!/Bwana!**	mzee/bwana
Please take (this/my)...	**Tafadhali chukua... (huu/wangu).**	tafaðalee chookoowa... (hoo-oo/wangoo)
luggage	**mizigo**	meezeego
suitcase	**sanduku/begi**	sandookoo/begee
(travelling) bag	**mkoba/shanta**	ⁿkoba/shanta
That one is mine.	**Hilo ni langu.**	heelo nee langoo
Take this luggage...	**Chukua mzigo huu, tafadhali...**	chookoowa ⁿzeego hoo-oo tafaðalee
to the bus	**kwenye basi**	kwenʸeh basee
to the luggage lockers	**kwenye kabati la mizigo**	kwenʸeh kabatee la meezeego
to the taxi	**kwenye teksi**	kwenʸeh teksee
How much is that?	**Hiyo ni bei gani?**	heeyo nee be-ee ganee
There's one piece missing.	**Mzigo mmoja umepungua.**	ⁿzeego ⁿmoja oomepoongoowa
Where are the luggage trolleys (carts)?	**Wapi nitapata vigari vya mizigo?**	wapee neetapata veegaree vya meezeego

Changing money *Kubadilisha pesa [fedha]*

Where's the currency exchange office?	**Wapi mahali pa kubadilisha pesa?**	wapee mahalee pa koobadeeleesha pesa
Can you change these traveller's cheques (checks)?	**Unaweza kubadilisha hizi cheki za safari?**	oonaweza koobadeeleesha heezee chekee za safaree
I want to change some dollars/pounds.	**Nataka kubadilisha dala za Kimarekani/pauni za Kiingereza.**	nataka koobadeeleesha dala za keemarekanee/paoonee za kee-eengereza
Can you change this into...?	**Unaweza kubadilisha hizi kwa...?**	oonaweza koobadeeleesha heezee kwa
Kenyan shillings	**Shilingi za Kenya**	sheeleengee za kenʸa
Tanzanian shillings	**Shilingi za Tanzania**	sheeleengee za tanzaneeya
Ugandan shillings	**Shilingi za Uganda**	sheeleengee za ooganda

BANK–CURRENCY, see page 129

| What's the exchange rate? | **Ni kiasi gani kuba-dilisha?** | nee keeyasee ganee koobadeeleesha |

Where is...? *Wapi...?*

Where is the...?	**Wapi iko...?**	wapee eeko
booking office	**ofisi ya kufanya buking [ofisi ya kuandikisha]**	ofeesee ya koofan'ya bookeeng [ofeesee ya koowandeekeesha]
duty (tax)-free shop	**duka lisilotoza ushuru**	dooka leeseelotoza ooshooroo
newsstand	**duka la magazeti/ muuza magazeti**	dooka la magazetee/moo-ooza magazetee
restaurant	**mkhawa/hoteli**	mkhawa/hotelee
How do I get to...?	**Vipi nitafika...?**	veepee neetafeeka
Is there a bus into town?	**Liko basi la kuenda mjini?**	leeko basee la kooenda mjeenee
Where can I get a taxi?	**Wapi nitapata teksi?**	wapee neetapata teksee
Where can I hire (rent) a car?	**Wapi naweza kukodi gari?**	wapee naweza kookodee garee

Hotel reservation *Uwekeshaji [Uwandikishaji] wa hoteli*

Do you have a hotel guide (directory)?	**Unayo orodha ya hoteli?**	oonayo oro∂a ya hotelee
Could you reserve a room for me?	**Unaweza kuniwe-keshea chumba?**	oonaweza kooneewekeshea choomba
in the centre	**katikati**	kateekatee
near the railway station	**karibu na stesheni ya reli**	kareeboo na stesheenee ya relee
a single room	**chumba cha mtu mmoja**	choomba cha mtoo ᵐmoja
a double room	**chumba cha watu wawili**	choomba cha watoo waweelee
not too expensive	**si cha ghali sana**	see cha ʀhalee sana
Where is the hotel/ guesthouse?	**Iko wapi hoteli/ nyumba ya wageni?**	eeko wapee hotelee/ n'oomba ya wagenee
Do you have a street map?	**Una ramani ya mitaa?**	oona ramanee ya meetaa

HOTEL/ACCOMMODATION, see page 22

Car hire (rental) *Kukodi [Gari za kukodi]*

At the airport you will find many international car-hire firms, as well as local operators. You will need a current driving licence or international driving licence. In Kenya you must also be over 23 years of age, and have held the licence for two years or more. You will need to take out insurance when you hire the car. In all three countries you drive on the left.

I'd like to hire (rent) a car.	**Nitapenda kukodi gari.**	neetapenda kookodee garee
small	**ndogo**	ndogo
medium-sized	**ya kiasi**	ya keeyasee
large	**kubwa**	koobwa
automatic	**bila gia/automatik**	beela geeya/aootomateek
with 2-wheel/4-wheel drive	**inayotumia nguvu ya magurudumu mawili/manne**	eenayotoomeeya ngoovoo ya magooroodoomoo maweelee/manneh
I'd like it for a day/a week.	**Naitaka kwa siku moja/wiki moja.**	naeetaka kwa seekoo moja/weekee moja
Are there any week-end arrangements?	**Kuna mipango maalumu mwisho wa wiki?**	koona meepango maaloomoo mweesho wa weekee
Do you have any special rates?	**Kuna malipo maalumu yoyote?**	koona maleepo maaloomoo yoyoteh
What's the charge per day/week?	**Kiasi gani kwa siku/wiki?**	keeyasee ganee kwa seekoo/weekee
Is mileage included?	**Ni pamoja na maili [masafa]?**	nee pamoja na maeelee [masafa]
What's the charge per kilometre?	**Ni kiasi gani kwa kilomita moja?**	nee keeyasee ganee kwa keelomeeta moja
I'd like to leave the car in...	**Ningependa kuacha gari ndani ya...**	neengependa koowacha garee ndanee ya
I'd like full insurance.	**Ningependa bima kamili.**	neengependa beema kameelee
How much is the deposit?	**Rubuni ni kiasi gani?**	rooboonee nee keeyasee ganee
I have a credit card.	**Nina kadi ya benki.**	neena kadee ya benkee
Here's my driving licence.	**Hii hapa leseni yangu.**	hee-ee hapa lesenee yangoo

CAR, see page 75

Taxi *Teksi*

There are several different types of taxi and few of them have meters, so it's a good idea to check the fare before you get in. Most taxis charge per kilometre. Long-distance taxis also operate. These are often shared and can be booked in advance.

Where can I get a taxi?	**Wapi naweza kupata teksi?**	wapee naweza koopata teksee
Where is the taxi rank (stand)?	**Mahali pa teksi pako wapi?**	mahalee pa teksee pako wapee
Could you get me a taxi?	**Nipatie teksi tafadhali? [Unaweza kunipatia teksi?]**	neepatee-eh teksee tafaᵭalee [oonaweza kooneepateeya teksee]
What's the fare to…?	**Nauli ni kiasi gani kwenda…?**	naoolee nee keeyasee ganee kwenda
How far is it to…?	**Ni umbali gani kwenda…?**	nee oombalee ganee kwenda
Take me to…	**Nipeleke…. tafadhali.**	neepelekeh…. tafaᵭalee
this address	**anuwani hii [mahali hapa]**	anoowanee hee-ee [mahalee hapa]
the airport	**uwanja wa ndege**	oowanja wa ndegeh
the town centre/downtown	**mjini [katikati ya mji]**	mjeenee [kateekatee ya mjee]
the… Hotel	**Hotelini…**	hoteleenee
the railway station	**stesheni ya reli [treni]**	stesheenee ya reᶥee [trenee]
Turn… at the next corner.	**Pinda [nenda]… kwenye kona ijayo.**	peenda [nenda]… kwenᵞeh kona eejayo
left/right	**kushoto/kulia**	kooshoto/kooleeya
Go straight ahead.	**Nenda moja kwa moja.**	nenda moja kwa moja
Please stop here.	**Simama hapa tafadhali.**	seemama hapa tafaᵭalee
I'm in a hurry.	**Nina haraka.**	neena haraka
Could you help me carry my luggage?	**Nisaidie [Unaweza kunisaidia] kubeba mizigo yangu?**	neesaeedee-eh [oonaweza kooneesaeedeeya] koobeba meezeego yangoo
Could you wait for me?	**Ningoje tafadhali? [Unaweza kuningoja?]**	neengojeh tafaᵭalee [oonaweza kooneengoja?]
I'll be back in 10 minutes.	**Nitarudi baada ya dakika kumi.**	neetaroodee baada ya dakeeka koomee

TIPPING, see inside back-cover

Hotel—Other accommodation

There is a wide range of accomodation available in East Africa, from Western-style luxury hotels to African thatched huts in the game parks. Hotel prices are often considerably discounted in the low season, but at peak times you will need to book well in advance.

Ya hali ya juu [Hoteli kabambe]
(ya halee ya joo-oo [hotelee kabambeh])

Hotel; in the game parks these are usually called "lodges". These vary enormously in price and facilities, from basic furnished rooms with running water to extravagant, de luxe suites.

Hoteli ndogo
(hotelee ndogo)

Motel; while there are very few, they do offer the motorist good accommodation, good food and many other services in a pleasant atmosphere.

Nyumba ya wageni
(nʸoomba ya wagenee)

Guest house; normally for a stay of several weeks or even months; offering board according to requirements.

Kijumba chenye vyombo vyote
(keejoomba chenʸeh vyombo vyoteh)

Furnished bungalow; usually located near a beach, sometimes also adjoining a large hotel.

Kitanda na chakula cha asubuhi
(keetanda na chakoola cha asooboohee)

"Board and lodging"; look out for signs placed at the roadside by families offering such accommodation. These establishments are not regulated, so standards can vary considerably.

Banda
(banda)

African thatched hut ; providing basic cooking facilities. Generally more suited to the independent traveller, they are often "self-help", requiring you to bring bedding, food and drink.

Hosteli ya vijana
(hostelee ya veejana)

Youth hostel; few and far between, perhaps the best of the youth hostels in the region is on Mount Kenya. Non-members are usually required to join the IYHA first.

Mahali maalumu pa kupiga kambi
(mahalee maaloomoo pa koopeega kambee)

Permanent tented camp; these permanently sited canvas tents are generally well furnished, offering a high degree of cuisine and provide an atmosphere of the old traditional safari.

Can you recommend a hotel/guesthouse?	**Nielekeze hoteli/ nyumba ya wageni?**	nee-elekezeh hotelee/ n^yoomba ya wagenee
Are there any flats (apartments) vacant?	**Kuna fleti zilio- tupu?**	koona fletee zeeleeotoopoo

Checking in—Reception *Mapokezi [Kuandikisha]*

My name is...	**Jina langu ni [Mimi ni/Naitwa]** ...	jeena langoo nee [**meemee** nee/**naeetwa**]
I have a reservation.	**Nimeekesha chumba.**	neemeekesha **choomba**
We've reserved 2 rooms.	**Tumeekesha vyumba viwili.**	toomeekesha **vyoomba** veeweelee
Here's the confirmation.	**Thibitisho hili hapa.**	theebeeteesho **heelee hapa**
Do you have any vacancies?	**Kuna vyumba vitupu?**	koona **vyoomba** veetoopoo
I'd like a...	**Ningependa** ...	neengependa
single room	**chumba cha mtu mmoja**	**choomba** cha mtoo mmoja
double room	**chumba cha watu wawili**	**choomba** cha **watoo waweelee**
We'd like a room...	**Tungependa chumba**	toongependa **choomba**
with twin beds	**chenye vitanda viwili**	chen^yeh veetanda veeweelee
with a double bed	**chenye kitanda cha watu wawili**	chen^yeh keetanda cha watoo waweelee
with a bath	**chenye bafu**	chen^yeh bafoo
with a shower	**chenye shawa**	chen^yeh shawa
with a balcony	**chenye roshani**	chen^yeh roshanee
with a view	**chenye mandhari**	chen^yeh man∂aree
at the front	**mbele**	^mbeleh
at the back	**nyuma**	n^yooma
It must be quiet.	**Lazima kiwe kimya.**	lazeema keeweh keemya
Is there...?	**Kuna/Imo** ...?	koona/eemo
air conditioning	**eyakandishan**	eyakandeeshan
a conference room	**chumba cha mku- tano**	**choomba** cha mkootano
a laundry service	**huduma za dobi**	hoodooma za **dobee**
a private toilet	**choo cha binafsi**	choo cha beenafsee
a radio/television in the room	**redio/televisheni ndani ya chumba**	redeeo/televeeshenee ndanee ya **choomba**
a swimming pool	**bwawa la kuogelea**	bwawa la koowogelea

CHECKING OUT, see page 31

hot water	**maji ya moto**	majee ya moto
room service	**huduma za chumbani**	hoodooma za choombanee
running water	**maji ya bomba**	majee ya bomba
Could you put an extra bed/a cot in the room?	**Unaweza kuongeza kitanda/kitanda cha mtoto chumbani?**	oonaweza koowongeza keetanda/keetanda cha mtoto choombanee

How much? *Kiasi gani?*

What's the price...?	**Bei gani...?**	be-ee ganee
per week	**kwa wiki [kwa juma]**	kwa weekee [kwa jooma]
for bed and breakfast	**kwa kulala na chakula cha asubuhi**	kwa koolala na chakoola cha asooboohee
excluding meals	**bila chakula**	beela chakoola
for full board (A.P.)	**kulala na chakula cha kutwa nzima**	koolala na chakoola cha kootwa nzeema
for half board (M.A.P.)	**kulala na chakula cha asubuhi na cha usiku tu**	koolala na chakoola cha asooboohee na cha ooseekoo too
Does that include...?	**Hiyo ni pamoja na...?**	heeyo nee pamoja na
breakfast	**chakula cha asubuhi**	chakoola cha asooboohee
service	**huduma**	hoodooma
value-added tax (VAT)	**pamoja na ijara**	pamoja na eejara
Is there any reduction for children?	**Mnapunguza bei kwa watoto?**	mnapoongooza be-ee kwa watoto
Do you charge for the baby?	**Mtoto mchanga analipishwa?**	mtoto mchanga analeepeeshwa
That's too expensive.	**Hiyo ni ghali sana.**	heeyo nee RHalee sana
Do you have anything cheaper?	**Kipo chumba cha rahisi kidogo?**	keepo choomba cha raheesee keedogo

How long? *Muda gani?*

We'll be staying...	**Tutakaa kwa...**	tootakaa kwa
overnight only	**usiku mmoja tu**	ooseekoo mmoja too
a few days	**siku chache**	seekoo chacheh
a week (at least)	**wiki moja (kwa uchache)**	weekee moja (kwa oochache)
I don't know yet.	**Sijui bado.**	seejooee bado

Decision *Uamuzi*

May I see the room?	**Naweza kukiona chumba?**	naweza kookeeona **choomba**
That's fine. I'll take it.	**Sawa. Nimekikubali.**	sawa. neemekeekoobalee
No. I don't like it.	**Hapana. Sikipendi.**	hapana. seekeependee
It's too...	**Ni... sana.**	nee... sana
cold/hot	**baridi/joto**	bareedee/joto
dark/small	**giza/kidogo**	geeza/keedogo
noisy	**kelele**	keleleh
I asked for a room with a bath.	**Nilitaka chumba chenye bafu.**	neeleetaka **choomba** chen^yeh bafoo
Do you have anything...?	**Una chumba...?**	oona **choomba**
better	**bora zaidi**	bora zaeedee
bigger	**kikubwa zaidi**	keekoobwa zaeedee
cheaper	**rahisi zaidi**	raheesee zaeedee
quieter	**kimya zaidi**	keemya zaeedee
Do you have a room with a better view?	**Kipo chumba chenye mandhari nzuri zaidi?**	keepo **choomba** chen^yeh man∂aree nzooree zaeedee

Registration *Kuandikisha*

Upon arrival at a hotel or guesthouse you'll be asked to fill in a registration form (*maandiskisho*).

Jina kamili	Name
Mji unaotoka/Mtaa/Namba ya nyumba	Home town/Street/Number
Uraiya/Kazi	Nationality/Occupation
Tarehe/Mahali pa kuzaliwa	Date/Place of birth
Unatoka.../Unakwenda...	Coming from.../Going to...
Nambari ya paspoti	Passport number
Mahali/Tarehe	Place/Date
Sahihi [Saini]	Signature

What does this mean?	**Hii ina mana gani?**	hee-ee eena mana ganee

Niangalie paspoti yako, tafadhali [Naweza kuangalia paspoti yako?]	May I see your passport, please?
Tafadhali jaza fomu hii ya kujiandikisha?	Would you mind filling in this registration form?
Tafadhali tia sahihi hapa. [Tafadhali saini hapa.]	Please sign here.
Utakaa kwa muda gani?	How long will you be staying?

What's my room number?	**Chumba changu nambari gani?**	choomba changoo nambaree ganee
Will you have our luggage sent up?	**Utatuma mizigo yetu juu?**	ootatooma meezeego yetoo joo-oo
Where can I park my car?	**Wapi naweza kue-gesha gari yangu?**	wapee naweza kooegesha garee yangoo
Does the hotel have a garage?	**Je hoteli ina garaji?**	jeh hotelee eena garajee
I'd like to leave this in the hotel safe.	**Nitapenda kuweka hii katika dhamana yenu.**	neetapenda kooweka hee-ee kateeka ðamana yenoo

Hotel staff *Wafanyakazi wa hoteli*

hall porter	**mbebaji mizigo**	ᵐbebajee meezeego
maid	**mfanyakazi wa kike**	mfanʸakazee wa keekeh
manager	**mkuu wa hoteli [meneja]**	mkoo-oo wa hotelee [meneja]
porter	**mchukuzi**	mchookoozee
receptionist	**mpokezi**	mpokezee
switchboard operator	**opereta [mfanyakazi wa simu]**	opereta [mfanʸakazee wa seemoo]
waiter	**mhudumu wa mkahawani**	mhoodoomoo wa mkahawanee
waitress	**msaidizi wa mkahawa**	msaeedeezee wa mkahawa

The polite way to call for a porter is *mzee!* or *bwana!* The polite way to address waiters is *mzee* or *ndugu*, and for a waitress it is *mama* or *dada*, depending on age.

TELLING THE TIME, see page 153

General requirements *Mahitaji ya yoyote*

The key to room..., please.	**Nipatie ufunguo wa chumba..., tafadhali.**	neepatee-eh oofoongoowo wa choomba ... tafaδalee
Could you wake me at... please?	**Niamshe saa... tafadhali?**	neeyamsheh saa ... tafaδalee
When is breakfast/ lunch/dinner served?	**Saa ngapi chakula cha asubuhi/ mchana/usiku hutolewa?**	sa-a ngapee chakoola cha asooboohee/mchana/ ooseekoo hootolewa
Is there a bath on this floor?	**Lipo bafu kwenye ghorofa hii?**	leepo bafoo kwenᵞeh RHorofa hee-ee
What's the voltage?	**Nguvu ya umeme ni ngapi hapa?**	ngoovoo ya oomemeh nee ngapee hapa
Where's the shaver socket (outlet)?	**Ipo wapi plagi ya mashini ya kunyo- lea?**	eepo wapee plagee ya masheenee ya koonᵞolea
Can you find me a...?	**Unaweza kunipa- tia?**	oonaweza kooneepateeya
babysitter	**mtu wa kuangalia mtoto**	mtoo wa koowangaleeya mtoto
typewriter	**mpiga mashini [mpiga taipu]**	mpeega masheenee [mpeega taeepoo]
May I have a/an/ some...?	**Nipatie...tafad- hali? [Naweza kupata...?]**	neepatee-eh ... tafaδalee [naweza koopata]
ashtray	**eshtrei**	eshtreee
bath towel	**taulo ya kuogea**	taoolo ya koo-ogea
(extra) blanket	**blangeti moja (zaidi)**	blangetee moja (zaeedee)
envelopes	**bahasha za barua**	bahasha za baroowa
(more) hangers	**vitundikia nguo (zaidi)**	veetoondeekeeya ngoo-o (zaeedee)
hot-water bottle	**chupa ya maji ya moto [mfuko wa maji ya moto]**	choopa ya majee ya moto [mfooko wa majee ya moto]
ice cubes	**barafu**	barafoo
needle and thread	**sindano na uzi**	seendano na oozee
(extra) pillow	**mto wa kulalia (zaidi)**	mto wa koolaleeya (zaeedee)
reading lamp	**taa ya kusomea**	taa ya koosomea
soap	**sabuni**	saboonee
writing paper	**karatasi za kuandi- kia**	karatasee za koowandeekeeya

BREAKFAST, see page 40

Where's the ...?	**Iko wapi ...?**	eeko wapee
bathroom	**bafu**	bafoo
dining-room	**chumba cha kulia**	choomba cha kooleeya
emergency exit	**mlango wa dharura**	mlango wa ∂aroora
	[mlango wa	[mlango wa
	kutumia wakati	kootoomeeya wakatee
	wa hatari]	wa hataree]
lift (elevator)	**lifti**	leeftee
Where are the	**Choo kiko wapi?**	choo **kee**ko wapee [vyoo
toilets?	**[Vyoo viko wapi?]**	**vee**ko wapee]

Telephone–Post (mail) *Simu–Barua*

Can you get me Kisumu 123-45-67?	**Unaweza kunipatia Kisumu 123-45-67?**	oona**we**za kooneepatee**ya** keesoomoo 123-45-67
Do you have any stamps?	**Unazo stempu?** **[Unauza stempu?]**	oo**na**zo **stem**poo [oona**oo**za **stem**poo]
Would you post this for me, please?	**Unaweza kunitilia posta, tafadhali?**	oona**we**za kooneetee**lee**ya posta tafa∂alee
Are there any letters for me?	**Kuna barua zangu?**	**koo**na ba**roo**wa zangoo
How much is my telephone bill?	**Hesabu [Bili] yangu ya simu ni kiasi gani?**	hesa**boo** [**bee**lee] yangoo ya **see**moo nee kee**ya**see ganee

Difficulties *Tabu [Shida]*

The ... doesn't work.	**... haifanyi kazi/... imeharibika.**	... haeefan^yee kazee/... eemehareebeeka
air conditioning	**eyakandishan [kiyoyozi]**	eyakandeeshan [keeyo**yo**zee]
fan	**panka [feni]**	panka [**fe**nee]
heating	**mtambo wa joto**	mtambo wa joto
light	**taa**	taa
radio	**redio**	re**dee**o
television	**televisheni**	tele**vee**shenee
The tap (faucet) is dripping.	**Bomba linavuja.**	bomba leena**voo**ja
There's no hot water.	**Hakuna maji ya moto.**	ha**koo**na majee ya moto
The washbasin is blocked.	**Beseni limeziba.**	be**se**nee leeme**zee**ba

POST OFFICE AND TELEPHONE, see page 132

The curtains are stuck.	**Mapazia yamenasa**.	mapazeeya yamenasa
The bulb is burned out.	**Globu imeungua**.	globoo eemeoongoowa
My bed hasn't been made up.	**Kitanda changu hakijatandikwa**.	keetanda changoo hakeejatandeekwa
The . . . is broken.	**. . . imevunjika**.	eemevoonjeeka
blind	**pazia**	pazeeya
lamp	**taa**	ta-a
plug	**plagi**	plagee
shutter	**mbao za dirisha**	ᵐbao za deereesha
switch	**swichi**	sweechee
Can you get it repaired?	**Unaweza kuitenge-neza?**	oonaweza kooeetengeneza

Laundry–Dry cleaner's *Dobi*

I'd like these clothes . . .	**Nitapenda nguo hizi . . .**	neetapenda ngoo-o heezee
cleaned	**kufuliwa [kusaf-ishwa]**	koofooleewa [koosafeeshwa]
ironed	**kupigiwa pasi**	koopeegeewa pasee
washed	**kufuliwa**	koofooleewa
When will they be ready?	**Zitakuwa tayari lini?**	zeetakoowa tayaree leenee
I need them . . .	**Ninazihitaji . . .**	neenazeeheetajee
today	**leo**	le-o
tonight	**leo usiku**	le-o ooseekoo
tomorrow	**kesho**	kesho
before Friday	**kabla ljumaa**	kabla eejoomaa
Can you . . . this?	**Unaweza . . . hii?**	oonaweza . . . hee-ee
mend	**kutengeneza**	kootengeneza
patch	**kutia kiraka**	kooteeya keeraka
stitch	**kushona**	kooshona
Can you sew on this button?	**Unaweza kutia kifungo hiki?**	oonaweza kooteeya keefoongo heekee
Can you get this stain out?	**Unaweza kutoa dowa hili?**	oonaweza kootowa dowa heelee
Is my laundry ready?	**Nguo zangu zisha-fuliwa?**	ngoo-o zangoo zeeshafooleewa
This isn't mine.	**Hii si yangu**.	hee-ee see yangoo
There's something missing.	**Kuna nguo ime-pungua**.	koona ngoowo eemepoongoowa
There's a hole in this.	**Kuna tundu humu**.	koona toondoo hoomoo

Hairdresser–Barber *Mtegenezaji nywele–Kinyozi*

Is there a hairdresser/beauty salon in the hotel?	Lipo kuna duka la kutengeneza nywele/duka la urembo?	leepo koona dooka la kootengeneza n^yweleh/dooka la oorembo
Can I make an appointment for Thursday?	Naweza kufanya miadi kwa Alhamisi? [Naweza kuja Alhamisi?]	naweza koofan^ya meeyadee kwa alhameesee [naweza kooja alhameesee]
I'd like a cut and blow dry.	Ningependa kukata na kuseti nywele.	neengependa kookata na koosetee n^yweleh
I'd like a haircut, please.	Ningependa kukata nywele, tafadhali.	neengependa kookata n^yweleh tafaðaalee
blow-dry	bloo drai	bloo draee
colour rinse	kutia rangi ya muda tu	kooteeya rangee ya mooda too
dye	rangi	rangee
hair gel	mafuta ya nywele	mafoota ya n^yweleh
manicure	kutengeneza makucha ya mikono	kootengeneza makoocha ya meekono
setting lotion	mafuta ya kuseti nywele	mafoota ya koosetee n^yweleh
shampoo and set with a fringe (bangs)	kuosha na kuchana ziteremke kwenye kipaji kidogo	koo-osha na koochana zeeteremkeh kwen^yeh keepajee keedogo
I'd like a shampoo for... hair.	Nitapenda shampuu ya nywele...	neetapenda shampoo-oo ya n^yweleh
normal/dry/greasy (oily)	za kawaida/kavu/zenye mafuta	za kawaeeda/kavoo/zen^yeh mafoota
Don't cut it too short.	Usikate fupi sana.	ooseekateh foopee sana
A little more off the...	Kata zaidi kidogo...	kata zaeedee keedogo
back	nyuma	n^yooma
neck	shingoni	sheengonee
sides	pembeni	pembenee
top	juu	joo-oo
I don't want any hairspray.	sitaki sprei ya nywele.	seetakee spre-ee ya n^yweleh
I'd like a shave.	Ningependa kunyoa ndevu.	neengependa koon^yowa ndevoo
Would you trim my..., please?	Unaweza kutengeneza... zangu tafadhali?	oonaweza kootengeneza... zangoo tafaðaalee

DAYS OF THE WEEK, see page 151

beard	**ndevu**	**nde**voo
moustache	**masharubu**	masharooboo
sideboards	**nywele za pembeni**	n'weleh za pembenee
(sideburns)		

Checking out *Malipo*

May I have my bill, please?	**Nipatie hesabu yangu, tafadhali?**	neepatee-eh hesaboo yangoo tafaðalee
I'm leaving early in the morning.	**Nitaondoka asu-buhi mapema kesho.**	neetaondoka asooboohee mapema kesho
Please have my bill ready.	**Tafadhali weka hesabu [bili] yangu tayari.**	tafaðalee weka hesaboo [beelee] yangoo tayaree
We'll be checking out around noon.	**Tutaondoka kama sa-a sita mchana.**	tootaondoka kama saa seeta mchana
I must leave at once.	**Lazima niende haraka.**	lazeema nee-endeh haraka
Is everything included?	**Je umetia kila kitu katika hesabu?**	jeh oometeeya keela keetoo kateeka hesaboo
Can I pay by credit card?	**Naweza kulipa kwa kadi ya benki?**	naweza kooleepa kwa kadee ya benkee
I think there's a mistake in the bill.	**Nafikiri kuna kosa katika hesabu.**	nafeekeeree koona kosa kateeka hesaboo
Can you get us a taxi?	**Tupatie teksi tafad-hali? [Unaweza kutupatia teksi?]**	toopatee-eh teksee tafaðalee [oonaweza kootoopateeya teksee]
Could you have our luggage brought down?	**Tuletee mizigo yetu chini tafad-hali? [Unaweza kutuletea mizigo yetu chini?]**	tooleeteeh meezeego yetoo cheenee tafaðalee [oonaweza kootooleetea meezeego yetoo cheenee]
Here's the forwarding address.	**Hii ni anwani ya huko niendako.**	hee-ee nee anwanee ya hooko nee-endako
You have my home address.	**Unayo anwani yangu ya nyum-bani.**	conayo anwanee yangoo ya n'oombanee
It's been a very enjoyable stay.	**Kwa kweli tum-estarehe sana na makaazi yetu.**	kwa kwelee toomestareheh sana na makaazee yetoo

TIPPING, see inside back-cover

Camping *Kupiga kambi*

Camping has become an increasingly popular way of seeing the region in recent years. Camp sites can be booked on the spot or from the town hall. Ask at the local tourist office for a list of sites. Be sure to find a site well before sunset, as it gets dark very rapidly in this part of the world.

Is there a camp site near here?	**Kuna mahali pa kupiga kambi karibu na hapa?**	koona mahalee pa koopeega kambee kareeboo na hapa
Can we camp here?	**Tunaweza kupiga kambi hapa?**	toonaweza koopeega kambee hapa
Do you have room for a tent/caravan (trailer)?	**Ipo nafasi ya kuweka hema/ karavani?**	eepo nafasee ya kooweka hema/karavanee
What's the charge…?	**Malipo ni kiasi gani kwa…?**	maleepo nee keeyasee ganee kwa
per day	**siku moja**	seekoo moja
per person	**mtu mmoja**	mtoo mmoja
for a car	**gari**	garee
for a tent	**hema**	hema
for a caravan (trailer)	**karavani**	karavanee
Is tourist tax included?	**Ni pamoja na ijara ya utalii?**	nee pamoja na eejara ya ootalee-ee
Is there/Are there (a)…?	**Kuna…?**	koona
drinking water	**maji ya kunywa**	majee ya koon^ywa
electricity	**umeme**	oomemeh
playground	**uwanja wa kuche-zea/michezo**	oowanja wa koochezea/ meechezo
restaurant	**mkahawa/hoteli**	mkahawa/hotelee
shopping facilities	**maduka**	madooka
swimming pool	**bwawa la kuogelea**	bwawa la koowogelea
Where are the showers/toilets?	**Wapi mahali pa kuogea/vyoo?**	wapee mahalee pa koowogea/vyoo
Where can I get butane gas?	**Wapi nitapata gesi ya butane?**	wapee neetapata gesee ya bootaneh
Is there a youth hostel near here?	**Iko hosteli ya vijana hapa karibu?**	eeko hostelee ya veejana hapa kareeboo

CAMPING EQUIPMENT, see page 106

Eating out

East Africa has a wide variety of eating and drinking places, ranging from the more familiar Western-style restaurants to more colourful establishments serving local food and drink.

Baa
(baa)

Bar which serves drinks and snacks

Baraza
(baraza)

Balcony of a café or a front porch of a house, serving hot drinks and sweet snacks. A place where the locals meet to exchange gossip and jokes over tea or coffee.

Mkahawa
(mkahawa)

A small café which serves various local dishes and non-alcoholic drinks. You can sit at the counter or at a table and enjoy the recorded local music while you eat.

Vioski
(veeoskee)

Serves cooked local dishes, salads and non-alcoholic hot and cold drinks. Usually located in working areas especially in the suburbs.

Baa ya dansi
(baa ya dansee)

A dance bar which plays recorded music or has live music in the evening and at weekends. It serves alcoholic and non-alcoholic drinks as well as snacks and light meals. Normally located in the city centre.

Mahali pa mishikaki
(mahalee pa meesheekakee)

An open-air eating place serving a variety of roasted meats – beef, lamb or chicken – with spicy sauces. A good place to meet local people.

Mkahawa wa kibaniani
(mkahawa wa keebaneeyanee)

An Indian restaurant serving a wide variety of vegetarian dishes using local produce.

Pcarnivro
(pcarneevro)

Indoor or outdoor eating place found in Nairobi, serving all sorts of barbecued game, accompanied by dips.

Eating habits *Dasturi za chakula*

Although hotels and most restaurants generally cater for a European style of dining, in homes and in many smaller local restaurants people still use their fingers for eating. A spoon is generally provided, but you may need to ask for a knife and fork.

Breakfast usually consists of bread and butter, although boiled eggs and omelets are sometimes served. Fresh fruit, too, is often eaten. But beware – tea (*chai*) is often brewed with milk, sugar and cardamon seeds, and coffee (*kahawa*) may be served black, sprinkled with ginger powder!

Lunch is the main meal of the day and may consist of meat or fish, accompanied by vegetable dishes or rice. You will find beef and chicken on the menu throughout the region, but if you are staying near the coast, the local fish and seafood is highly recommended. Beans and sweet potatoes are common, as are cassava, maize and plantains.

Afternoon tea usually consists of tea and cake.

The evening meal is a lighter affair than lunch, and may consist of flat bread or rice fritters. Fish, chicken or vegetable dishes may also be served.

Meal times *Nyakati za chakula*

Breakfast (*chakula cha asubuhi* – cha**koo**la cha asoo**boo**hee) is usually served from 7 a.m. to 9.30 a.m. in restaurants, but in homes between 7 a.m. and 8 a.m.

Lunch (*chakula cha mchana* – cha**koo**la cha m**cha**na) is served in restaurants from noon until 2.30 p.m., in homes between 1 p.m. and 2 p.m.

Afternoon tea (*chai ya alasiri* – chaee ya ala**see**ree) is served between 3.30 p.m. and 5.30 p.m. in restaurants, but between 4.30 p.m. and 5 p.m. in homes.

Evening meal (*chakula cha usiku* – cha**koo**la cha oo**see**koo) is generally served in restaurants from 7 p.m. to 9.30 p.m. but at home between 8 p.m. and 9.30 p.m.

East African cuisine *Mapishi ya Afrika mashariki*

Although many hotels cater for Western tastes, do try the local cuisine, which, in the cities particularly, is an interesting mixture of African, Indian and Arab influences.

The traditional African staples of maize (corn), cassava, plantains, beans and okra feature heavily in East African cooking. However, the Tanzanians in particular tend to be more versatile than the rest of the continent in their use of ingredients.

Inland is a cattle-rearing area and the local beef is recommended. It is often served roasted or barbecued. If you're staying near the coast then don't miss out on the superb fish and seafood – especially lobsters and prawns.

Ungependa kula nini?	What would you like?
Mimi naona bora ule...	I recommend this.
Ungependa kunywa nini?	What would you like to drink?
Hakuna [Hatuna]...	We don't have...
Ungependa...?	Would you like...?

Hungry? *Una njaa?*

I'm hungry/thirsty.	**Nina njaa/Nina kiu.**	neena njaa/neena keeoo
Can you recommend a good restaurant?	**Nielekeze mkahawa unaouza chakula kizuri?**	nee-elekezeh mkahawa oonaoooza chakoola keezooree
Are there any inexpensive restaurants around here?	**Kuna mikahawa ya rahisi karibu na hapa?**	koona meekahawa ya raheesee kareeboo na hapa

If you want to be sure of getting a table in a well-known restaurant, it may be better to book in advance.

I'd like to reserve a table for 4.	**Nataka kuekesha meza kwa watu wanne, tafadhali.**	nataka kooekesha meza kwa watoo wanneh tafadaalee
We'll come at 8.	**Tutakuja saa mbili usiku.**	tootakooja saa ᵐbeelee ooseekoo

Could we have a table...?	**Tunaweza kupata meza?**	toonaweza koopata meza
in the corner	**iliyo pembeni**	eeleeyo pembenee
by the window	**karibu na dirisha**	kareeboo na deereesha
outside	**nje**	njeh
on the terrace	**barazani**	barazanee
in a non-smoking area	**kwenye sehemu isiyovutwa sigara**	kwen^yeh sehemoo eeseeyovootwa seegara

Asking and ordering *Kuuliza na kuagiza*

Waiter/Waitress!	**Bwana!/Bibi!**	bwana/beebee
I'd like something to eat/drink.	**Nataka chakula/ kinywaji, tafadhali.**	nataka chakoola/ keen^ywajee tafaðalee
May I have the menu, please?	**Nipatie orodha ya chakula, tafadhali?**	neepatee-eh oroða ya chakoola tafaðalee
Do you have a set menu/local dishes?	**Iko orodha maalumu ya chakula/ chakula cha kienyeji?**	eeko oroða maaloomoo ya chakoola/chakoola cha kee-en^yejee
What do you recommend?	**Chakula gani unakiona kizuri, niambie?**	chakoola ganee oonakeeona keezooree neeyambee-eh
Do you have anything ready quickly?	**Kiko chakula kiliyo tayari, sasa hivi?**	keeko chakoola keeleeyo tayaree sasa heevee
I'm in a hurry.	**Nina haraka [ninakimbilia]**	neena haraka [neenakeembeeleeya]
I'd like...	**Ningependa...**	neengependa
Could we have a/ an..., please?	**Tupatie [Tunaomba]...**	toopatee-eh [toonaomba]
ashtray	**eshtrei**	eshtre-ee
cup	**kikombe**	keekombeh
fork	**uma**	ooma
glass	**gilasi [bilauli]**	geelasee [beelaoolee]
knife	**kisu**	keesoo
napkin (serviette)	**kitambaa cha kulia**	keetambaa cha kooleeya
plate	**sahani**	sahanee
spoon	**kijiko**	keejeeko
May I have some...?	**Nipatie [Naomba] ..., tafadhali?**	neepatee-eh [naomba]... tafaðalee
bread	**mkate**	mkateh
butter	**siagi**	seeyagee
ketchup	**tomato sosi**	tomato sosee
lemon	**limau**	leemaoo

oil	**mafuta**	mafoota
pepper	**pilipili manga**	peeleepeelee manga
salt	**chumvi**	choomvee
seasoning	**viungo**	veeoongo
sugar	**sukari**	sookaree
vinegar	**siki**	seekee

Special diet *Chakula maaluum*

Some useful expressions for those with special requirements:

I'm on a diet.	**Nafanya dayat.**	nafanʸa dayat
I'm vegetarian.	**Nakula vyakula vya mboga mboga.**	nakoola vyakoola vya ᵐboga ᵐboga
I don't drink alcohol.	**Silewi [sitimii pombe].**	seelewee [seeteemee-ee pombeh]
I don't eat meat.	**Sili nyama.**	seelee nʸama
I mustn't eat food containing...	**Nisile chakula chenye...**	neeseeleh chakoola chenʸeh
flour/fat	**unga/mafuta**	oonga/mafoota
salt/sugar	**chumvi/sukari**	choomvee/sookaree
Do you have... for diabetics?	**Una... kwa wagonjwa wa kisukari?**	oona kwa wagonjwa wa keesookaree
cakes	**keki**	kekee
fruit juice	**maji [jus] ya matunda**	majee [joos] ya matoonda
a special menu	**chakula maalumu**	chakoola maaloomoo
Do you have any vegetarian dishes?	**Kuna vyakula vya mboga mboga?**	koona vyakoola vya ᵐboga ᵐboga
Could I have... instead of dessert?	**Naweza kupata... badala ya vitamutamu?**	naweza koopata... badala ya veetamootamoo

And...

I'd like some more.	**Ningependa zaidi.**	neengependa zaeedee
Can I have more..., please?	**Nipatie... zaidi, tafadhali.**	neepatee-eh... zaeedee tafaðalee
Just a small portion.	**Kidogo tu.**	keedogo too
Nothing more, thanks.	**Sitaki kitu zaidi, asante.**	seetakee keetoo zaeedee asanteh
Where are the toilets?	**Choo kiko wapi? [Vyoo vi wapi?]**	choo keeko wapee [vyoo vee wapee]

What's on the menu? *Mna chakula gani?*

Under the headings below you'll find alphabetical lists of dishes that might be offered on an East African menu with their English equivalents. You can simply show the book to the waiter. If you want some fruit for example, let *him* point to what's available on the appropriate list. Use pages 36 and 37 for ordering in general.

Reading the menu *Kusoma oradha ya chakula*

aina moja tu	set menu
kwa kuagiza tu	made to order
spesheli ya leo	dish of the day
spesheli yetu	speciality of the house
... zaidi	... extra

aiskrimu	aeeskreemoo	ice cream
baga	baga	burgers
bia [pombe]	beeya [pombeh]	beer
kuku	kookoo	poultry
matunda	matoonda	fruit
mboga	ᵐboga	vegetables
nyama	nʸama	game
saladi	saladee	salads
samaki	samakee	fish
supu	soopoo	soups
vitamutam	veetamootam	desserts
vyakula vya bahari	vyakoola vya baharee	seafood
vyakula vya mayai	vyakoola vya mayaee	egg dishes

Breakfast *Chakula cha asubuhi*

An East African breakfast consists simply of bread and butter, sometimes beans and tea. However, most hotels also provide an English or American breakfast.

On the coast, soup is a popular breakfast meal. Restaurants will offer "special morning soup", generally made from goat meat.

I'd like breakfast, please.	**Nataka chakula cha asubuhi, tafadhali.**	nataka chakoola cha asooboohee tafaᵭalee
I'll have a/an/ some...	**Nataka...**	nataka
bacon and eggs	**nyama ya nguruwe na mayai**	nʸama ya ngoorooweh na mayaee
beans	**maharagwe**	maharagweh
boiled egg	**yai la kuchemsha**	yaee la koochemsha
hard/soft	**gumu/laini**	goomoo/laeenee
medium	**uji**	oojee
cereal	**la kiasi**	la keeyasee

eggs	mayai	mayaee
fried eggs	ya kukaanga	ya kooka-anga
scrambled eggs	ya kuvuruga	ya koovoorooga
poached eggs	ya kupika bila	ya koopeeka beela
omelet	mfuta kiwanda	mfoota keewanda
(fruit) juice	maji (ya matunda)	majee (ya matoonda)
coconut	... madafu	madafoo
grapefruit	... ya balungi	ya baloongee
lime	... ya ndimu	ya ndeemoo
mango	... ya embe	ya embeh
orange	... ya machu-ngwa	ya machoongwa
tamarind	... ya ukwaju	ya ookwajoo
ham and eggs	nyama ya nguruwe na mayai	nʸama ya ngoorooweh na mayaee
jam	jamu	jamoo
marmalade	mamiledi	mameeledee
omelet	kimanda/kiwanda	keemanda/keewanda
toast	tosti	tostee
yoghurt	maziwa ya kuganda/lala	mazeewa ya kooganda/lala
May I have some...?	Nipatie [Naomba]... tafadhali?	neepatee-eh [naomba]... tafaðalee
bread	mkate	mkateh
butter	siagi	seeyagee
coffee	kahawa	kahawa
decaffeinated	isiyokuwa kali	eeseeyokoowa kalee
black/with milk	bila maziwa/na maziwa	beela mazeewa/na mazeewa
without sugar	bila sukari	beela sookaree
with ginger	na tangawizi	na tangaweezee
honey	asali	asalee
hot chocolate	chokleti ya ya kunywa	chokletee ya ya koonʸwa
milk	maziwa	mazeewa
cold/hot	ya baridi/ya moto	ya bareedee/ya moto
pepper	pilipili manga	peeleepeelee manga
rolls	mikate	meekateh
salt	chumvi	choomvee
tea	chai	chaee
with milk	ya maziwa	ya mazeewa
with lemon	na limau	na leemaoo
without milk	bila maziwa	beela mazeewa
lemon grass	mchaichai	mchaeechaee
(hot) water	maji (ya moto)	majee (ya moto)

Snacks *Vitafunio*

Starters or appetizers are not common in East African cuisine, since dishes are usually brought to the table all at once. However, you will find a wide range of snacks available at the many open-air snack bars. For a further list of items suitable for a picnic, see page 64.

I'd like...	**Nitapenda**...	neetapenda
What would you recommend?	**Wewe unaona nile nini?**	weweh oonaona neeleh neenee
bajia	bajeeya	spiced fried balls made from bean flour
biringani	beereenganee	egg plant
chaza	chaza	oysters
chipsi za muhogo	cheepsee za moohogo	cassava chips
embe	embeh	mango
mbichi	ᵐbeechee	unripe
kaa	kaa	crab meat
kababu	kababoo	meat balls
kamba	kamba	prawns/shrimp/lobster/crayfish
korosho	korosho	cashew nuts
maini ya kuku	maeenee ya kookoo	chicken liver
mayai yaliotokoswa sana	mayaee yaleeotokoswa sana	hard boiled eggs
mayai ya samaki	mayaee ya samaki	caviar
mbatata za urojo	ᵐbatata za oorojo	potatoes in tamarind sauce
mhogo	mhogo	cassava
mhogo wa kuchoma	mhogo wa koochoma	roast cassava
mkate wa kusukuma	mkateh wa koosookooma	fried flat wheat bread
mkunga	mkoonga	eel
mkunga aliokaushwa	mkoonga aleeokaooshwa	dried eel
nyama baridi	nʸama bareedee	cold meat
paja la nguruwe	paja la ngoorooweh	pig's thigh
paja la nguruwe liliotokoswa	paja la ngoorooweh leeleeotokoswa	boiled pig's thigh
samaki tamvu	samakee tamvoo	herring
samaki tamvu na ukwaju	samakee tamvoo na ookwajoo	herring marinated in citrus juice
samaki tamvu waliokaushwa	samakee tamvoo waleeokaooshwa	smoked herring

tikiti maji	teekeetee majee	melon
tini (kavu)	teenee (kavoo)	(dry) figs
uyoga	ooyoga	mushrooms
zeituni	ze-eetoonee	olives
zeituni zenye pilipili	ze-eetoonee zenʸeh peeleepeelee	stuffed olives

mkate wa ufuta (mkateh wa oofoota)	flat wheat bread, sprinkled with sesame seeds and baked
mshikaki (msheekakee)	shish kebab; pieces of meat roasted on a skewer and often served in a roll
sambusa (samboosa)	*sambusa* or *samosa* is a triangular, spiced meat/vegetable pastry popular throughout East Africa; on the coast, it's often served with lime

Egg dishes *Vyakula vya mayai*

I'd like an omelet.	**Nataka kiwanda.**	nataka keewanda
kiwanda cha jibini	keewanda cha jeebeenee	cheese omelet
kiwanda cha kamba kamba	keewanda cha kamba kamba	shrimp omelet
kiwanda chenye viungo	keewanda chenʸeh veeoongo	spiced omelet
kiwanda na nyanya	keewanda na nʸanʸa	tomato omelet
mayai ya bata	mayaee ya bata	duck eggs
mayai ya kukaangwa	mayaee ya kookaangwa	fried eggs
mayai ya kuchemshwa	mayaee ya koochemshwa	boiled eggs
mayai ya kuvuruga	mayaee ya koovooroogwa	scrambled eggs
mayai yaliyotokoswa laini	mayaee yaleeyotokoswa laeenee	soft-boiled eggs
mayai mabichi tumboni (mayaee mabeechee toombonee)	unlaid eggs: a rare dish of eggs removed from the hen before they are laid	

Salads *Saladi*

What salads do you have?	**Una saladi aina gani?**	**oo**na saladee a**ee**na **ga**nee
Can you recommend a local speciality?	**Unaweza kunifisia saladi ya mahali?**	oona**we**za kooneefee**see**ya saladee ya ma**ha**lee
biringani iliyokaushwa	beeree**nga**nee eeleeyoka**oo**shwa	smoked aubergine (eggplant)
nyanya zilizokaushwa na nanaa	n**y**an**y**a zeeleezoka**oo**shwa na **na**naa	smoked tomato and mint
saladi ya figili	saladee ya fee**gee**lee	lettuce salad
saladi ya majani	saladee ya ma**ja**nee	green salad
saladi ya mbatata	saladee ya ᵐba**ta**ta	potato salad
saladi ya mzizi wa figili	saladee ya m**zee**zee wa fee**gee**lee	radish salad, with onions and lemon

embe mbichi (embeh ᵐ**bee**chee)	grated green mango, with onions, garlic, pepper and lemon
kachumbari (kachoo**mba**ree)	sliced onions and chopped tomatoes, with salt, pepper and lemon juice
matango (ma**ta**ngo)	cucumber salad, with onions, tomatoes and lemon juice
nanaa (**na**naa)	mint salad (with garlic, black pepper, salt and lemon

Soups *Supu*

Soups are common in hotels, but are less popular in local cuisine. However, you will find "local soup" in the many open-air bars. Made from beef, bones and cartilages, this highly spiced soup goes down very well with beer.

Do you have...?	**Unayo...?**	oo**na**yo
kisusio	kee**soo**see**o**	goat meat soup
konsome	kon**so**meh	consommé
mchuzi mwepesi wa mbonga	mchoo**zee** mwe**pe**see wa ᵐ**bo**nga	vegetable soup
mchuzi mwepesi wa ngombe	mchoo**zee** mwe**pe**see wa **ngo**mbeh	consommé
mchuzi mzito wa kuku	mchoo**zee** m**zee**to wa **koo**koo	cream of chicken soup

mchuzi mzito wa ngano ya kusagwa	mchoozee mzeeto wa ngano ya koosagwa	semolina soup
mchuzi wa malenge	mchoozee wa malengeh	pumpkin soup
mchuzi wa nazi	mchoozee wa nazee	cream of coconut soup
mchuzi wa ngano	mchoozee wa ngano	barley soup
mchuzi wa nyanya	mchoozee wa nᵛanᵛa	tomato soup
mchuzi wa pojo	mchoozee wa pojo	green pea soup
mchuzi wa viazi vya mviringo	mchoozee wa veeyazee vya ᵐveereengo	potato soup
mchuzi wa wali	mchoozee wa walee	cream of rice soup
mtori	mtoree	cream of plantain or banana soup
supu ya raizoni	soopoo ya raeezonee	calf's foot soup
supu ya mafupa	soopoo ya mafoopa	cow bone soup
supu ya kuku	soopoo ya kookoo	chicken soup
supu ya njiwa	soopoo ya njeewa	pigeon soup
supu ya papai	soopoo ya papaee	paw-paw soup

Fish and seafood *Samaki wa aina mbali mbali*

Fish and seafood are plentiful and good in the coastal regions. The shellfish such as lobster and crab is particularly recommended.

Inland, you may come across freshwater fish around Lake Victoria and other large lakes.

I'd like some fish.	**Ningetaka samaki.**	neengetaka samakee
What kind of seafood do you have?	**Mna aina gani ya chakula cha baharini?**	mna aeena ganee ya chakoola cha bahareenee
aina ya kaa	aeena ya kaa	crayfish
changu	changoo	white mackerel
chaza	chaza	oysters
dagaa	dagaa	sardines
jodari	jodaree	salmon
kaa	kaa	crab
kamba	kamba	lobster
kamba kamba	kamba kamba	shrimp
kibuwa	keeboowa	mackerel

kolekole	kolekoleh	trevally (a local game fish)
mkizi	mkeezee	cod
mkunga	mkoonga	eel
mkunga wa kukaushwa	mkoonga wa kookaaooshwa	smoked eel
nguru	ngooroo	king fish
nguru wa kukaushwa	ngooroo wa kookaaooshwa	smoked king fish
papa	papa	trout
perege	peregeh	herring
peshi	peshee	perch
samoni	samonee	salmon
samoni wa kukaushwa	samonee wa kookaaooshwa	smoked salmon
sumbururu	soomboorooroo	tunny (tuna)
tasi	tasee	herring
tilapia	teelapeeya	tilapia (a local salt-water fish)

There are many ways of preparing fish:

baked	**aliyepalizwa**	aleeyepaleezwa
barbecued	**aliyechomwa kwa makaa**	aleeyechomwa kwa makaa
fried	**aliyekaangwa**	aleeyekaangwa
deep fried	**aliyekaangwa mafutani**	aleeyekaangwa mafootanee
grilled	**aliyechomwa**	aleeyechomwa
poached	**aliyechemshwa**	aleeyechemshwa
raw	**mbichi**	ᵐbeechee
smoked	**aliyekaushwa**	aleeyekaooshwa
steamed	**aliyepikwa**	aleeyepeekwa
stewed	**aliyetokoswa**	aleeyetokoswa

Your fish may also be prepared with different ingredients:

bia [pombe]	beeyah [pombeh]	beer
mayai	mayaee	eggs
maziwa	mazeewa	milk
siki	seekee	vinegar
unga	oonga	flour

Fish and seafood specialities *Mapishi spesheli ya samaki*

aina ya kaa wa kuchemshwa	aeena ya kaa wa koochemshwa	local dish of crayfish or lobster
kaa wa kuchemshwa	kaa wa koochemshwa	crab dish with local seasoning
kamba wa kukaanga mafutani	kamba wa kookaanga mafootanee	deep-fried prawns
katlesi	katlesee	fish cutlet
kombe	kombeh	shellfish
mchuzi wa chaza	mchoozee wa chaza	oyster sauce in coconut milk
mchuzi wa kamba	mchoozee wa kamba	lobster/crayfish sauce
mkunga wa kukaanga	mkoonga wa kookaanga	deep-fried eel
ngisi wa kukaanga	ngeesee wa kookaanga	fried squid
pweza mkavu	pweza mkavoo	dried octopus
pweza wa kuchoma	pweza wa koochoma	roast octopus
samaki mkavu	samakee mkavoo	dried fish
samaki wa kukaanga	samakee wa kookaanga	fried fish, often served with chips
samaki wa kukausha	samakee wa kookaoosha	fish stewed or baked with spices
tango ya papa	tango ya papa	dried fish with cucumbers and pickles
tilapia wa kukaangwa mafutani	teelapeeya wa kookaa-ngwa mafootanee	deep-fried tilapia

papa mbichi
(papa ᵐbeechee)
sun-dried trout, marinated and served with lemon, raw onions and tomatoes

samaki wa chukuchuku
(samakee wa chookoochookoo)
fish cooked in curry sauce, served with rice

samaki wa kupaka
(samakee wa koopaka)
fish baked in coconut milk with spices. Often served with chapatis or pancakes.

samaki wa nazi
(samakee wa nazee)
coconut fish curry. Made with salmon, tuna or trevally, this creamy curry is a popular dish along the Tanzanian coast, served with boiled or fried rice.

Meat *Nyama*

The inland part of East Africa is known for its cattle raising and it is well worth seeking out a beef steak. You can order pork in major cities but areas with predominantly Moslem population won't offer it due to religious reasons.

Lamb is popular in the northern part of Kenya as well as throughout Uganda and certain parts of Tanzania.

What kind of meat do you have?	**Aina gani ya nyama unayo?**	aeena ganee ya nˠama oonayo
beef	**nyama ya ngombe**	nˠama ya ngombeh
lamb	**nyama ya kondoo**	nˠama ya kondoo
pork	**nyama ya nguruwe**	nˠama ya ngoorooweh
veal	**nyama ya ndama**	nˠama ya ndama
baga ya bifu	baga ya beefoo	beef burger
baga ya jibini	baga ya jeebeenee	cheese burger
kondoo	kondoo	mutton
mafigo	mafeego	kidneys
mbuzi	ᵐboozee	goat
maini	maeenee	liver
nyama ya kuponda	nˠama ya kooponda	minced meat
nyama ya nguruwe iliyohifadhiwa	nˠama ya ngoorooweh eeleeyoheefaᵭeewa	bacon
paja la nguruwe	paja la ngoorooweh	(smoked) ham
soseji	sosejee	sausage
steki	stekee	steak
steki ya mbuzi	stekee ya ᵐboozee	goat steak
steki ya ngombe	stekee ya ngombeh	beef steak
ubongo	oobongo	brains
ulimi	ooleemee	tongue

baked	**iliyookwa**	eeleeyookwa
barbecued	**iliyochomwa kwa makaa**	eeleeyochomwa kwa makaa
boiled	**iliyochemshwa**	eeleeyochemshwa
braised	**iliyopashwa**	eeleeyopashwa
fried	**iliyokaangwa**	eeleeyokaangwa
grilled	**iliyochomwa**	eeleeyochomwa
roast	**iliyokaushwa**	eeleeyokaooshwa
stewed	**mchuzi**	mchoozee
stuffed	**iliyojazwa**	eeleeyojazwa
underdone (rare)	**iliyoiva kidogo**	eeleeyoeeva keedogo
medium	**ya kuiva kiasi**	ya kooeeva keeyasee
well-done	**iliyoiva sawa sawa**	eeleeyoeeva sawa sawa

East African meat dishes *Vyakula vya nyama vya Afrika mashariki*

kababu	kababoo	meatballs
kima iliyokaangwa	keema eeleeyo-kaangwa	fried minced meat
matumbo	matoombo	tripe with seasonings
mchuzi wa kima	mchoozee wa keema	curried minced meat
mchuzi wa kondoo	mchoozee wa kondoo	lamb curry
mshikaki wa maini	msheekakee wa maeenee	liver kebabs
ndama aliyechomwa	ndama aleeyechomwa	roast veal
ngombe aliyechomwa	ngombeh aleeyechomwa	roast beef
nyama ya kuponda	nʸama ya kooponda	minced meat
soseji na mkate wa tanuri	sosejee na mkateh wa tanooree	sausage wrapped in a pancake

biriani
(beereeanee)
fried meat in a thick sauce of spices, tomatoes and yoghurt, served on a bed of saffron rice

katlesi ya ngombe
(katlesee ya ngombeh)
beef fillet covered with hashed brown potatoes

mchicha na nyama
(mcheecha na nʸama)
beef and spinach, flavoured with ginger and sweet peppers and served with *ugali*

msanif
(msaneef)
small batter pancakes filled with spicy minced meat

mtabak
(mtabak)
pie filled with spicy meat, onions and slices of egg

ndizi ya na nyamo
(ndeezee ya na nʸamo)
a filling stew of diced beef, tomatoes, coconut milk and plantain cubes

pilau
(peelaoo)
fried rice mixed with meat and different spices; cummin, cardamom, cinnamon, garlic, onions and fresh ginger

sukuma wiki
(sookooma weekee)
a stew of leftover meat, onions, sweet peppers and spinach, served with *ugali*, rice or plantain. A popular traditional dish, also available in most Kenyan restaurants.

viazi vya nyama
(veeazee vya nʸama)
sweet potatoes cooked in coconut milk and served with chunks of beef

Game and poultry *Nyama na kuku*

Chicken is very often on the menu throughout the region, though its quality can vary. A wide variety of game is also eaten. However, the more exotic dishes may not be available in the westernized restaurants on the coast and in major cities. For a full list of game, see page 86.

I'd like some game/ fowl.	**Ninataka nyama ya mwituni/kanga.**	neenataka n'ama ya mwee mweetoonee/kanga
baga ya kuku	**baga ya kook**oo	chicken burger
bata	**bata**	duck
bata mchanga	**bata mchanga**	duckling
bata mzinga	**bata mzeenga**	goose
bata mzinga wa kukausha	**bata mzeenga wa kookaoosha**	roast duck
dikidiki	**deekeedeekee**	dikdiki (a kind of antelope)
kanga	**kanga**	guinea fowl
kongoni	**kongonee**	hartebeest (a kind of antelope)
kuku	**kook**oo	chicken
kuru	**koor**oo	waterbuck (a kind of antelope)
maini ya kuku	**maeenee ya kook**oo	chicken liver
mbuni	**ᵐboonee**	pheasant
mguu wa paa	**mgoo wa paa**	leg of venison
ndege	**ndeg**eh	bird
ndege wa pwani	**ndeg**eh wa **pwan**ee	seagull
nguruwe dume	**ngooroow**eh **doom**eh	wild boar
njiwa	**njee**wa	pigeon
nyati	**n'at**ee	buffalo
paa	**paa**	venison
pavu la paa	**pavoo la paa**	venison tenderloin
pofu	**pof**oo	antelope
pugi	**poog**ee	a kind of pigeon
sungura wa mjini	**soongoor**a wa **mjee**nee	rabbit
sungura wa pori	**soongoor**a wa **por**ee	hare
swala	**swal**a	impala (a kind of antelope)
tandala mkubwa	**tandala mkoo**bwa	kudu (a kind of antelope)

Game and fowl dishes *Vyakula vya nyama na kuku*

Due to Indian influence, East Africa is renowned for its curry specialities, such as chicken curry (*mchuzi wa kuku*), which is normally prepared with carrots, onions and tomatoes. Genuine curry comprises no less than seventy different spices.

bata wa kukaanga	bata wa kookaanga	fried duck
bata wa kukausha	bata wa kookaoosha	roast duck
bata mzinga wa kukausha	bata mzeenga wa kookaoosha	roast goose
biriani ya kuku	beereeyanee ya kookoo	delicately spiced chicken with rice
kuku aliyejazwa	kookoo aleeyejazwa	baked chicken stuffed with rice
kuku mchanga	kookoo mchanga	spring chicken
kuku na mayai yake	kookoo na mayaee yakeh	roast chicken stuffed with eggs
kuku wa kuchemsha	kookoo wa koochemsha	boiled chicken
kuku wa kuchoma	kookoo wa koochoma	roast chicken
kuku wa kukaanga	kookoo wa kookaanga	fried chicken
kuku wa kupaka	kookoo wa koopaka	chicken cooked in spicy coconut milk
mchuzi wa kuku	mchoozee wa kookoo	chicken curry
njiwa aliyekaangwa	njeewa aleeye kaangwa	fried pigeon
njiwa aliyekaushwa	njeewa aleeyekaooshwa	roast chicken
paa aliyekaangwa	paa aleeyekaangwa	fried venison steaks
pavu la paa	pavoo la paa	venison tenderloin
pilau ya kuku	peelaoo ya kookoo	spicy fried rice with chicken

katlesi ya kuku (katlesee ya kookoo)	breast of chicken covered with hashed brown potatoes
kuku aliyepakwa (kookoo aleeyepakwa)	roast chicken with a sauce of coconut milk, often served with pancakes

Vegetables *Mboga*

Maize (corn) is widely grown in East Africa and forms the basis of *ugali*, a stiff porridge or semolina and a cheap staple part of the diet. It's prepared in such a way that the cook is able to gather a ball of it in his hand, make a hole inside and serve it with a broth or a sauce; sometimes, it's also sliced like cake.

Another prevalent vegetable is *mchicha*, similar to spinach and often used in soups, casseroles, salads and pies or served with *ugali*.

aina ya mzizi	aeena ya mzeezee	turnips
bamiya	bameeya	okra
biringani	beereenganee	aubergine (eggplant)
bitiruti	beeteerootee	beetroot
dengu	dengoo	peas
dodoki	dodokee	pumpkin
hadesi	hadesee	lentils
kabeji	kabejee	cabbage
karoti	karotee	carrots
kaulifulawa	kaooleefoolawa	cauliflower
kiukamba ya tango	keeookamba ya tango	gherkins
liki	leekee	leeks
mahindi	maheendee	corn
mhogo	mhogo	cassava
mtama	mtama	millet
mumunye	moomoonⁿeh	vegetable marrow
nyanya za mshumaa	nyanya za mshumaa	green tomatoes
mboga	ᵐboga	spinach
majimbi	majeembee	sweet potatoes (yams)
nyanya	nⁿanⁿa	tomatoes
tango	tango	cucumber
tungule	toongoole	cherry tomatoes
seleri	seleree	celery
uyoga	ooyoga	mushrooms
viazi vitamu	veeyazee veetamoo	sweet potatoes (yams)
viazi vya kiingereza	veeyazee vya kee-eengereza	potatoes
viazi vyekundu	veeyazee vyekoondoo	radishes
vitunguu	veetoongoo-oo	onions
wali	walee	rice
wanga	wanga	arrowroot

Vegetable dishes *Vyakula vya mboga*

Since meat is rather expensive for the average East African, vegetable dishes form the main constituent of the local diet. This means that there is a wide choice available, particularly in Indian restaurants and small local eating places.

bamiya	bameeya	okra boiled with spices
chipsi za mhogo	cheepsee za mhogo	cassava chips
dodoki la sukari	dodokee la sookaree	pumpkin cooked in coconut milk
kachori ya samaki [nyama]	kachoree ya samakee [n'ama]	cassava dumplings with fish or meat
makopa ya tangawizi	makopa ya tangaweezee	sun-dried cassava cooked with ginger
matoke na achari	matokeh na acharee	cooked green bananas with pickles
matoke na matumbo ya mbuzi	matokeh na matoombo ya mboozee	green bananas cooked with lamb tripe
mbaazi	mbaazi	peas cooked in coconut milk
mchicha wa maji	mcheecha wa majee	boiled spinach
mhogo wa kuchoma na nanaa	mhogo wa koochoma na nanaa	fried cassava with mint
mkono wa tembo	mkono wa tembo	ripe plantain cooked in coconut milk
mseto na samaki	mseto na samakee	mixed rice and lentils with fish
sambusa ya vitunguu	samboosa ya veetoongoo-oo	onion samosas (pastries)
viazi vya kuchemshwa kwa nyanya na nanaa	veeyazee vya koochemshwa kwa n'an'ya na nanaa	boiled potatoes with tomatoes and mint
vitumbua	veetoombooa	fritters made from ground rice

Keep a look out for these specialities:

iriyo (eereeyo)	potato, cabbage and beans mashed together, sometimes flavoured with herbs and spices; can be stuffed into vegetables, served by itself or as an addition to fish or meat dishes

kisamvu (keesamvoo)		pounded cassava leaves cooked in coconut milk with onions and spices
maharagwe (maharagweh)		kidney beans cooked with onions and tomatoes
mboga ya kisamvu [mayugwa] (ᵐboga ya keesamvu [mayoogwa])		cassava leaves mixed with tomatoes and cooked in yoghurt
mayugwa (mayoogwa)		yam leaves cooked in coconut milk with onions and spices
mchicha (mchicha)		spinach cooked with onions and tomatoes
mchicha wa nazi (mcheecha wa nazee)		spinach cooked in coconut milk and fried with onions, tomatoes and curry powder
mtori (mtoree)		green bananas or plantains steamed with a touch of oil, cooked with beef
mtoriro (mtoreero)		sweet potato leaves cooked with beans and sardines
sukuma wiki (sookooma weekee)		a kind of cabbage boiled with tripe and spices
ugali [sima] na mtoriro (oogalee [seema] na mtoreero)		cassava and maize meal with yam (sweet potato) leaves

Sauces *Mchuzi*

East African sauces (*mchuzi*) are similar to curries or soups, rather than what we might expect.

mchuzi wa ngombe	mchoozee wa ngombeh	beef sauce
mchuzi wa kuku	mchoozee wa kookoo	chicken sauce
mchuzi wa kamba	mchoozee wa kamba	lobster sauce

Pasta *Pasta*

makaronya	makaronᵞa	macaroni
mkate wa tambi	mkateh wa tambee	vermicelli cake
tambi	tambee	vermicelli
tambi za kukaanga	tambee za kookaanga	fried vermicelli with sultanas
tambi za mchele	tambee za mcheleh	rice flour vermicelli
tambi za nazi	tambee za nazee	vermicelli in coconut milk with cardamon seeds

Herbs and spices *Viungo*

East Africa is famous for its spices – Zanzibar is the largest producer of cloves in the world. Different kinds of peppers and curry spices are also grown and used widely.

With cold plates, but sometimes also with other dishes, a selection of pickled vegetables and spices are provided – to which you help yourself. However, before heaping them joyfully onto your plate you'd better take just a tiny sample of each first, to make sure they aren't too hot for you ... and don't overestimate your possibilities.

Mango, lemon, paprika with lemon slices in vinegar, Indian spices (curry, Cayenne pepper, cardimom, dried pepper), cloves, are all known under the generic name of *viungo*.

achari	acharee	mixed pickles
chatne ya embe	chatneh ya embeh	grated coconut and sour-mango chutney
chatne ya karoti na ndimu	chatneh ya karotee na ndeemoo	carrot and lemon chutney
haradali	haradalee	strong local mustard
karafuu	karafoo-oo	cloves
mastadi	mastardee	mustard
mchuzi	mchoozee	curry
pilipili	peeleepeelee	pepper
pilipili isiyokali	peeleepeelee eeseeyokalee	black
pilipili kali	peeleepeelee kalee	chilli
siki	seekee	vinegar
zafarani	zafaranee	saffron

Fruit and nuts *Matunda na njugu mbali mbali*

Fresh fruit is found in abundance throughout East Africa. Take the opportunity to try some of the more exotic varieties.

In Tanzania, fruit is often used to add an exotic taste to dishes. Plantains, which resemble large bananas, are particularly common in cooking but are best not eaten raw.

Do you have any fresh fruit?	**Unayo matunda freshi?**	oonayo matoonda freshee
I'd like very ripe ones.	**Nataka yaliyoiva sana.**	nataka yaleeyoeeva sana
Not too ripe, please.	**Yasiyoiva sana, tafadhali.**	yaseeyoeeva sana tafaðalee
I'd like some sugar, please.	**Nataka sukari pamoja na tunda.**	nataka sookaree pamoja na toonda

aprikoti	apreekotee	apricots
balungi	baloongee	grapefruit
chenza	chenza	tangerine
chungwa	choongwa	orange
doriani	doreeyanee	dorian fruit
embe	embeh	mango
embe za boribo	embeh za boreebo	large mango
embe za kufyonza	embeh za koofyonza	small sweet mango
kangaja	kangaja	clementine
komamanga	komamanga	pomegranate
korosho	korosho	cashews
kunazi	koonazee	jujube fruit
lozi	lozi	almonds
mapera	mapera	guavas
matufaha	matoofaha	Swahili apples
muwa	moowa	sugar cane
nanasi	nanasee	pineapple
nazi	nazee	coconut
ndimu	ndeemoo	lemon
ndimu tamu	ndeemoo tamoo	sweet lemon
njugu karanga	njoogoo karanga	groundnuts
ndizi	ndeezee	banana
njugu nyasa	njoogoo n'asa	peanuts
peya	peya	avocado
strawberi	strawberee	strawberries

tende	tendeh	dates
tikiti	teekeetee	watermelon
tini	teenee	figs
zabibu mbichi	zabeeboo ᵐbeechee	grapes
zabibu nyekundu	zabeeboo nʸekoondoo	sultanas
zambarau	zambaraoo	velvet plums

These are some of the more exotic fruits you may encounter:

dafu
(dafoo)
unripe coconut; often sold in streets on the coast, its sweet juice is refreshing in the hot climate and the thin fleshy part can be eaten.

fenesi
(fenesee)
jack-fruit (a kind of large melon). Inside the texture is chewy and pleasantly astringent in small doses.

mzuzu
(mzoozoo)
plantain; a kind of green-skinned banana. Used green and cooked as a vegetable, their taste resembles that of mashed potatoes.

papai
(papaee)
paw paw (papaya) – fairly well known and readily available in the West; large yellow-skinned fruit tasting a little like mango but is more solid.

satafeli
(satafelee)
custard apple; contains a tangy, soft interior under a warty hide. They are ripe when they give slightly under the pressure of your thumb.

shelisheli
(sheleeshelee)
bread-fruit; usually eaten baked or roasted, it has a texture like bread, as the name suggests.

shokishoki
(shokeeshokee)
rambutan; a small fruit with red chunky skin; eat the flesh inside and throw away the pit; juicy and sweet like a lychee.

stafeli
(stafelee)
mango-shaped fruit with a hard skin; it is sweet with plenty of seeds inside.

ubuyu
(oobooyoo)
baobab fruit; gourd-like with an edible pulp called monkey bread.

Desserts—Pastries *Vitamu tamu*

In addition to Western desserts served in hotel restaurants, you may be tempted by the local specialities. Some Asian restaurants also serve delicious desserts.

I'd like a dessert, please.	**Tafadhali ninge-penda chakula cha mwisho.**	tafaðalee neengependa chakoola cha **mwee**sho
What do you recommend?	**Unapendekeza kitu gani?**	oonapendeke**za keetoo ganee**
Something light, please.	**Kitu chepesi tafad-hali.**	**keetoo** chepesee tafaðalee
Just a small portion.	**Kiasi kidogo tu.**	keeyasee keedogo too
Nothing more, thanks.	**Imetosha, asante.**	eemetosha asanteh

aiskrimu ya embe	aee**skree**moo ya embeh	mango ice cream
aiskrimu ya vanila	aee**skree**moo ya vaneela	vanilla ice cream
barafu ya kirimu	barafoo ya kee**ree**moo	ice-cream
biskuti	bees**koo**tee	biscuits
farne	farneh	ground rice with milk
keki	kekee	cakes
keki ya tunda	kekee ya **toon**da	apple pie
miksi	**meek**see	ice cream with fruit salad
mkate wa kumimina [sinia]	mkateh wa koomee**mee**na [see**nee**ya]	rice cake
mkate wa mayai	mkateh wa ma**yaee**	sponge cake
ndizi za kukaanga	**ndee**zee za kookaanga	fried plantains
pudini	**poo**deenee	cream caramel
pudini ya mchele	**poo**deenee ya mcheleh	rice pudding, served with either sugar or jam
tunda ndani ya asali	**toon**da ndanee ya **asa**lee	fruit in syrup
tunda ndani ya asali na speriti	**toon**da ndanee ya **asa**lee na spe**ree**tee	fruit in syrup laced with liquor
vileja	vee**le**ja	rice biscuits
visheti	vee**she**tee	sugar-coated pastry

chapati ya ndizi tamu   fritters made from hot, mashed bananas;
(cha**pa**tee ya **ndee**zee   common throughout Africa
tamoo)

faluda   a kind of jelly, made of milk or water, jelly
(fa**loo**da)   leaves and cardamom or rose essence

haluwa   sweetmeat, similar to Turkish delight, gener-
(ha**loo**wa)   ally eaten with coffee

kaimati   a kind of doughnut rolled in small balls and
(ka**ee**matee)   soaked in syrup

kashata   swahili fudge made of nuts, almonds or
(ka**sha**ta)   grated coconut

kitumbua   oily cakes made of rice flour and palm sap
(keetoom**boo**wa)

ndizi tamu za kupika   sweet bananas cooked in coconut milk; espe-
(**ndee**zee **ta**moo za   cially good are the large variety, called *mkono*
koo**pee**ka)   *wa tembo* (elephant's leg)

Drinks *Vinywaji*

The locals tend to drink beer or spirits with their meals, rather
than wine, although tourist hotels obviously cater for Western
tastes.

Beer *Biya*

East African beer is excellent and inexpensive. The local
brands include *Tusker*, *Premium*, *White Cap* and *Safari*. *Tusker*
lager was so named by a brewery founder back in the 1920s in
memory of his brother, who was killed by a stampeding
elephant.

There are also some local brews (*pombe*), made from less
conventional ingredients. In particular, look out for *moshi*,
made of millet, maize or banana. These potent tipples can be
found in rural villages, rather than cities.

I'd like a (cold) beer.	**Tafadhali nataka bia [pombe] (baridi).**	tafaḏalee nataka **bee**ya [**pom**beh] (ba**ree**dee)
local beer	**bia [pombe] ya kienyeji**	**bee**ya [**pom**beh] ya kee-en^yejee
imported beer	**bia [pombe] ya nje**	**bee**ya [**pom**beh] ya njeh
non-alcoholic beer	**bia isiyo ya kulevya**	**bee**ya ee**see**yo ya koo**lev**ya
palm-tree beer	**bia ya mnazi**	**bee**ya ya m**na**zee

> **KARIBU, TUNYWE**
> CHEERS

Wine *Mvinyo/Divai*

Many tourist restaurants do serve imported wine, but this very often expensive, and not always kept under the best conditions. There are some locally produced wines, particularly from the area around Dodoma, which you might like to try.

For those of a more adventurous nature, why not try the local wines made with papaya, plantain, pineapple or passion fruit, or even the very potent palm wine.

I would like a bottle of white/red wine.	**Nataka chupa ya divai nyeupe/nye-kundu.**	nataka **choo**pa ya dee**va**ee n^ye**oo**peh/n^ye**koon**doo
How much is a bottle of...?	**Kima [Kiasi] gani chupa ya...?**	**kee**ma [**kee**yasi] **ga**nee **choo**pa ya
Please bring me another...	**Tafadhali niletee... zaidi.**	tafaḏalee neelete-eh... za**yee**dee
glass/carafe/bottle	**bilauri/jagi/chupa**	beela**oo**ree/**ja**gee/**choo**pa
Where does this wine come from?	**Divai hii imetoka wapi?**	dee**va**ee hee-ee eeme**to**ka **wa**pee
red/white wine	**mvinyo [divai] nyeupe/nye-kundu**	^m**vee**n^yo [dee**va**ee] n^ye**oo**peh/n^ye**koon**doo

Local alcoholic beverages *Ulevi*

There are a few interesting national specialities, including *Kenya Cane* (a kind of rum), *Tanzanian Konyagi* (a kind of brandy) and *Waragi*, a spirit from Uganda. But beware – they can be very strong!

In some banana-growing areas you will also find a kind of banana brandy. For drinking after dinner, you could also try a local coffee liqueur called *Kenya Gold*.

The consumption of certain drinks, such as *chang'aa* (usually made from the fruit of the loofah plant), *kanga* (distilled from local grain and/or vegetables) and *mutukuru* (distilled from maize or wheat), is prohibited in Kenya because of their high alcoholic content.

Are there any local specialities?	**Je, kipo kinywaji cha hapa kwenu?**	jeh **kee**po keen^y**wa**jee cha hapa kwe**noo**
Please bring me a bottle of palm-tree toddy.	**Tafadhali niletee chupa ya tembo.**	tafa∂a**lee** neele**te**-eh **choo**pa ya **te**mbo
single (shot)	**pegi moja**	pe**gee mo**ja
double (shot)	**pegi mbili**	pe**gee** ᵐ**bee**lee
glass	**bilauri**	beela**oo**ree
bottle	**chupa**	**choo**pa
Africoco	afree**co**coa	liqueur from Tanzania
buzaa (kanga)	**boo**za-a (kanga)	Nubian gin
Kenya Cane	ken^ya cayn	white rum
waragi	wara**gee**	Ugandan brandy

chibuku (chee**boo**koo)	a drink made from millet (Tanzania)
konyagi (kon^ya**gee**)	a kind of brandy made from a mixture of fruit (Tanzania)
tembo (**te**mbo)	literally "elephant": palm-tree toddy, often very hot, due to the spices which are added to it
tende (**ten**deh)	a strong, fermented drink (contents vary from region to region)

Non-alcoholic drinks *Vinywaji*

Try *sharubati* (milk-coloured sherbet with herbs) or *maziwa ya lozi* (fresh milk with almonds).

fizzy drink (soda)	**soda**	**so**da
lemonade	**soda ya ndimu**	**so**da ya **ndee**moo
orangeade	**soda ya machungwa**	**so**da ya ma**choo**ngwa
fruit juice	**maji ya matunda [jus]**	ma**jee** ya ma**too**nda [joos]
grapefruit juice	**maji ya mabalungi**	ma**jee** ya maba**loo**ngee
iced tea	**chai baridi**	**chaee** ba**ree**dee
lemon juice	**maji ya ndimu**	ma**jee** ya **ndee**moo
mango juice	**maji ya maembe**	ma**jee** ya ma**embeh**
milk	**maziwa**	ma**zee**wa
orange juice	**maji ya machungwa**	ma**jee** ya ma**choo**ngwa
tomato juice	**maji ya nyanya**	ma**jee** ya nʸanʸa
tonic water	**maji ya tonik**	ma**jee** ya **to**neek
maji ya mapeya	ma**jee** ya ma**pe**ya	avocado juice
maji ya mapera	ma**jee** ya ma**pe**ra	guava juice
maji ya ndimu	ma**jee** ya **ndee**moo	lime juice
maji ya ukwaju	ma**jee** ya oo**kwa**joo	tamarind juice
togwa	**to**gwa	cold millet drink
uji wa kunde	**oo**jee wa **koo**ndeh	porridge made from *aduki* beans
uji wa ngano	**oo**jee wa **nga**no	porridge made from cracked wheat
uji wa tapo	**oo**jee wa **ta**po	porridge made from *tapo* nuts

Hot beverages *Vinywaji vimoto*

Tea is the national beverage, drunk at breakfast and as refreshment throughout the day: a brew of milk, hot water, tea leaves and lots of sugar.

Kenya has a well-developed coffee industry and its beans are exported all over the world. Amongst coastal people in both Kenya and Tanzania, the Arab influence has made coffee popular. Up country, though, coffee drinking is not common.

(hot) chocolate	**chakleti**	chakletee
coffee	**kahawa**	kahawa
with cream	**kahawa na maziwa mtindi**	kahawa na mazeewa mteendee
espresso coffee	**kahawa ya espresso**	kahawa ya espresso
tea	**chai**	chaee
with milk/lemon	**na maziwa/ ndimu**	na mazeewa/ndeemoo
without milk	**chai kavu**	chaee kavoo

Or you may come across:

| **tangawizi** | tangaweezee | hot ginger drink |

Complaints *Nung'uniko*

That's not what I ordered.	**Hicho sicho nili- choagiza.**	heecho seecho neeleechowageeza
I asked for...	**Niliomba nipa- tiwe...**	neeleeomba neepateeweh
May I change this?	**Naweza kubadi- lisha hii?**	naweza koobadeeleesha hee-ee
The meat is...	**Hyama hii...**	hyama hee-ee
overdone	**imepikwa sana**	eemepeekwa sana
underdone	**imepikwa kidogo**	eemepeekwa keedogo
too rare	**haijapikwa sana**	haeejapeekwa sana
too tough	**ngumu sana**	ngoomoo sana
This is too... bitter/salty/sweet	**Hii ni... sana. kakasi/chungu/ tamu mno**	hee-ee nee... sana kakasee/choongoo/tamoo mno
The food is cold.	**Chakula kimepoa.**	chakoola keemepowa
This isn't fresh.	**Hii si safi.**	hee-ee see safee
What's taking you so long?	**Nini kinachoku- weka muda wote huo?**	neenee keenachokooweka mooda woteh hoo-oo
Have you forgotten our drinks?	**Vipo wapi vinywaji vyetu?**	veepo wapee veenʸwajee vyetoo
This isn't clean.	**Hii si safi.**	hee-ee see safee
Would you ask the head waiter to come over?	**Unaweza kumwita msimamizi wa utumishi aje hapa?**	oonaweza koomweeta mseemameezee wa ootoomeeshee ajeh hapa

The bill (check) *Hesabu*

I'd like to pay.	**Nataka kulipa.**	nataka kooleepa
May I please have the bill (check)?	**Unaweza kunipa jumla ya hesabu?**	oonaweza kooneepa joomla ya hesaboo
We'd like to pay separately.	**Fanya hesabu kila mtu pekee.**	fanᵞa hesaboo keela mtoo peke-eh
I think there's a mistake in this bill.	**Nafikiri umefanya makosa katika hesabu hii.**	nafeekeeree oomefanᵞa makosa kateeka hesaboo hee-ee
What's this amount for?	**Jumla hii ni ya kitu gani?**	joomla hee-ee nee ya keetoo ganee
Is service included?	**Je, ni pamoja na malipo ya utumishi?**	jeh nee pamoja na maleepo ya ootoomeeshee
Is the cover charge included?	**Pamoja na malipo ya mwanzo?**	pamoja na maleepo ya mwanzo
Is everything included?	**Hiyo ni jumla vyote?**	heeyo nee joomla vyoteh
Do you accept traveller's cheques?	**Utakubali malipo kwa hawala ya safari?**	ootakoobalee maleepo kwa hawala ya safaree
Do you accept credit cards?	**Unapokea kadi za benki?**	oonapokea kadee za benkee
Thank you, this is for you.	**Asante, na hii kwaajili yako.**	asanteh na hee-ee kwaajeelee yako
Keep the change.	**Chukua hizo zilobakia.**	chookoowa heezo zeelobakeeya
That was delicious.	**Chakula hicho kilikua kizuri sana.**	chakoola heecho keeleekooa keezooree sana
We enjoyed it, thank you.	**Tumefurahi, asante.**	toomefoorahee asanteh

> **PAMOJA NA UTUMISHI**
> SERVICE INCLUDED

TIPPING, see inside back-cover

Snacks—Picnic *Vitafunio—Mandari*

| I'll have one of those, please. | **Tafadhali nipe ile moja.** | tafaðalee neepeh eeleh moja |
| to the left/right | **kushoto/kulia** | kooshoto/kooleeya |

Here's a basic list of food and drink that might come in useful when shopping for a picnic. For traditional East African snacks, found at snack bars throughout the region, see page 41.

I'd like a/an/some...	**Nipe...**	neepeh
biscuits (Br.)	**biskuti**	beeskootee
beer	**bia**	beea
bread	**mkate**	mkateh
brown bread	**mkate wa ngano nzima**	mkateh wa ngano nzeema
butter	**siagi**	seeagee
candy	**peremende**	peremendeh
canned beef	**nyama ya ng'ombe ya mkebeni**	n'ama ya ng'ombe ya mkebenee
cheese	**jibini**	jeebeenee
chocolate bar	**kipande cha chakleti**	keepandeh cha chakletee
cookies	**biskuti**	beeskootee
ice-cream	**sikirimu**	seekeereemoo
milk	**maziwa**	mazeewa
rolls	**andazi**	andazee
salt	**chumvi**	chumvee
soft drink (soda)	**soda**	soda
sugar	**sukari**	sookaree
toast	**tosti**	tostee

---

1 kilogram or kilo (kg.) = 1000 grams (g.)

| 100 g. = 3.5 oz. | ½ kg. = 1.1 lb. |
| 200 g. = 7.0 oz. | 1 kg. = 2.2 lb. |

1 oz. = 28.35 g.

1 lb. = 453.60 g.

---

1 litre (l.) = 0.88 imp. quarts = 1.06 U.S. quarts

| 1 imp. quart = 1.14 l. | 1 U.S. quart = 0.95 l. |
| 1 imp. gallon = 4.55 l. | 1 U.S. gallon = 3.8 l. |

Travelling around

There are many package tours to East Africa nowadays, some of which include full safari itineraries, whereas others are based mainly on the coast. For the independent traveller in addition to the regular scheduled flights it is sometimes possible to buy flight-only tickets on holiday charter flights.

Buses are the main form of public transport across most of the region, but some of the main cities are linked by railways or internal flights.

Plane *Ndege*

Internal air services operate on a fairly regular basis across East Africa. Kenya boasts the busiest domestic flight network in Africa, with over 200 scheduled flights a week arriving from 15 destinations.

Is there a flight to Mombasa?	**Kuna [Iko] ndege ya kwenda Mombasa?**	koona [eeko] ndegeh ya kwenda mombasa
Is it a direct flight?	**Iko [Kuna] ndege ya moja kwa moja?**	eeko [koona] ndegeh ya moja kwa moja
When's the next flight to Zanzibar?	**Saa ngapi [Wakati gani] iko ndege nyengine ya kwenda Zanzibar?**	saa ngapee [wakatee ganee] eeko ndegeh n^yengeeneh ya kwenda zanzeebar
Is there a connection to Entebbe?	**Iko [Kuna] ndege inayoelekea Entebe?**	eeko [koona] ndegeh eenayoelekea entebeh
I'd like to book a ticket to Kampala.	**Nataka [Ningependa] kuekesha tikti ya kwenda Kampala?**	nataka [neengependa] kooekesha teektee ya kwenda kampala
single (one-way)	**kwenda tu**	kwenda too
return (round trip)	**kwenda na kurudi**	kwenda na kooroodee
business class	**daraja ya pili**	daraja ya peelee
aisle seat	**kiti cha ujiani**	keetee cha oojeeyanee
window seat	**kiti cha dirishani**	keetee cha deereeshanee
What time do we take off?	**Kuruka saa ngapi? [Tutaruka saa ngapi?]**	koorooka saa ngapee [tootarooka saa ngapee]

What time should I check in?	**Saa ngapi nifike uwanja wa ndege? [Saa ngapi kufika kiwanjani?]**	saa **nga**pee neefeekeh oowanja wa **nde**geh [saa **nga**pee koo**fee**ka keewanjanee]
Is there a bus to the airport?	**Liko basi la [Kuna matatu/daladala] kwenda uwanja wa ndege?**	**lee**ko ba**see** la [**koo**na matatoo/daladala] kwenda oowanja wa ndegeh
What's the flight number?	**Nambari ya flaiti ni ngapi? [Flaiti nambari ngapi?]**	nambaree ya fla**ee**tee nee **nga**pee [fla**ee**tee nambaree **nga**pee]
What time do we arrive?	**Saa ngapi tutafika [kufika]?**	saa **nga**pee tootafeeka [koo**fee**ka]
I'd like to... my reservation.	**Nataka ku... safari yangu.**	nataka koo... safaree yangoo
cancel	**kukensel [kuvunja]**	kookensel [koo**voo**nja]
change	**kubadilisha**	koobadee**lee**sha
confirm	**kuhakikisha [kuthibitisha]**	koohakee**kee**sha [kootheebee**tee**sha]

| **KUWASILI [KUFIKA]**
ARRIVAL | **KUONDOKA**
DEPARTURE |

Train *Treni*

There are two main railway lines in the region. One links Mombasa on the coast with the inland cities of Nairobi, Kampala and Kasese. The other runs inland across Tanzania, from Dar es Salaam to Dodoma, Tabora and Kigoma.

There is usually a choice of first, second and third class. In Kenya, modern first- and second-class rolling stock provide comfortable accommodation convertible for night travel.

The first class service is good and reasonably priced. The trains are normally well provided with dining cars and sleeping cars, but thefts on trains are common, so keep an eye on your luggage. Time-tables, though, are of variable reliability.

Comparatively low rail fares ensure the popularity of certain routes, which require you to pre-book at least one week in advance by calling the ticket office.

To the railway station *Kwenda stesheni ya reli [treni]*

Where's the railway station?	**Iko wapi stesheni ya reli [treni]?**	eeko wapee steshenee ya relee [trenee]
Taxi!	**Teksi!**	teksee
Take me to the…	**Tafadhali nipe-leke…**	tafaðalee neepelekeh
main railway station	**kituo kikuu cha reli [steshini kuu ya reli]**	keetoo-o keekoo-oo cha relee [stesheenee koo-oo ya relee]
What's the fare?	**nauli ni kiasi gani?**	naoolee nee keeyasee ganee

KUINGIA	ENTRANCE
KUTOKA	EXIT
MAJUKWA/MAPLETFOM	TO THE PLATFORMS
MAELEZO	INFORMATION

Where's the…? *Iko wapi…?*

Where is/are (the)…?	**Iko wapi…? Ziko wapi…?**	eeko wapee/zeeko wapee
bar	**baa**	baa
booking office	**ofisi ya kuekesha tikti**	ofeesee ya kooekesha teektee
currency exchange office	**ofisi ya kubadilisha [kuvunja] pesa**	ofeesee ya koobadeeleesha [koovoonja] pesa
left-luggage office (baggage check)	**ofisi ya kuweka mizigo**	ofeesee ya kooweka meezeego
lost property (lost and found) office	**ofisi ya mizigo iliyopotea [ofisi ya mizigo iliyoo-nekana]**	ofeesee ya meezeego eeleeyopotea [ofeesee ya meezeego eeleeyoonekana]
luggage lockers	**makabati ya kuweka mizigo**	makabatee ya kooweka meezeego
newsstand	**mahali pa kununua magazeti**	mahalee pa koonoonoowa magazetee
platform 7	**jukwaa [pletfom] 7**	jookwaa [pletfom] saba

TAXI see page 21

reservations office	**ofisi ya kuekesha tikiti za safari**	ofeesee ya kooekesha teekeetee za safaree
restaurant	**mkahawa**	mkahawa
snack bar	**mahali wanauza vitafunio [vyakula vidogo vidogo]**	mahalee wanaooza veetafoonee-o [vyakoola veedogo veedogo]
ticket office	**ofisi ya tikiti**	ofeesee ya teektee
waiting room	**chumba cha kungojea [chumba cha kusubiri]**	choomba cha koongojea [choomba cha koosoobeeree]
Where are the toilets?	**Choo kiko wapi?/ Msalani ni wapi?**	choo keeko wapee/ msalanee nee wapee

Inquiries *Uliza hapa [Maulizo]*

When is the... train to Kasese?	**Saa ngapi [Wakati gani]... treni ya kasese?**	saa ngapee [wakatee ganee]... trenee ya kaseseh
first/last/next	**ya kwanza/ya mwisho/nyengine**	ya kwanza/ya mweesho/ n^{y}engeeneh
What time does the train to Nairobi leave?	**Wakati gani huondoka [Saa ngapi inaondoka] treni ya Nairobi?**	wakatee ganee hooondoka [saa ngapee eenaondoka] trenee ya naeerobee
What's the fare to Dar es Salaam?	**Nauli ya Daresalam ni shilingi ngapi? [Kiasi gani nauli ya Dar?]**	naoolee ya daresalam nee sheeleengee ngapee [keeyasee ganee naoolee ya dar]
Is it a through train?	**Treni hii inakwenda moja kwa moja?**	trenee hee-ee eenakwenda moja kwa moja
Is there a connection to...?	**Hubadilishi mahali ...?**	hoobadeeleeshee mahalee
Do I have to change trains?	**Lazima nibadilishe treni?**	lazeema neebadeeleesheh trenee
Is there enough time to change?	**Kuna wakati wa [saa ya] kutosha kubadilisha treni?**	koona wakatee wa [saa ya] kootosha koobadeeleesha trenee
Is the train running on time?	**Treni inakwenda kwa wakati? [Treni inachelewa?]**	trenee eenakwenda kwa wakatee [trenee eenachelewa]
What time does the train arrive in Kigoma?	**Saa ngapi treni itafika Kigoma?**	saa ngapee trenee eetafeeka keegoma

Is there a dining car/ sleeping car on the train?	**Kuna behewa la chakula/behewa la kulala?**	**koo**na behewa la cha**koo**la/ behewa la **koo**lala
Does the train stop in Tabora?	**Treni husimama Tabora?**	**tre**nee hoo**see**mama tabora
I'd like a time-table.	**Nipatie saa za [Nipatie ratiba ya] safari, tafadhali.**	neepa**tee**eeh saa za [neepa**tee**-eh ra**tee**ba ya] safaree tafa**d**alee

---

Lazima ubadilishe utapofika...	You have to change at...
Badilisha utapofika... na panda treni nyengine.	Change at... and get a local train.
Jukwaa nambari 7 liko...	Platform 7 is...
kule/juu [panda ngazi]	over there/upstairs
kushoto/kulia	on the left/on the right
Iko treni ya kwenda... saa...	There's a train to... at...
Treni yenu itaondoka kutoka pletfomu nambari nane.	Your train will leave from platform 8.
Itachelewa kwa dakika...	There will be a delay of... minutes.
Klasi [daraja] kwanza iko mbele/ kati kati/nyuma.	First class at the front/in the middle/at the rear.

Tickets *Tikti*

I'd like a ticket to Tabora.	**Nataka tikti ya kwenda Tabora.**	nataka **tee**ktee ya **kwe**nda tabora
single (one-way)	**ya kwenda tu**	ya **kwe**nda too
return (round trip)	**kwenda na kurudi**	**kwe**nda na koo**roo**dee
first/second class	**klasi ya kwanza/pili**	kla**see** ya **kwa**nza/**pee**lee
half price	**nusu bei**	**noo**soo **bee**-e

Reservation *Kuekesha tikti*

I'd like to reserve a...	**Nataka kue- kesha...**	nataka koo**e**kesha
seat (by the window)	**kiti (karibu na dirisha)**	**kee**tee (ka**ree**boo na dee**ree**sha)
berth	**kitanda**	**kee**tanda
upper	**cha juu**	cha **joo**-oo
middle	**cha kati**	cha **ka**tee
lower	**cha chini**	cha **chee**nee

All aboard *Pandeni nyote*

Is this the right train to Kampala?	**Hii ndiyo treni inayokwenda Kampala?**	hee-ee **ndee**yo **tre**nee eenayokwenda kampala
Excuse me. Could I get past?	**Samahani, nataka kupita [Hebu nipishe].**	samahanee nataka koo**pee**ta [**he**boo neepee**sheh**]
Is this seat taken?	**Kuna mtu kwenye kiti hiki?**	**koo**na mtoo kwen^yeh **kee**tee **hee**kee

| **WAVUTAO SIGARA** SMOKER | **WASIOVUTA SIGARA** NONSMOKER |

I think that's my seat.	**Unafikiri hicho ni kiti changu.**	oonafeek**kee**ree **hee**cho nee **kee**tee changoo
Would you let me know before we get to Jinja?	**Tafadhali niambie kabla kufika Jinja?**	tafaðalee neeyam**bee**-eh kabla koo**fee**ka **jeen**ja
What station is this?	**Ni stesheni gani hii? [Ni kituo gani hiki?]**	nee stesh**enee ganee hee-ee [nee keetoo-o ganee heekee]
How long does the train stop here?	**Kwa muda gani treni husimama hapa?**	kwa **moo**da **ga**nee **tre**nee hoo**see**mama hapa
When do we arrive in Nairobi?	**Wakati gani tutafika Nairobi?**	wa**ka**tee **ga**nee toota**fee**ka naeero**bee**

Sleeping *Kulala*

Are there any free compartments in the sleeping car?	**Kuna nafasi kwenye behewa la kulala?**	**koo**na nafa**see** kwen^yeh behewa la koo**lala**
Where's the sleeping car?	**Liko wapi behewa la kulala?**	**lee**ko wa**pee** behewa la koo**lala**
Where's my berth?	**Kitanda changu kiko wapi?**	kee**tanda** changoo **kee**ko wa**pee**
I'd like a lower berth.	**Nitapenda kitanda cha chini.**	neeta**penda** kee**tanda** cha **chee**nee

| Would you make up our berths? | **Tafadhali tutandikie kitanda chetu?** | tafaðalee tootandeekee-eh keetanda chetoo |
| Would you wake me at 7 o'clock? | **Tafadhali niamshe saa moja asubuhi?** | tafaðalee neeyamsheh saa moja asooboohee |

Eating *Kula*

There's usually a dining-car on long-distance trains where meals and drinks are available. On many trains, depending on the class, an attendant comes around with snacks, biscuits and soft drinks. However, on certain services restaurant cars can be unpredictable, so it may be advisable to carry your own food.

| Where's the dining-car? | **Liko wapi behewa la chakula?** | leeko wapee behewa la chakoola |

Baggage—Porters *Mizigo–Wachukuzi*

Porter!	**Bwana! [Mzee!]/ Bibi! [Mama!]**	bwana [mze-eh]/beebee [mama]
Can you help me with my luggage?	**Tafadhali nisaidie mizigo?**	tafaðalee neesaeedee-eh meezeego
Where are the luggage trolleys (carts)?	**Viko wapi vigari vya kuchukulia mizigo?**	veeko wapee veegaree vya koochookooleeya meezeego
Where are the luggage lockers?	**Yako wapi makabati ya mizigo?**	yako wapee makabatee ya meezeego
Where's the left-luggage office (baggage check)?	**Iko wapi ofisi ya kuweka mizigo?**	eeko wapee ofeesee ya kooweka meezeego
I'd like to leave my luggage, please.	**Nataka kuweka mizigo yangu, tafadhali.**	naataka kooweka meezeego yangoo tafaðalee
I'd like to register (check) my luggage.	**Nataka kuandikisha mizigo yangu.**	nataka koowandeekeesha meezeego yangoo

> **KUANDIKISHA MIZIGO**
> REGISTERING (CHECKING) BAGGAGE

PORTERS, see also page 18

Coach (long-distance bus) *Basi*

Many bus companies and transport operators run inter-city buses and express passenger saloon car services. These are swift and economic in well-maintained vehicles.

For long-distance coach journeys you need to book in advance in order to reserve a seat.

When's the next coach/matatu to...?	**Wakati gani kuna basi jengine/ matatu nyengine...?**	wakatee ganee koona basee jengeeneh/matatoo nᵛengeeneh
Does this coach stop at...?	**Basi hili linasimama...?**	basee heelee leenaseemama
Does this coach go to Mount Kilimanjaro?	**Basi hili linakwenda Kilimanjaro?**	basee heelee leenakwenda keeleemanjaro
Where do I change for...?	**Wapi nibadilishe...?**	wapee neebadeeleesheh
How long does the journey (trip) take?	**Safari inachukua masaa mangapi [muda gani?]**	safaree eenachookoowa masaa mangapee [mooda ganee]
Which platform does the coach to the Maasai Mara National Reserve leave from?	**Basi la Masai Mara linaondokea wapi [pletfomu gani]?**	basee la masaee mara leenaondokea wapee [pletfomoo ganee]
Which platform does the coach from Kisumu arrive at?	**Basi kutoka Kisumu linasimama wapi?**	basee kootoka keesoomoo leenaseemama wapee
Is this the right platform for the coach to Lamu?	**Hapa ndipo basi la Lamu linapoondokea?**	hapa ndeepo basee la lamoo leenapoondokea

Note: Most of the phrases on the previous pages can be used or adapted for travelling on local transport.

Bus *Basi*

The bus is the cheapest form of domestic transport. For local journeys you can buy your ticket on the bus. Just give the conductor your destination and he'll tell you the fare. Departure begins once the bus is overcrowded, and the use of bus services between 9.30 a.m. and 3.00 p.m. may have you fighting to get on and off.

Matatus are privately owned adapted mini vans which augment the overstretched bus services. Fares are generally more expensive and they are often poorly maintained and driven at terrifying speeds.

I'd like a booklet of tickets.	**Nataka kijitabu cha tikti.**	nataka keejeetaboo cha **teek**tee
Which bus goes to the town centre?	**Basi gani linakwenda mjini?**	**ba**see **ga**nee leena**kwe**nda mjeenee
Where can I get a bus to the National Museum?	**Wapi nitapata basi la kwenda Makumbusho ya Taifa?**	**wa**pee neeta**pa**ta **ba**see la **kwe**nda ma**koo**mbo**o**sho ya ta**ee**fa
Which bus do I take to Parliament Square?	**Nipande basi gani kwenda Parliament Square?**	nee**pa**ndeh **ba**see **ga**nee **kwe**nda parlament skweh
Where's the bus stop?	**Kituo cha basi kiko wapi?**	kee**too**-o cha **ba**see **kee**ko **wa**pee
When is the... bus to Machakos?	**Saa ngapi... basi la Machakos?**	saa **nga**pee... **ba**see la macha**kos**
first/last/next	**la kwanza/mwisho/lingine [jengine]**	la **kwa**nza/**mwee**sho/ leen**gee**neh [jen**gee**neh]
How much is the fare to...?	**Shilingi ngapi [Kiasi gani] nauli...?**	shee**lee**ngee **nga**pee [kee**ya**see **ga**nee] na**oo**lee
Do I have to change buses?	**Jee, nibadilishe basi?**	je-eh neeba**dee**lee**shee**sheh **ba**see
How many bus stops are there to...?	**Kuna vituo vingapi kabla ya...?**	**koo**na vee**too**-o veen**ga**pee **kabl**a ya
How often do buses go to Bagamoyo?	**Mara ngapi mabasi huenda Bagamoyo?**	**ma**ra **nga**pee ma**ba**see ho**oe**nda bagamoyo
Every 20 minutes.	**Baada ya kila dakika ishirini.**	**ba**ada ya **kee**la da**kee**ka eeshee**ree**nee
Will you tell me when to get off?	**Utaniambia wapi niteremke?**	ootanee**ya**mbee**ya wa**pee neete**re**mkeh
I want to get off at the Aga Khan mosque.	**Nataka kuteremka msikiti wa Agakhan.**	na**ta**ka koote**re**mka msee**kee**tee wa aga**kh**an

KITUO CHA BASI   BUS STOP

Boat service *Safari za meli [boti]*

The are regular coastal services to Zanzibar, Pembu and the Lama islands. Ferries also operate across Lake Victoria. Ask a travel agent for details.

An alternative way of travelling between the islands is by *dhow*, a large sailing-boat typical of this part of Africa.

When does the next boat for Zanzibar leave?	**Meli nyengine ya Zanzibar itaondoka saa ngapi?**	melee n'engeeneh ya zanzeebar eetaondoka saa ngapee
Where's the embarkation point?	**Wapi mahali pa kupandia?**	wapee mahalee pa koopandeeya
How long does the crossing take?	**Muda gani huchukua kuvuka?**	mooda ganee hoochookoowa koovooka
Which port(s) do we stop at?	**Bandari gani tunasimama?**	bandaree ganee toonaseemama
I'd like to take a cruise/ tour of the harbour.	**Ningependa kusafiria meli/kutembelea bandarini.**	neengependa koosafeereeya melee/ kootembelea bandareenee
boat	**meli**	melee
cabin single/double	**kebin/chumba cha mtu moja/ cha watu wa wawili**	kebeen/choomba cha mtoo moja/cha watoo wa waweelee
deck	**deki**	dekee
ferry	**feri [pantoni]**	feree [pantonee]
hydrofoil	**meli ya haidrofoili**	melee ya haeedrofoeelee
life belt/boat	**laif belti/boti**	laeef beltee/botee
port	**bandari**	bandaree
reclining seat	**kiti cha kukunja**	keetee cha kookoonja
river cruise	**matembezi ya mtoni**	matembezee ya mtonee
ship	**meli**	melee
steamer	**stima**	steema

Other means of transport *Usafiri wa aina nyengine*

Hitch-hiking is not the most practical way of getting around in the region, as lifts may be few and far between in some areas.

to hitchhike	**kuomba usafiri [lifti]**	koo-omba oosafeeree [leeftee]
to walk	**kutembea [kwenda] kwa miguu**	kootembea [kwenda] kwa meegoo-oo

| Can you give me/us a lift, please? | **Naomba usafiri?** [**Nisaidie lifti, tafadhali?**] | naomba oosafeeree [neesaeedee-eh leeftee tafaðalee] |

Or perhaps you prefer:

cable car	**gari ya kebul**	garee ya keboool
donkey riding	**kupanda punda**	koopanda poonda
helicopter	**helikopta**	heleekopta
horseback riding	**kupanda farasi**	koopanda farasee
moped	**kipikipiki**	keepeekeepeekee
motorbike/scooter	**pikipiki/skuta**	peekeepeekee/skoota
sailing-boat	**boti ya safari**	botee ya safaree

Bicycle hire *Kukodi baskeli*

I'd like to hire a... bicycle.	**Nataka kukodi baskeli...**	nataka kookodee baskelee
5-gear	**5 giya**	tano geeya
mountain	**mlima**	mleema

Car *Gari*

Driving conditions in this part of the world are not good, although roads are being improved all the time. Apart from the main highways, many of the roads are dirt tracks which can quickly turn to mud when it rains.

If you do hire a car, check it over before setting out on a long journey – make sure you have a good spare tyre and a set of tools – as breakdowns in remote areas can be at best inconvenient, at worst dangerous. If you're planning any off-road driving, a four-wheel drive vehicle is the best choice.

In Kenya, motorists drive on the left and overtake (pass) on the right.

In national parks, speed limits are restricted to 20-30 m.p.h so as not to frighten the animals.

| Where's the nearest (self-service) filling station? | **Kiko wapi kituo cha karibu cha petroli?** | keeko wapee keetoo-o cha kareeboo cha petrolee |
| Fill it up, please. | **Jaza, tafadhali.** | jaza tafaðalee |

CAR HIRE, see page 20

Give me... litres of petrol (gasoline).	Nipatie... lita za petroli.	neepatee-eh... leeta za petrolee
super (premium)/regular	ya supa [daraja ya kwanza]/kawaida	ya soopa [daraja ya kwanza]/kawaeeda
unleaded/diesel	ambayo haina lead/dizeli	ambayo haeena led/deezelee
Please check the...	Tafadhali [Hebu] angalia...	tafaðalee [heboo] angaleeya
battery	betri	betree
brake fluid	fluid ya breki	flooeed ya brekee
oil/water	mafuta/maji	mafoota/majee
Would you check the tyre pressure?	Tafadhali pima pumzi ya taya?	tafaðalee peema poomzee ya taya
1.6 front, 1.8 rear.	1.6 mbele, 1.8 nyuma	1.6 mbele 1.8 nyooma
Please check the spare tyre, too.	Tafadhali angalia taya ya speya.	tafaðalee angaleeya taya ya speya
Can you mend this puncture (fix this flat)?	Tafadhali nifiksiye pancha.	tafaðalee neefeekseeyeh pancha
Would you change the... please?	Tafadhali badil-isha...	tafaðalee badeeleesha
bulb	globu	globoo
fan belt	fenibelti	feneebeltee
spark(ing) plugs	spaki plagi	spakee plagee
tyre (tire)	taya/tairi	taya/taeeree
wipers	waipa	waeepa
Would you clean the windscreen (windshield)?	Tafadhali safisha windiskrini [kiyoo]?	tafaðalee safeesha weendeeskreenee [keeyoo]

Asking the way—Street directions *Kuuliza njia–Kuelekezwa mtaa*

Can you tell me the way to...?	Tafadhali niambie njia ya kwenda...?	tafaðalee neeyambee-eh njeeya ya kwenda
In which direction is...?	... iko upande gani?	eeko oopandeh ganee
How do I get to...?	Vipi unafika...?	veepee oonafeeka
Are we on the right road for...?	Hii ndiyo barabara ya kwenda...?	hee-ee ndeeyo barabara ya kwenda
How far is the next village?	Umbali gani kufika kijiji cha pili?	oombalee ganee koofeeka keejeejee cha peelee
How far is it to... from here?	Umbali gani kwenda... kutoka hapa?	oombalee ganee kwenda... kootoka hapa

Is there a motorway (expressway)?	**Iko barabara kuu [kubwa]?**	eeko barabara koo-oo [koobwa]
How long does it take by car/on foot?	**Masaa mangapi kwa gari/kwa miguu?**	masaa mangapee kwa garee/kwa meegoo-oo
Can you tell me where... is?	**Tafadhali niambie... iko wapi?**	tafaðalee neeyambee-eh ... eeko wapee
How can I find this place/address?	**Vipi nitafika mahali hapa/anwani hii?**	veepee neetafeeka mahalee hapa/anwanee hee-ee
Where's this?	**Ni wapi hapa? [Tuko wapi?]**	nee wapee hapa [tooko wapee]
Can you show me on the map where I am?	**Hebu nionyeshe niko wapi kwenye ramani hii?**	heboo nee-on'esheh neeko wapee kwen'eh ramanee hee-ee
Where are the nearest public toilets?	**Kiko wapi choo cha serikali kilio karibu?**	keeko wapee choo cha sereekalee keeleeo kareeboo

Uko kwenye barabara siyo.	You're on the wrong road.
Nenda moja kwa moja.	Go straight ahead.
Iko kule chini kushoto/kulia.	It's down there on the left/right.
mbele yako/nyuma yako...	opposite/behind...
karibu na.../baada ya...	next to/after...
kaskazini/kusini	north/south
mashariki/magharibi	east/west
Nenda kwenye njia panda ya kwanza/ya pili.	Go to the first/second crossroads (intersection).
Pinda kushoto kwenye taa za trafik.	Turn left at the traffic lights.
Nenda kulia kwenye kona ya pili.	Turn right at the next corner.
Nenda njia hii...	Take the... road.
Barabara ya upande mmoja.	It's a one-way street.
Lazima urudi nyuma...	You have to go back to...
Fuata alama ya Nakuru.	Follow signs for Nakuru.

Parking *Kuegesha gari*

Where can I park?	**Niegeshe wapi gari? [Wapi naweza kuegesha gari?]**	neeegesheh **wa**pee **ga**ree [**wa**pee na**we**za koo**e**gesha **ga**ree]
Is there a car park nearby?	**Kuna mahala pa karibu pa kuegesha gari?**	**koo**na mahala pa ka**ree**boo pa koo**e**gesha **ga**ree
May I park here?	**Niegeshe gari hapa?**	nee-e**ge**sheh **ga**ree **ha**pa
How long can I park here?	**Kwa muda gani naweza kuegesha gari hapa?**	kwa **moo**da **ga**nee na**we**za koo**e**gesha **ga**ree **ha**pa
What's the charge per hour?	**Unalipa shilingi ngapi kwa saa?**	oona**lee**pa shee**lee**ngee **nga**pee kwa saa
Do you have some change for the parking meter?	**Una chenji [pesa ndogo ndogo] za kutia kwenye mita?**	**oo**na **chen**jee [**pe**sa **ndo**go **ndo**go] za koo**tee**ya **kwen**Yeh **mee**ta

Breakdown—Road Assistance *Kuharibika gari*

If you're planning a long-distance car journey, it's well worth contacting the local Automobile Association who will give you useful advice on road conditions, and information on how to obtain help in case of a breakdown.

Where's the nearest garage?	**Gareji ya karibu iko wapi?**	gare**jee** ya ka**ree**boo **ee**ko **wa**pee
My car has broken down.	**Gari yangu imeharibika.**	**ga**ree **yan**goo eemeha**ree**beeka
Where can I make a phone call?	**Wapi ntaweza kupata simu?**	**wa**pee nta**we**za koo**pa**ta **see**moo
I've had a breakdown at...	**Gari langu limeharibika...**	**ga**ree **lan**goo leemeha**ree**beeka
Can you send a mechanic?	**Tafadhali nipatie fundi [makenika]?**	tafa∂a**lee** neepa**tee**-eh **foon**dee [make**nee**ka]
My car won't start.	**Gari langu halitaki kuingia moto.**	**ga**ree **lan**goo halee**ta**kee koo**een**geeya **mo**to
The battery is dead.	**Betri imekufa.**	**bet**ree eeme**koo**fa
I've run out of petrol (gasoline).	**Petroli imeniishia.**	petro**lee** eemenee-**ee**sheeya

I have a flat tyre.	**Tairi limetoboka.**	taeeree leemetoboka
The engine is over-heating.	**Injini inafoka.**	eenjeenee eenafoka
There's something wrong with the...	**Kuna kitu kimehari-bika katika...**	koona keetoo keemehareebeeka kateeka
brakes	**breki**	brekee
carburettor	**kabureta**	kabooreta
exhaust pipe	**egsozi paipu**	egsozee paeepoo
radiator	**rediyeta**	redeeyeta
wheel	**gurudumu**	gooroodoomoo
Can you send a break-down van (tow truck)?	**Unaweza kunileta gari la kukokota?**	oonaweza kooneeletea garee la kookokota
How long will you be?	**Muda gani utachu-kua kufika?**	mooda ganee ootachookoowa koofeeka
Can you give me an estimate?	**Unaweza kuniam-bia itafika shilingi ngapi?**	oonaweza kooneeyambeeya eetafeeka sheeleengee ngapee

Accident—Police *Ajali—Polisi*

Please call the police.	**Tafadhali mwite polisi.**	tafaðalee mweeteh poleesee
There's been an accident. It's about 2 km. from...	**Kumetokea ajali. Imetokea kiasi cha kilomita mbili kutoka...**	koometokea ajalee. eemetokea keeyasee cha keelomeeta ᵐbeelee kootoka
Where's there a telephone?	**Simu iko wapi?**	seemoo eeko wapee
Call a doctor/an ambulance quickly.	**Mwite daktari/ambalesi haraka, tafadhali.**	mweeteh daktaree/ambalesee haraka tafaðalee
There are people injured.	**Kuna watu wameu-mia[wamejeru-hiwa].**	koona watoo wameoomeeya [wamejerooheewa]
Here's my driving licence.	**Hii leseni yangu.**	hee-ee lesenee yangoo
What's your name and address?	**Jina lako ni nani/na anwani yako?**	jeena lako nee nanee/na anwanee yako
What's your insurance company?	**Kampuni yako ya bima ni ipi?**	kampoonee yako ya beema nee eepee

Sightseeing

It's a good idea to visit your local tourist office to see if they have any useful maps or information on local attractions. If you want to go on a sightseeing tour or excursion, many hotels will organise these, or call in at a reputable local travel agent.

Where's the tourist office?	Ofisi ya watalii iko wapi?	ofeesee ya watalee-ee eeko wapee
What are the main points of interest?	Mahali gani kuzuri kwa mtu kwenda kutembea?	mahalee ganee koozooree kwa mtoo kwenda kootembea
We're here for...	Tuko hapa kwa...	tooko hapa kwa
only a few hours	saa chache	sa-a chache
a day	siku moja	seekoo moja
a week	wiki moja	weekee moja
Can you recommend a sightseeing tour/an excursion?	Tafadhali nipatie jina la kampuni ya utaalii?	tafaðalee neepatee-eh jeena la kampoonee ya ootaalee-ee
Where do we leave from?	Tutaondokea wapi?	tootaondokea wapee
Will the bus pick us up at the hotel?	Basi litakuja kutuchukua kutoka hotelini?	basee leetakooja kootoochookoowa kootoka hoteleenee
How much does the tour cost?	Kiasi gani malipo ya safari?	keeyasee ganee maleepo ya safaree
What time does the tour start?	Saa ngapi safari itaanza?	saa ngapee safaree eetaanza
Is lunch included?	Malipo ni pamoja na chakula cha mchana?	maleepo nee pamoja na chakoola cha mchana
What time do we get back?	Saa ngapi tutarejea? [Kurudi saa ngapi?]	saa ngapee tootarejea [kooroodee saa ngapee]
Do we have free time in...?	Tutakuwa na wakati wetu...?	tootakoowa na wakatee wetoo
Is there an English-speaking guide?	Yuko mtu wa kutuongoza anayesema Kizungu [Kiingereza]?	yooko mtoo wa kootooongoza anayesema keezoongoo [keeeengereza]
Do I need to hire a ranger/scout?	Itanilazimu nimkodi mtu wa kutuongoza?	eetaneelazeemoo neemkodee mtoo wa kootoo-ongoza

Where is/Where are the...?	Iko/Ziko wapi...?	eeko/zeeko wapee
aquarium	tangi la kuweka samaki	tangee la kooweka samakee
art gallery	jumba la sanaa	joomba la sanaa
botanical gardens	bustani ya mimeya ya kila aina	boostanee ya meemeya ya keela aeena
building	jengo [jumba]	jengo [joomba]
business district	madukani [sehemu ya biashara]	madookanee [sehemoo ya beeyashara]
castle	kasri [jumba la mfalme]	kasree [joomba la mfalmeh]
cathedral	kanisa kuu	kaneesa koo-oo
cave	pango	pango
cemetery	kiunga cha kuzikia [makaburini]	keeoonga cha koozeekeeya [makabooreenee]
city centre	mjini	mjeenee
church	kanisa	kaneesa
concert hall	jumba la muziki	joomba la moozeekee
court house	mahakama [korti]	mahakama [kortee]
cultural centre	jumba la utamaduni	joomba la ootamadoonee
downtown area	mitaani	meetaanee
exhibition	maonyesho	maon'esho
factory	kiwanda	keewanda
fair	maonyesho	maon'esho
flea market	soko la mitumba	soko la meetoomba
fortress	ngome	ngomeh
fountain	chemchem	chemchem
game sanctuary	mahali pa kutunza wanyama	mahalee pa kootoonza wan'yama
gardens	bustani	boostanee
harbour	gati [bandari]	gatee [bandaree]
library	maktaba	maktaba
market	soko	soko
monument	ukumbusho	ookoomboosho
mosque	msikiti	mseekeetee
museum	makumbusho	makoomboosho
national park	bustani	boostanee
park	bustani ya kupunga upepo	boostanee ya koopoonga oopepo
parliament building	Jengo la bunge	jengo la boongeh
planetarium	pleniterium	pleneetereeoom
presidential palace	Ikulu [jumba la rais]	eekooloo [joomba la raees]
royal palace	kasri la mfalme	kasree la mfalme
ruins	magofu	magofoo

shopping area	**madukani [sehemu ya maduka]**	madookanee [sehemoo ya madooka]
stadium	**uwanja wa miche-zo [stediyum]**	oowanja wa meechezo [stedeeyoom]
statue	**sanamu**	sanamoo
stock exchange	**soko la fedha**	soko la fe∂a
temple	**hekalu**	hekaloo
tomb	**kaburi**	kabooree
tower	**mnara**	mnara
town hall	**ofisi ya baraza la mji**	ofeesee ya baraza la mjee
university	**chuo kikuu**	**choo**-o **kee**koo-oo
zoo	**bustani ya wanyama**	boostanee ya wanᵞama

Admission *Kiingilio*

Is...open on Sundays?	**...hufunguliwa Jumapili?**	hoofoongoo**lee**wa joomapeelee
What are the opening hours?	**Saa gani hufungu-liwa? [Saa za kazi?]**	saa ganee hoofoongoo**lee**wa [saa za **ka**zee]
When does it close?	**Saa ngapi hufungwa?**	saa **nga**pee hoo**foon**gwa
How much is the entrance fee?	**Kiingilio kiasi gani?**	kee-eengee**lee**-o keeyasee **ga**nee
Is there any reduction for...?	**Iko bei nafuu kwa...?**	**ee**ko be-ee nafoo-oo kwa
children	**watoto**	watoto
disabled	**vilema/walemavu**	veelema/walemavoo
groups	**vikundi**	vee**koon**dee
pensioners	**wazee**	**wa**zee
students	**wanafunzi**	wanafoonzee
Do you have a guide-book (in English)?	**Unacho kitabu cha uwongozi cha Kizungu/Kiinge-reza?**	oonacho keetaboo cha oowongozee cha keezoongoo/kee-eengereza
Can I buy a catalogue?	**Nataka kununua katalogi?**	nataka koonoonoowa katalogee
Is it all right to take pictures?	**Ni ruhusa kupiga picha?**	nee roohoosa koopeega **pee**cha

| **KIINGILIO BILA MALIPO [BURE]** | ADMISSION FREE |
| **SI RUHUSA KUPIGA PICHA** | NO CAMERAS ALLOWED |

Who—What—When? *Nani?–Nini?–Lini?*

What's that building?	**Ni jengo [jumba] gani lile?**	nee jengo [joomba] **ganee leeleh**
Who was the...?	**Nani aliye...?**	nanee aleeyeh
architect	**chora ramani ya majengo [majumba]**	chora ramanee ya majengo [majoomba]
artist	**msanii**	msanee-ee
painter	**mchora picha**	mchora peecha
sculptor	**mchongaji masa-namu [vinyago]**	mchongajee masanamoo [veen^vago]
When was it built?	**Lilijengwa [ili-jengwa] lini?**	leeleejengwa [eeleejengwa] leenee
Where's the house where... lived?	**Nyumba ali-yoishi... iko wapi?**	n^voomba aleeyoeeshee... eeko wapee
We're interested in...	**Tunapenda...**	toonapenda
antiques	**vitu vya zamani**	veetoo vya zamanee
archaeology	**magofu [athari za kale]**	magofoo [atharee za kaleh]
art	**sanaa**	sanaa
botany	**mambo ya mimea**	mambo ya meemea
ceramics	**vigae vya kila aina**	veegaeh vya keela aeena
coins	**sarafu**	sarafoo
fine arts	**sanaa za kila aina**	sanaa za keela aeena
geology	**sayansi ya mawe udongo na ardhi**	sayansee ya maweh oodongo na ar∂ee
handicrafts	**vitu vilivotenge-nezwa kwa mkono [sanaa]**	veetoo veeleevotengenezwa kwa mkono [sanaa]
history	**historia**	heestoreeya
music	**muziki [ngoma]**	moozeekee [ngoma]
national costume	**nguo za kitaifa**	ngoo-o za keetaeefa
natural history	**historia ya viumbe/ wanyama wa kale**	heestoreeya ya veeoombeh/wan^vama wa kaleh
ornithology	**sayansi ya ndege**	sayansee ya ndegeh
painting	**picha za kuchora**	peecha za koochora
pottery	**ufinyanzi**	oofeen^vanzee
religion	**dini**	deenee
sculpture	**kuchonga vinyago/ sanamu**	koochonga veen^vago/sanamoo
wild life	**wanyama pori**	wan^vama poree
wood carving	**vinyago**	veen^vago
zoology	**sayansi ya wanyama**	sayansee ya wan^vama

It's...	Ni...	nee
amazing	**inashangaza**	eenashangaza
awful	**ᵐbaya**	ᵐbaya
beautiful	**safi/nzuri**	safee/nzooree
gloomy	**imejiinamia**	eemejee-eenameeya
impressive	**inavutia**	eenavooteeya
interesting	**inapendeza**	eenapendeza
pretty	**nzuri**	nzooree
strange	**ya ajabu**	ya ajaboo
superb	**ya hali ya juu**	ya halee ya joo-oo
terrifying	**inatisha [inaogo-pesha]**	eenateesha [eenaogopesha]
tremendous	**kabambe**	kabambe
ugly	**haipendezi/mbaya**	haeependezee/ᵐbaya

Churches—Religious services *Makanisa ibada za kidini*

Roughly half the population of East Africa are Christian, with both Protestant and Catholic traditions more or less equally represented. In the towns, many of the services are conducted in English. Details of church services can be found in the newspaper on Saturdays.

There are large Moslem communities, particularly in the coastal regions, with other faiths also represented in the cities. Inland, especially in the country areas, traditional local religious practices are often followed.

Is there a... near here?	**Liko/Uko... karibu na hapa?**	leeko/ooko... kareeboo na hapa
Catholic church	**kanisa la kikatoliki**	kaneesa la keekatoleekee
Protestant church	**kanisa la kiprotesenti**	kaneesa la keeprotesentee
mosque	**msikiti**	mseekeetee
synagogue	**hekalu la kiyahudi**	hekaloo la keeyahoodee
What time is...?	**... ni saa ngapi?**	nee saa ngapee
mass/the service	**misa/sala**	meesa/sala
Where can I find a... who speaks English?	**Wapi naweza kupata... anayesema Kizungu [Kiingereza]?**	wapee naweza koopata... anayesema keezoongoo [kee-eengereza]
priest/minister/rabbi	**kasisi [fadhai]/rabai**	kaseesee [fa∂aee]/rabaee
I'd like to visit the church.	**Nataka kutembelea kanisani.**	nataka kootembelea kaneesanee

In the countryside Mashamba [Mikoani]

How far is it to...?	Ni umbali gani kwenda...?	nee oombalee ganee kwenda
Is it safe to walk there?	Ni salama kwenda kwa miguu huko? [Ni salama kutembea huko?]	nee salama kwenda kwa meegoo-oo hooko [nee salama kootembea hooko]
What kind of... is that?	Ni kitu gani kile...?[Ni nini ile...?]	nee keetoo ganee keeleh [nee neenee eeleh]
animal/bird	mnyama/ndege	mnʸama/ndegeh
flower/tree	mauwa/mti	maoowa/mtee

bridge	daraja	daraja
cliff	mlima mdogo	mleema mdogo
farm	shamba	shamba
field	konde	konde
footpath	njia ya miguu	njeeya ya meegoo-oo
forest	msitu	mseetoo
garden	bustani	boostanee
hill	bonde [kilima]	bondeh [keeleema]
house	nyumba	nʸoomba
jungle	pori	poree
lake	ziwa	zeewa
mountain	mlima	mleema
mountain range	milimani	meeleemanee
nature reserve	hifadhi ya mazingira	heefaðee ya mazeengeera
oasis	kijiji kati ya jangwa	keejeejee katee ya jangwa
path	njia	njeeya
peak	kilele	keeleleh
plantation	shamba	shamba
pond	kidimbwi	keedeembwee
river	mto	mto
road	barabara	barabara
savannah	mbuga	ᵐbooga
sea	bahari	baharee
spring	chemchem	chemchem
swamp	mikoko	meekoko
track	njia	njeeya
village	kijiji	keejeejee
volcano	jabali la volkeno	jabalee la volkeno
wall	ukuta	ookoota
waterfall	mporomoko wa maji	mporomoko wa majee
wood	mbao	ᵐbao

On safari *Kwenda safari*

Wildlife parks and game reserves are numerous in East Africa and safaris are very popular. Organized trips offer many opportunities for photographing and filming. The independent traveller will require a ticket or permit.

Here is a list of some of the animals you may spot.

antelope	**pofu**	pofoo
baboon	**nyani**	nᵛanee
boar	**nguruwe dume**	ngoorooweh **doomeh**
buffalo	**nyati**	nᵛatee
bushbaby	**kombo**	kombo
cheetah	**duma**	dooma
crocodile	**mamba**	mamba
duck	**bata**	bata
elephant	**tembo [ndovo]**	tembo [ndovo]
flamingo	**korongo**	korongo
gazelle	**swala**	swala
gecko	**mjusi**	mjoosee
giraffe	**twiga**	tweega
hartebeest	**kongoni**	kongonee
hippopotamus	**koboko**	koboko
honey badger	**nyerege**	nᵛeregeh
hyena	**fisi**	feesee
impala	**swala**	swala
jackal	**mbweha**	ᵐbweha
kudu	**tandala**	tandala
leopard	**chui**	chooee
lion/lioness	**simba/simba jike**	seemba/seemba jeeke
lizard	**kenge**	kengeh
mongoose	**nguchiro**	ngoocheero
monkey	**nyani**	nᵛanee
ostrich	**mbuni**	ᵐboonee
porcupine	**nungunungu**	noongoonoongoo
python	**chatu**	chatoo
rhinoceros	**kifaru**	keefaroo
serval cat	**mondo**	mondo
snake	**nyoka**	nᵛoka
steinbok	**tondoro**	tondoro
tortoise/turtle	**kobe/kasa**	kobeh/kasa
warthog	**ngiri**	ngeeree
waterbuck	**kuku**	kookoo
wildebeest	**nyumbu**	nᵛoomboo
wild cat	**paka wa mwitu**	paka wa **mwee**too
zebra	**punda milia**	poonda meeleeya

Relaxing

Cinema (movies)—Theatre *Sinema—Thiyeta*

Most films screened in cinemas are in English, though some may be in Swahili with English subtitles. You can find out what's on from newspapers and billboards.

What's on at the cinema tonight?	**Leo wanaonyesha filam [mchezo] gani snema?**	leo wanao**nʸ**esha fee**lam** [m**chezo**] gan**ee** s**nema**
What's playing at the ... Theatre?	**Kuna mchezo gani katika thiyeta ya ...?**	ko**ona** m**chezo** gan**ee** kate**eka** the**eyeta** ya
What sort of play is it?	**Ni mchezo wa aina gani?**	nee m**chezo** wa a**eena** gan**ee**
Who's it by?	**Nani kauandika-[kautunga]?**	nan**ee** kaooo**andeeka** [ka**ootoonga**]
Can you recommend a ...?	**Nielekeze ...?**	nee-e**lekezeh**
good film (movie)	**filam nzuri**	fee**lam** n**zooree**
comedy	**mchezo wa kuchekesha**	m**chezo** wa koo**chekesha**
musical	**mchezo wenye nyimbo**	m**chezo** wen**ʸeh** n**ʸeembo**
pantomime	**mchezo wa watoto**	m**chezo** wa wa**toto**
Is there a pantomime show on somewhere?	**Kuna mchezo wa watoto-popote?**	ko**ona** m**chezo** wa watoto-po**poteh**
What time does it begin?	**Saa ngapi unaanza?**	saa **ngapee** oo**naanza**
Are there any seats for tonight?	**Kuna tikiti zozote kwa leo usiku?**	ko**ona** tee**keetee** zozo**teh** kwa **leo** oo**seekoo**
How much are the seats?	**Kiasi gani tikiti?**	kee**yasee** gan**ee** tee**keetee**
I'd like to reserve 2 seats for the show on Friday evening.	**Nataka kuekesha tikiti mbili za mchezo wa ljumaa.**	na**taka** koo**ekesha** tee**ktee** ᵐbee**lee** za m**chezo** wa ee**joomaa**
Can I have a ticket for the matinée on Tuesday?	**Nataka tikiti za mchezo wa Jumanne mchana.**	na**taka** tee**keetee** za m**chezo** wa ee**joomaa** mchana
I'd like a seat in the stalls (orchestra).	**Nataka tikiti ya kukaa sehemu ya chini.**	na**taka** tee**keetee** ya ko**okaa** se**hemoo** ya chee**nee**
Not too far back.	**Isiwe nyuma sana.**	ee**seeweh** n**ʸooma** sana

DAYS OF THE WEEK, see page 151

Somewhere in the middle.	Iwe ya katikati.	eeweh ya kateekatee
How much are the seats in the circle (mezzanine)?	Kiasi gani tikti uki-taka kukaa sehemu ya juu?	keeyasee ganee teektee ookeetaka kookaa sehemoo ya joo-oo
May I have a programme, please?	Nipatie ratiba [pro-gramu] tafadhali?	neepateeeh rateeba [programoo] tafaдalee
Where's the cloakroom?	Choo kiko wapi?	choo keeko wapee

Samahani, tikiti zimekwisha. [Samahani hakuna tikiti kabisa.] — I'm sorry, we're sold out.

Viko viti vichache tu vimebaki sehemu ya juu kabisa. — There are only a few seats left in the circle (mezzanine).

Hebu niangalie tikiti yako. — May I see your ticket?
Hiki ni kiti chako. — This is your seat.

Opera—Concert *Nyimbo na ngoma za kienyeji [utamaduni]*

As you would expect, this kind of entertainment is not common in the region, but is occasionally found in the larger cities.

Can you recommend a(n)...?	Hebu nielekeze kwenye...?	heboo nee-elekezeh kwen'eh
concert	muziki	moozeekee
opera	tarabu	taraboo
Where's the opera house/the concert hall?	Wapi wanapiga tarabu/muzik?	wapee wanapeega taraboo/moozeek
Who's singing/dancing?	Nani anayeimba/cheza?	nanee anaye-eemba/cheza
Which orchestra is playing?	Kikundi gani kina-piga leo?	keekoondee ganee keenapeega leo
What are they playing?	Wanatoa mpya gani leo?	wanatowa mpya ganee leo

Local dances *Ngoma za kienyeji*

Many of the traditional local dances are performed to celebrate special occasions. You may be lucky enough to come across the following.

beni	benee	wedding dance
bomu	bomoo	fancy dress dance prior to the wedding night
unyago	oon'ago	initiation dance for girls
ndege (ndegeh)		umbrella dance; women in colourful outfits, waving matching umbrellas, sing and dance their way round town
May I photograph you?	**Naweza kukupiga picha?**	naweza kookoopeega peecha

Nightclubs–Discos *Vilabu–Madisko*

Found mainly in the larger cities, nightclubs often feature local professional bands performing Western-style pop music.

Can you recommend a good nightclub?	**Hebu niambie klabu gani nzuri kwenda?**	heboo neeyambee-eh klaboo ganee nzooree kwenda
Is there a floor show?	**Kuna maonyesho leo usiku?**	koona maon'yesho leo ooseekoo
What time does the show start?	**Maonyesho huanza saa ngapi?**	maon'yesho hoowanza saa ngapee
Is evening dress required?	**Lazima kuvaa nguo rasmi?**	lazeema koovaa ngoo-o rasmee
Where can we go dancing?	**Wapi tunaweza kwenda kudansi?**	wapee toonaweza kwenda koodansee
Is there a discotheque in town?	**Kuna disko mjini?**	koona deesko mjeenee
Would you like to dance?	**Utapenda kudansi?**	ootapenda koodansee

Sports *Michezo*

Football is the main spectator sport in this part of the world. Golf and tennis facilities are available at many large hotels.

With many spectacular mountains and hills spread across the region, hill walking is an increasingly popular activity, holding the special attraction of the still untamed great outdoors.

| Is there a football (soccer) match anywhere this Saturday? | **Kuna mechi ya futboli popote Jumamosi hii?** | koona mechee ya footbolee popoteh joomamosee hee-ee |

basketball	mpira wa mikono	mpeera wa meekono
boxing	ndondi	ndondee
car racing	mbio za magari	ⁿbee-o za magaree
cycling	kuendesha baskeli	kooendesha baskelee
football (soccer)	futboli [kandanda]	footbolee [kandanda]
hill walking	kutembea kwenye milima	kootembea kwenʸeh meeleema
horse racing	mashindano ya farasi	masheendano ya farasee
(horse-back) riding	kupanda farasi	koopanda farasee
mountaineering	kupanda milima	koopanda meeleema
swimming	kuogelea	koo-ogelea
tennis	kucheza tenis	koocheza tenees
volleyball	kucheza voliboli	koocheza voleebolee

Which teams are playing?	Timu zipi zina-cheza?	teemoo zeepee zeenacheza
Can you get me a ticket?	Unaweza kunipatia tikti?	oonaweza kooneepateeya teektee
What's the admission charge?	Kiingilio kiasi gani?	kee-eengeeleeo keeyasee ganee
Where's the nearest golf course?	Uwanja wa gofu wa karibu uko wapi?	oowanja wa gofoo wa kareeboo ooko wapee
Where are the tennis courts?	Uwanja wa tenis uko wapi?	oowanja wa tenees ooko wapee
What's the charge per...?	Malipo kiasi gani kwa...?	maleepo keeyasee ganee kwa
day/round/hour	siku/duru/saa	seekoo/dooroo/saa
Can I hire (rent) rackets?	Naweza kukodi reket?	naweza kookodee reket
Where's the race course (track)?	Uwanja wa mshin-dano uko wapi?	oowanja wa msheendano ooko wapee
Is there any good fishing/hunting around here?	Kuna mahali pazuri pa kuvua/kuwinda karibu na hapa?	koona mahalee pazooree pa koovoowa/kooweenda kareeboo na hapa
Do I need a permit?	Nahitaji kibali [ruhusa]?	naheetajee keebalee [roohoosa]
Where can I get one?	Nitakipata wapi?	neetakeepata wapee
Can one swim in the lake/river?	Mtu anaweza kuo-gelea kwenye ziwa/mto?	mtoo anaweza koo-ogelea kwenʸeh zeewa/mto
Is there a swimming pool here?	Kuna bwawa la kuogelea hapa?	koona bwawa la koo-ogelea hapa

Is it open-air or indoor?	**Liko nje au ndani?**	leeko njeh aoo ndanee
Is it heated?	**Maji yake ni ya moto?**	majee yakeh nee ya moto
What's the temperature of the water?	**Maji yake yana umoto gani?**	majee yakeh yana oomoto ganee
Is there a sandy beach?	**Kuna pwani yenye mchanga safi?**	koona pwanee yenᶜeh mchanga safee

On the beach *Pwani*

The coastal waters are perfect for swimming and watersports. Unlike the inland rivers and lakes, they are largely unpolluted. Snorkelling and scuba-diving is popular on the Kenyan coral reefs – the sharks tend to stay outside the reef! Some resorts also offer water-skiing and windsurfing.

Note that nudity is illegal and topless sunbathing acceptable, possibly, only in the close vicinity of your hotel.

Is it safe to swim here?	**Hakuna hatari kuogelea humo?**	hakoona hataree koo-ogelea hoomo
Is there a lifeguard?	**Yuko mtu wa kuku-okoa [kukusaidia] ukizama?**	yooko mtoo wa kookoo-okowa [kookoosaeedeeya] ookeezama
Is it safe (for children)?	**Ni salama kwa watoto?**	nee salama kwa watoto
I want to hire (rent) a/an/ some...	**Nataka kukodi...**	nataka kookodee
bathing hut (cabana)	**kibanda cha kuoga [kabana]**	keebanda cha koo-oga [kabana]
deck chair	**kiti cha kukunja**	keetee cha kookoonja
motorboat	**mataboti**	matabotee
rowing-boat	**ngarawa**	ngarawa
sailing boat	**mashua**	mashoowa
skin-diving equipment	**vifaa vya kuzamia mbizi**	veefaa vya koozameeya ᵐbeezee
sunshade (umbrella)	**mwavuli**	mwavoolee
water-skis	**wota-skis**	wota-skees
windsurfer	**windsufa**	weendsoofa

| PWANI YA MTU BINAFSI | PRIVATE BEACH |
| SI RUHUSA KUOGELEA | NO SWIMMING |

Making friends

Introductions *Kujulishana*

On the whole, East Africans are very friendly and easy-going. In the cities people are rather more formal than in the smaller towns and countryside. In the more remote country areas you may find yourself a bit of a curiosity.

May I introduce…?	**Hebu nikujulishe na…?**	heboo neekoojooleesheh na
John, this is…	**Joni, huyu ni…**	jonee **hoo**yoo nee
My name is…	**Jina langu ni [Naitwa]…**	jeena langoo nee [naeetwa]
Pleased to meet you!	**Nimefurahi kukutana nawe!**	neemefoorahee kookootana naweh
What's your name?	**Jina lako nani? [Unaitwaje?]**	jeena lako nanee [oonaeetwajeh]
How are you?	**Hujambo? [Habari gani?]**	hoojambo [habaree ganee]
Fine, thanks. And you?	**Sijambo, wewe? [Nzuri, habari zako/yako?]**	seejambo weweh [nzooree habaree zako/yako]

Follow up *Kuendeleza mazungumzo*

How long have you been here?	**Muda gani mko hapa?**	mooda ganee mko hapa
We've been here a week.	**Tuko hapa wiki sasa.**	tooko hapa weekee sasa
Is this your first visit?	**Hii ni safari yako ya kwanza?**	hee-ee nee safaree yako ya kwanza
No, we came here last year.	**A-a, tulifika mwaka jana.**	a-a tooleefeeka mwaka jana
Are you enjoying your stay?	**Mnastarehe? [Mnapapenda?]**	mnastareheh [mnapapenda]
Yes, I like it very much.	**Ndiyo, ninapapenda sana.**	ndeeyo neenapapenda sana
I like the scenery a lot.	**Naipenda sana mandhari ilivyo.**	naeependa sana mandaree eeleevyo
What do you think of the country?	**Unaionaje nchi hii na watu wake?**	oonaee-onajeh nchee hee-ee na watoo wakeh

Where do you come from?	Unatoka wapi [nchi gani]?	oonatoka wapee [nchee ganee]
I'm from...	Natoka...	natoka
What nationality are you?	U mwananchi wa wapi wewe?	oo mwananchee wa wapee weweh
I'm...	Mimi ni [Miye]...	meemee nee [meeyeh]
American	Mmarekani [Mwa-merika]	mmarekanee [mwamereeka]
British	Raiya wa Uinge-reza	raeeya wa ooeengereza
Canadian	Mkanada	mkanada
English	Mwingereza	mweengereza
Irish	Mwairish	mwaeereesh
Where are you staying?	Umefikia wapi?	oomefeekeeya wapee
Are you on your own?	Uko peke yako?	ooko pekeh yako
I'm with my...	Niko pamoja na... wangu/yangu.	neeko pamoja na... wangoo/yangoo
wife	mke [bibi]	mkeh [beebee]
husband	mume [bwana]	moomeh [bwana]
family	familia	fameeleeya
children	watoto	watoto
parents	wazazi	wazazee
boyfriend/girlfriend	rafiki yangu	rafeekee yangoo

father/mother	baba/mama	baba/mama
son/daughter	mtoto/mtoto	mtoto/mtoto
brother/sister	kaka/dada	kaka/dada
uncle/aunt (paternal)	mjomba/shangazi	mjomba/shangazee
uncle/aunt (maternal)	baba mdogo/mama mdogo	baba mdogo/mama mdogo
nephew/niece	mtoto wa dada/kaka	mtoto wa dada/kaka
cousin	jamaa	jamaa

Are you married?	Umeoa/Umeo-lewa?	oomeowa/oomeolewa
Are you single?	Hujaoa/Hujaolewa?	hoojaowa/hoojaolewa
Do you have children?	Una watoto?	oona watoto
What do you do?	Unafanya kazi gani?	oonafan'ya kazee ganee

COUNTRIES, see page 146

I'm a student.	(Mimi) mwana-funzi.	(meemee) mwanafoonzee
What are you studying?	Unasomea nini?	oonasomea neenee
I'm here on a business trip/on holiday.	Niko hapa kwa kazi [biashara]/likizo?	neeko hapa kwa kazee [beeyashara]/leekeezo
Do you travel a lot?	Unasafiri sana?	oonasafeeree sana
Do you play cards/chess?	Unacheza karata/dama?	oonacheza karata/dama

The weather *Hali ya hewa*

What a lovely day!	Leo kuzuri!	leo koozooree
What awful weather!	Hali ya hewa mbaya! [Kubaya leo!]	halee ya hewa [koobaya leo]
Isn't it cold/hot today?	Si baridi/joto [moto] leo?	see bareedee/joto [moto] leo
Is it usually as dusty as this?	Siku zote huwa vumbi namna hii?	seekoo zoteh hoowa voombee namna hee-ee
Do you think it's going to... tomorrow?	Unafikiri itakuwa... kesho?	oonafeekeeree eetakoowa... kesho
be a nice day	siku nzuri	seekoo nzooree
be hot	joto	joto
rain	mvua	mvoowa
What's the weather forecast?	Nini utabiri wa hali ya hewa?	neenee ootabeeree wa halee ya hewa

cloud	mawingu	maweengoo
frost	umande	oomande
ice	barafu	barafoo
lightning	umeme	oomemeh
moon	mwezi	mwezee
rain	mvua	mvoowa
long rains	mvua kali [masika]	mvoowa kalee [maseeka]
short rains	mvua kidogo [vuli]	mvoowa keedogo [voolee]
sky	mbingu	mbeengoo
star	nyota	nvota
sun	jua	joowa
thunder	radi	radee
thunderstorm	dharuba	ðarooba
wind	upepo	oopepo

Invitations Mialiko [Kualikwa]

Would you like to have dinner with us on…?	**Karibu kwetu kwa chakula cha usiku …?**	kareeboo kwetoo kwa chakoola cha ooseekoo
May I invite you to lunch?	**Nakualika chakula cha mchana?**	nakoowaleeka chakoola cha mchana
Can you come round for a drink this evening?	**Utaweza kuja nyumbani leo usiku tujiburudishe?**	ootaweza kooja n^yoombanee leo ooseekoo toojeebooroodeesheh
There's a party. Are you coming?	**Kuna karamu [pati]. Utaweza kuja?**	koona karamoo [patee]. ootaweza kooja
That's very kind of you.	**Asante sana. [Nakushukuru.]**	asanteh sana [nakooshookooroo]
Great. I'd love to come.	**Uzuri, ntapenda sana kuja.**	oozooree ntapenda sana kooja
What time shall we come?	**Saa ngapi tuje?**	saa ngapee toojeh
May I bring a friend?	**Ni sawa nikija na rafiki yangu?**	nee sawa neekeeja na rafeekee yangoo
I'm afraid we have to leave now.	**Samahani lazima twende sasa hivi.**	samahanee lazeema twendeh sasa heevee
Next time you must come to visit us.	**Lazima ututembe-lee mara nyingine.**	lazeema ootootembele-eh mara n^yeengeeneh
Thanks for the evening. It was great.	**Asante sana. Tumefurahi sana.**	asanteh sana. toomefoorahee sana

Dating Kupangana

Do you mind if I smoke?	**Ni Sawa nikivuta sigara? [Hujali nikivuta sigara?]**	nee sawa neekeevoota seegara [hoojalee neekeevoota seegara]
Would you like a cigarette?	**Utapenda sigara?**	ootapenda seegara
Do you have a light, please?	**Unacho kibiritri, kwa hisani yako?**	oonacho keebeereetree kwa heesanee yako
Why are you laughing?	**Mbona unacheka? [Unacheka nini?]**	^mbona oonacheka [oonacheka neenee]
Is my Swahili that bad?	**Hivi kiswahili changu kibaya hivyo?**	heevee keeswaheelee changoo keebaya heevyo

DAYS OF THE WEEK, see page 151

Do you mind if I sit here?	Ni sawa nikikaa hapa?	nee sawa neekeekaa hapa
Can I get you a drink?	Nikupatie kinywaji?	neekoopatee-eh keenʸwajee
Are you waiting for someone?	Unamngoja [Unamsubiri] mtu?	oonamngoja [oonamsoobeeree] mtoo
Are you free this evening?	Una nafasi [Unafanya nini] leo jioni?	oona nafasee [oonafanʸa neenee] leo jee-onee
Would you like to go out with me tonight?	Utapenda tutoke pamoja leo usiku?	ootapenda tootokeh pamoja leo ooseekoo
Would you like to go dancing?	Utapenda kwenda kwenye dansa?	ootapenda kwenda kwenʸeh dansa
I know a good discotheque.	Nakujua kwenye disko zuri.	nakoojoowa kwenʸeh deesko zooree
Shall we go to the cinema (movies)?	Twende snema?	twendeh snema
Would you like to go for a drive?	Utapenda kweda kutembea kwa gari?	ootapenda kweda kootembea kwa gareh
Where shall we meet?	Tukutane wapi?	tookootaneh wapee
I'll pick you up at your hotel.	Nitakupitia hoteli.	neetakoopeeteeya hotelee
I'll call for you at 8.	Nitakupigia simu saa mbili usiku.	neetakoopeegeeya seemoo saa ᵐbeelee ooseekoo
May I take you home?	Nikupeleke nyumbani?	neekoopelekeh nʸoombanee
Can I see you again tomorrow?	Tunaweza kukutana tena, kesho?	toonaweza kookootana tena kesho
I hope we'll meet again.	Natumai tutakutana tena.	natoomaee tootakootana tena

...and you might answer:

I'd love to, thank you.	Nitafurahi, asante.	neetafoorahee asanteh
Thank you, but I'm busy.	Asante, sina nafasi. [nina kazi]	asanteh seena nafasee [neena kazee]
No, I'm not interested, thank you.	A-a, sitapendelea, asante.	a-a seetapendelea asanteh
Leave me alone, please!	Usinisumbue, tafadhali!	ooseeneesoomboooeh tafaᵭalee
Thank you, it's been a wonderful evening.	Asante, nimefurahi sana jioni hii.	asanteh neemefoorahee sana jee-onee hee-ee
I've enjoyed myself.	Nimestarehe.	neemestareheh

Shopping Guide

This shopping guide is designed to help you find what you want with ease, accuracy and speed. It features:

1. A list of all major shops, stores and services (p.98).

2. Some general expressions required when shopping to allow you to be specific and selective (p.100).

3. Full details of the shops and services most likely to concern you. Here you'll find advice, alphabetical lists of items and conversion charts listed under the headings below.

LAUNDRY, see page 29/HAIRDRESSER'S, see page 30

Shops, stores and services *Aina ya maduka na huduma zake*

Smaller shops are usually open from around 8.30. a.m. to 8.00 p.m., often closing for lunch between noon and 3.00 p.m. Larger stores in the cities normally stay open at lunch time. All shops are open on Saturdays until 2.00 p.m., but very few shops open on Sundays.

The outdoor markets are well worth a visit, and here haggling over prices is expected. Bargaining can well bring prices down by at least half. However, marked prices generally indicate that prices are fixed—*bei moja*.

Where's the nearest...?	... ya [la] karibu liko [iko] wapi?	ya [la] kareeboo leeko [eeko] wapee
antique shop	duka la vitu vya kizamani	dooka la veetoo vya keezamanee
art gallery	jumba la sanaa	joomba la sanaa
baker's	duka la mikate	dooka la meekateh
bank	benki	benkee
barber's	kinyozi	keenʸozee
beauty salon	duka la urembo wa kike	dooka la oorembo wa keekeh
bookshop	duka la vitabu	dooka la veetaboo
butcher's	duka la nyama	dooka la nʸama
camera shop	duka la kamera	dooka la kamera
chemist's	duka la dawa	dooka la dawa
dairy	duka la maziwa	dooka la mazeewa
dentist	daktari wa meno	daktaree wa meno
department store	duka kubwa [dipat-ment stoo]	dooka koobwa [deepatment sto-o]
drugstore	duka la dawa	dooka la dawa
dry cleaner's	dobi	dobee
fishmonger's	duka la samaki	dooka la samakee
florist's	duka la mauwa	dooka la maowa
furrier's	duka la vitu vya manyoya	dooka la veetoo vya manʸoya
greengrocer's	duka la mboga	dooka la mboga
grocer's	duka la chakula	dooka la chakoola
hairdresser's (ladies/men)	mtengenezaji nywele (wana-wake/wanaume)	mtengenezajee nʸweleh (wanawakeh/wanaoomeh)
hardware store	duka la vitu vya ujenzi	dooka la veetoo vya oojenzee
health food shop	duka la vyakula vya siha	dooka la vyakoola vya seeha

hospital	**hospitali**	hospeetalee
ironmonger's	**duka la vyombo vya chuma**	dooka la **vyo**mbo vya **choo**ma
jeweller's	**sonara**	sonara
launderette	**mahali pa kufulia**	mahalee pa koofooleeya
laundry	**dobi**	dobee
library	**maktaba**	maktaba
market	**soko**	soko
newsstand	**muuza magazeti**	moo-**oo**za magazetee
optician	**mpima miwani**	mpeema meewanee
pastry shop	**duka la keki**	dooka la kekee
photographer	**mpiga picha**	mpeega peecha
police station	**kituo cha polisi**	keetoo-o cha poleesee
post office	**posta**	posta
second-hand shop	**duka la mitumba**	dooka la meetoomba
shoemaker's (repairs)	**mshonaji viatu (mtengenezaji viatu)**	mshonajee veeyatoo (mtengenezajee veeyatoo)
shoe shop	**duka la viatu**	dooka la veeyatoo
shopping centre (mall)	**madukani**	madookanee
souvenir shop	**duka la kitalii**	dooka la keetalee-ee
sporting goods shop	**duka la vitu vya michezo**	dooka la veetoo vya meechezo
stationer's	**muuzaji kalamu nakaratasi**	moo-oozajee kalamoo nakaratasee
supermarket	**supamaket**	soopamaket
sweet shop	**duka la peremende**	dooka la peremendeh
tailor's	**mshoni**	mshonee
telegraph office	**ofisi ya simu**	ofeesee ya seemoo
tobacconist's	**muuza sigara**	moo-ooza seegara
toy shop	**duka la vitu vya kuchezea**	dooka la veetoo vya koochezea
travel agency	**wakala**	wakala
vegetable store	**duka la mboga**	dooka la ᵐboga
veterinarian	**daktari wa wanyama**	daktaree wa wanʸama
watchmaker's	**fundi wa saa**	foondee wa saa
wine merchant	**muuza mvinyo [pombe]**	moo-ooza ᵐveenʸo [pombeh]

KUINGIA	ENTRANCE
KUTOKA	EXIT
MLANGO WA DHARURA	EMERGENCY EXIT

Maslezo juu ya maduka

General expressions *Masuala ya kawaida [kufaa]*

Where? *Wapi?*

Where's there a good...?	**Wapi kuna... zuri/ nzuri/mzuri/ kizuri*?**	wapee koona... zooree/ nzooree/mzooree/ keezooree
Where can I find a...?	**Wapi naweza kupata...?**	wapee naweza koopata
Where's the main shopping area?	**Madukani ni wapi?**	madookanee nee wapee
Is it far from here?	**Ni mbali kutoka hapa?**	nee ᵐbalee kootoka hapa
How do I get there?	**Nitafikaje huko?**	neetafeekajeh hooko

SELI   SALE

Service *Huduma*

Can you help me?	**Nisaidie tafadhali?**	neesaeedee-eh tafaðalee
I'm just looking.	**Naangalia [Nata- zama] tu.**	na-angaleeya [natazama] too
Do you sell...?	**Unauza...?**	oonaooza
I'd like to buy...	**Nataka kununua...**	nataka koonoonoowa
I'd like...	**Ningependa...**	neengependa
Can you show me some...?	**Unaweza kunio- nesha...?**	oonaweza kooneeonesha
Do you have any...?	**Kuna...?**	koona
Where's the... department?	**Sehemu ya... iko wapi?**	sehemoo ya... eeko wapee
Where is the lift (elevator)?	**Lifti iko wapi?**	leeftee eeko wapee

That one *Ile pale*

Can you show me...?	**Unaweza kunio- nesha...?**	oonaweza kooneeonesha
this/that	**hii/ile**	hee-ee/eeleh
the one in the window/in the display case	**ile iliyomo dirishani/katika sanduku**	eeleh eeleeyomo deereeshanee/kateeka sandookoo

* See GRAMMAR, page 160

Defining the article *Kuelezea vyema*

I'd like a ... one.	**Nitapenda ...**	neetapenda
big	**kubwa**	koobwa
cheap	**rahisi**	raheesee
dark	**nyeusi**	nᵞeoosee
good	**nzuri**	nzooree
heavy	**nzito**	nzeeto
large	**kubwa**	koobwa
light (weight)	**nyepesi**	nᵞepesee
light (colour)	**ya mwangaza**	ya mwangaza
oval	**ya mviringo**	ya ᵐveereengo
rectangular	**ya pembe nne**	ya pembeh nneh
round	**ya duwara**	ya doowara
small	**ndogo**	ndogo
square	**pembe nne**	pembeh nneh
sturdy	**pana**	pana
I don't want anything too expensive.	**Sitaki kitu cha ghali.**	seetakee keetoo cha RHalee

Preference *Chagua [Kuchagua]*

Can you show me some others?	**Unaweza kunionesha nyenginezo?**	oonaweza kooneeonesha nᵞengeenezo
Don't you have anything ...?	**Unayo ...?**	oonayo ...
cheaper/better	**ya rahisi/bora zaidi**	ya raheesee/bora zaeedee
larger/smaller	**kubwa zaidi/ndogo zaidi**	koobwa zaeedee/ndogo zaeedee

How much *Kiasi gani?*

How much is this?	**Hii bei gani?**	hee-ee be-ee ganee
How much are they?	**Hizo bei gani?**	heezo be-ee ganee
I don't understand.	**Sifahamu [Sielewi].**	seefahamoo [see-elewee]
Please write it down.	**Tafadhali niandikie.**	tafaẟalee neeyandeekee-eh
That's too much.	**Bei yako ghali.**	be-ee yako RHalee
I don't want to spend more than ... shillings.	**Sitaki kutumia zaidi ya shilingi ...**	seetakee kootoomeeya zaeedee ya sheeleengee

Decision *Kukata shauri*

It's not quite what I want.	**Hii siyo ninayoitaka.**	hee-ee seeyo neenayoeetaka

COLOURS, see page 113

| No, I don't like it. | **A-a, siipendi hii.** | a-a see-eependee hee-ee |
| I'll take it. | **Nitainunua.** | neetaeenoonoowa |

Ordering *Kuagiza*

| Can you order it for me? | **Unaweza kuniagizishia?** | oonaweza kooneeyageezeesheeya |
| How long will it take? | **Itachukua muda gani?** | eetachookoowa mooda ganee |

Delivery *Kupeleka*

I'll take it with me.	**Nitaichukua mwenyewe.**	neetaeechookoowa mwen'eweh
Deliver it to the... Hotel.	**Ipeleke hoteli ya...**	eepelekeh hotelee ya
Please send it to this address.	**Tafadhali ipeleke anwani hii.**	tafaðalee eepelekeh anwanee hee-ee
Will I have any difficulty with the customs?	**Nitapata matatizo na watu wa forodha?**	neetapata matateezo na watoo wa foroða

Paying *Kulipa*

How much is it?	**Bei gani? [Kiasi gani?]**	be-ee ganee [keeyasee ganee]
Can I pay by traveller's cheque?	**Naweza kulipa kwa hundi za msafiri?**	naweza kooleepa kwa hoondee za msafeeree
Do you accept dollars/pounds?	**Unapokea dala/pauni?**	oonapokea dala/paoonee
Do you accept credit cards?	**Unapokea kadi za benki?**	oonapokea kadee za benkee
Do I have to pay the VAT (sales tax)?	**Lazima nilipe kodi [ijara] ya mauzo?**	lazeema neeleepeh kodee [eejara] ya maoozo
I think there's a mistake in the bill.	**Nafikiri mna makosa katika hesabu [bili] hiyo.**	nafeekeeree mna makosa kateeka hesaboo [beelee] heeyo

Anything else? *Unataka kitu kingine [Nini zaidi]*

| No, thanks, that's all. | **A-a, asante, inatosha.** | a-a asanteh eenatosha |
| Yes, I'd like... | **Asante, ningependa...** | asanteh neengependa |

Can you show me...?	**Unaweza kunio-nesha...?**	oonaweza kooneeoonesha
May I have a bag, please?	**Nipatie mfuko tafadhali? [Naomba mfuko?]**	neepatee-eh mfooko tafaдalee [naomba mfooko]
Could you wrap it up for me, please?	**Nifungie kwa hisani yako(tafad-hali)?**	neefoongee-eh kwa heesanee yako (tafaдalee)
May I have a receipt?	**Nipatie risiti.**	neepatee-eh reeseetee

Dissatisfied? *Kutoridhisha*

Can you exchange this, please?	**Unaweza kuniba-dilisha hii, tafad-hali?**	oonaweza kooneebadeeleesheeya hee-ee tafaдalee
I want to return this.	**Nataka kurudisha hii.**	nataka kooroodeesha hee-ee
I'd like a refund. Here's the receipt.	**Nataka munire-jeshee pesa zangu. Hii risiti.**	nataka mooneerejesheeh pesa zangoo. hee-ee reeseetee

---

Nikusaidie nini?	Can I help you?
Utapenda nini?	What would you like?
... gani utapenda?	What... would you like?
rangi/shepu/kwaliti	colour/shape/quality
Samahani hatuna kabisa.	I'm sorry, we don't have any.
Zimetuishia.	We're out of stock.
Tukuagizishie?	Shall we order it for you?
Utaichukua mweyewe au tukutumie?	Will you take it with you or shall we send it?
Nini zaidi? [Unataka kitu kingine?]	Anything else?
Hizo ni shilingi..., tafadhali.	That's... shillings, please.
Sehemu ya malipo ile pale.	The cash desk is over there.

Bookshop–Stationer's *Duka la vitabu vya kusomea na kuandikia*

English-language newspapers and magazines are readily available in the cities. They can be bought either from newsagents' shops or from one of the many newsstands.

Where's the nearest...?	**Liko wapi... la karibu?**	leeko wapee... la kareeboo
bookshop	**duka la vitabu**	dooka la veetaboo
stationer's	**duka la vitabu vya kuandikia**	dooka la veetaboo vya koowandeekeeya
newsstand	**duka la magazeti**	dooka la magazetee
Where can I buy an English-language newspaper?	**Wapi naweza kununua gazeti la Kizungu [Kiingereza]?**	wapee naweza koonoonoowa gazetee la keezoongoo [keeeengereza]
Where's the guide-book section?	**Iko wapi sehemu ya vitabu vya mwongozo?**	eeko wapee sehemoo ya veetaboo vya mwongozo
Where do you keep the English books?	**Wapi unaweka vitabu vya Kiingereza [kizungu]?**	wapee oonaweka veetaboo vya keeeengereza [keezoongoo]
Have you any of...'s books in English?	**Kuna vitabu vya... kwa Kiingereza ?**	koona veetaboo vya... kwa keeeengereza
Do you have second-hand books?	**Kuna vitabu vilivyoshatumiwa?**	koona veetaboo veeleevyoshatoomeewa
I want to buy a/an/some...	**Nataka kununua...**	nataka koonoonoowa
address book	**kitabu cha anwani**	keetaboo cha anwanee
adhesive tape	**gundi**	goondee
ball-point pen	**kalamu (peni)**	kalamoo (penee)
book	**buku [kitabu]**	bookoo [keetaboo]
calendar	**kalenda**	kalenda
carbon paper	**karatasi ya kukopia**	karatasee ya kookopeeya
crayons	**penseli za rangi**	penselee za rangee
dictionary	**kamusi**	kamoosee
Swahili-English	**kamusi la Kiswahili kwa Kiingereza**	kamoosee la keeswaheelee kwa keeeengereza
pocket	**kamusi dogo**	kamoosee dogo
drawing paper	**karatasi za kuchorea**	karatasee za koochorea
drawing pins	**pini za kupachikia**	peenee za koopacheekeeya
envelopes	**bahasha za barua**	bahasha za baroowa
eraser	**raba**	raba

exercise book	**daftari [kitabu cha kuandikia]**	daftaree [keetaboo cha koowandeekeeya]
fountain pen	**peni ya wino**	penee ya weeno
glue	**gundi**	goondee
grammar book	**kitabu cha sarufi**	keetaboo cha saroofee
ink	**wino**	weeno
black/red/blue	**mweusi/mwe-kundu/bluu**	mweoosee/ mwekoondoo/bloo-oo
magazine	**magazeti**	magazetee
map	**ramani [mepu]**	ramanee [mepoo]
street map	**ramani ya mji**	ramanee ya mjee
road map of...	**ramani ya barab-ara**	ramanee ya barabara
newspaper	**gazeti**	gazetee
American/English	**la kimarekani/la kiingereza**	la keemarekanee/la kee-eengereza
notebook	**kijidaftari [kijitabu]**	keejeedaftaree [keejeetaboo]
note paper	**karatasi ya kuandi-kia**	karatasee ya koowandeekeeya
paintbox	**kisanduku cha rangi**	keesandookoo cha rangee
paper	**karatasi**	karatasee
paperback	**karatasi [gamba] laini**	karatasee [gamba] laeenee
paperclips	**vibanio vya kara-tasi**	veebaneeo vya karatasee
paste	**gundi**	goondee
pen	**kalamu [peni]**	kalamoo [penee]
pencil	**penseli**	penselee
pencil sharpener	**cha kuchongea penseli**	cha koochongea penselee
playing cards	**karata**	karata
pocket calculator	**kalkuleta ndogo**	kalkooleta ndogo
postcard	**postkadi**	postkadee
propelling pencil	**penseli maalumu**	penselee ma-aloomoo
refill (for a pen)	**kalamu ya kujalizia**	kalamoo ya koojaleezeeya
rubber	**raba**	raba
ruler	**rula**	roola
string	**uzi**	oozee
travel guide	**kitabu cha maelezo ya safari**	keetaboo cha maelezo ya safaree
wrapping paper	**karatasi za kufun-gia vitu**	karatasee za koofoongee a veetoo
writing pad	**karatasi za kuandi-kia**	karatasee za koowandeekeeya

Camping and sports equipment *Vifaa vya michezo na kupigia kambi*

I'd like a/an/ some . . .	Nataka . . .	nataka
air bed (mattress)	kitanda (godoro)	keetanda (godoro)
axe	shoka	shoka
backpack	shanta [mfuko wa safari]	shanta [mfooko wa safaree]
butane gas	gesi ya kibutane	gesee ya keebootaneh
campbed	kitanda cha kam- bini	keetanda cha kambeenee
(folding) chair	kiti (cha kukunja)	keetee (cha kookoonja)
charcoal	mkaa [makaa]	mkaa [makaa]
compass	dira	deera
cool box	sanduku la kuhi- fadhi chakula cha baridi	sandookoo la kooheefaᶁee chakoola cha bareedee
deck chair	viti vya deki	veetee vya dekee
fire lighters	vibiriti [kuni]	veebeereetee [koonee]
fishing tackle	mshipi	msheepee
flashlight	taa	taa
groundsheet	turubali	tooroobalee
hammock	kitanda cha wavu [kamba]	keetanda cha wavoo [kamba]
ice pack	kifuko cha barafu	keefooko cha barafoo
insect spray (killer)	dawa ya wadudu	dawa ya wadoodoo
kerosene	mafuta ya taa	mafoota ya taa
lamp/lantern	taa/kandili	taa/kandeelee
mallet	nyundo	nʸoondo
matches	vibiriti	veebeereetee
(rubber) mattress	godoro	godoro
mosquito net	chandarua	chandaroowa
paraffin	mafuta ya taa	mafoota ya ta-a
picnic basket	kikapu cha mandar	keekapoo cha mandar
primus stove	jiko la mafuta	jeeko la mafoota
pump	pampu/bomba	pampoo/bomba
rope	kamba	kamba
rucksack	shanta	shanta
sheathknife	kisu chenye ala	keesoo chenʸeh ala
sleeping bag	mfarishi	mfareeshee
(folding) table	meza (ya kukunja)	meza (ya kookoonja)
tent	hema	hema
tent pegs	vishikio vya hema	veesheekeeo vya hema
tent pole	boriti za hema	boreetee za hema
torch	tochi	tochee
windsurfer	windsufa	weendsoofa
water flask	chupa ya maji	choopa ya majee

CAMPING, see page 32

Chemist's (drugstore) *Duka la dawa*

Finding a pharmacy in any of the cities is no problem, and they will usually have a rota system for staying open late. You can find out the details from local newspapers. Pharmacies at major hospitals stay open 24 hours a day.

The smaller chemist's shops often sell medical goods only, but the larger ones may well offer a full range of toiletries.

General *Mazungumzo ya jumla*

Where's the nearest (all-night) chemist's?	**Liko wapi duka la dawa (ambalo halifungwi) la karibu?**	leeko wapee dooka la dawa (ambalo haleefoongwee) la kareeboo
What time does the chemist's open/close?	**Saa ngapi hufunguliwa/hufungwa duka la dawa?**	saa ngapee hoofoongooleewa/hoofoongwa dooka la dawa

1—Pharmaceutical *Madawa*

I'd like something for...	**Nataka dawa ya...**	nataka dawa ya
a cold/a cough	**mafua/kikohozi**	mafoowa/keekohozee
hay fever	**kamasi**	kamasee
insect bites	**kuumwa na mdudu**	koo-oomwa na mdoodoo
sunburn	**kuunguzwa na jua kali**	koo-oongoozwa na joowa kalee
travel sickness	**mkunguru wa safari**	mkoongooroo wa safaree
an upset stomach	**maumivu ya tumbo**	maoomeevoo ya toombo
Can you prepare this prescription for me?	**Unaweza kunitayarishia dawa hii?**	oonaweza kooneetayareesheeya dawa hee-ee
Can I get it without a prescription?	**Naweza kuipata bila cheti?**	naweza kooeepata beela chetee
Shall I wait?	**Nisubiri?**	neesoobeeree
Can I have a/an/some...?	**Naweza kupata...?**	naweza koopata...
adhesive plaster	**palasta/plasta**	palasta/plasta

analgesic	**dawa ya kupunguza maumivu**	dawa ya koopoongooza maoomeevoo
antiseptic cream	**malhamu ya kupunguza maumivu**	malhamoo ya koopoongooza maoomeevoo
aspirin	**aspirini**	aspeereenee
bandage	**bendeji**	bendejee
chlorine tablets	**vidonge vya klorin**	veedongeh vya kloreen
condoms	**makondom**	makondom
contraceptives	**dawa ya kuzuia uzazi**	dawa ya koozooeeya oozazee
corn plasters	**palasta ya ndunda**	palasta ya ndoonda
cotton wool (absorbent cotton)	**pamba**	pamba
cough drops	**dawa ya kifua**	dawa ya keefoowa
disinfectant	**dawa ya wadudu**	dawa ya wadoodoo
ear drops	**dawa ya masikio**	dawa ya maseekeeo
eye drops	**dawa ya macho**	dawa ya macho
first-aid kit	**kisanduku cha fasteid**	keesandookoo cha fasteeed
flea powder	**podari ya kiroboto**	podaree ya keeroboto
gauze	**pamba**	pamba
insect repellent/spray	**dawa ya kujikinga na vidudu**	dawa ya koojeekeenga na veedoodoo
iodine	**aidini**	aeedeenee
laxative	**haluli [msahala]**	haloolee [msahala]
mouthwash	**dawa ya kusukutua**	dawa ya koosookootoowa
nose drops	**dawa ya pua**	dawa ya poowa
quinine tablets	**vidonge vya kwinini**	veedongeh vya kweeneenee
sanitary towels (napkins)	**mapedi**	mapedee
sleeping pills	**dawa za usingizi**	dawa za ooseengeezee
suppositories	**vidonge vya kutia nyuma**	veedongeh vya kooteeya nᵛooma
... tablets	**vidonge [tembe] ...**	veedongeh [tembeh]
tampons	**pedi za wanawake**	pedee za wanawakeh
thermometer	**cha kupimia homa**	cha koopeemeeya homa
throat lozenges	**dawa za koo**	dawa za koo
tranquillizers	**dawa za kutuliza hali**	dawa za kootooleeza haleh
vitamin pills	**vidonge vya kutia nguvu**	veedongeh vya kooteeya ngoovoo

---

SUMU   POISON

2—Toiletries *Vitu vya urembo na usafi wa muvili*

I'd like a/an/some ...	**Nitapenda** ...	neetapenda
after-shave lotion	**dawa ya kunyolea**	dawa ya koon^yolea
astringent	**maji ya kusafishia uso**	majee ya koosafeesheeya ooso
bath salts	**chumvi ya kutia kwenye maji ya kuogea**	choomvee ya kooteeya kwen^yeh majee ya koowogea
blusher (rouge)	**rangi ya mashavu**	rangee ya mashavoo
bubble bath	**urembo wa kuogea**	oorembo wa koowogea
cream	**kirimu**	keereemoo
cleansing cream	**kirimu ya kusafishia ngozi**	keereemoo ya koosafeesheeya ngozee
foundation cream	**vipodozi**	veepodozee
moisturizing cream	**kirimi ya kurutubisha ngozi**	keereemee ya koorootoobeesha ngozee
night cream	**kirimu ya kujipaka unapolala**	keereemoo ya koojeepaka oonapolala
deodorant	**mafuta ya kukata jasho**	mafoota ya kookata jasho
eyebrow pencil	**wanja wa nyusi**	wanja wa n^yoosee
eyeliner	**wanja wa macho**	wanja wa macho
eye shadow	**aishedo**	aeeshedo
face powder	**podari ya uso**	podaree ya ooso
foot cream	**kirimu ya miguu**	keereemoo ya meegoo-oo
hand cream	**kirimu ya mikono**	keereemoo ya meekono
lipsalve	**kirimu ya mdomo**	keereemoo ya mdomo
lipstick	**rangi ya mdomo**	rangee ya mdomo
make-up remover	**vya kufutia vipodozi**	vya koofooteeya veepodozee
pads	**vijipamba**	veejeepamba
nail brush	**brashi ya kucha**	brashee ya koocha
nail clippers	**cha kukatia kucha**	cha kookateeya koocha
nail file	**cha kuchongea kucha**	cha koochongea koocha
nail polish	**rangi ya kucha**	rangee ya koocha
nail scissors	**mkasi wa kukatia makucha**	mkasee wa kookateeya makoocha
perfume	**mafuta mazuri**	mafoota mazooree
powder	**podari**	podaree
powder puff	**uwa la kutilia podari**	oowa la kooteeleeya podaree
razor	**wembe [kijembe]**	wembeh [keejembeh]
razor blades	**vijembe**	veejembeh
rouge	**rangi ya mashavu**	rangee ya mashavoo
safety pins	**pini**	peenee

shaving brush	**brashi ya kunyolea**	brashee ya koon'olea
shaving cream	**kirimu ya kunyolea**	keereemoo ya koon'olea
soap	**sabuni**	saboonee
sponge	**spanji**	spanjee
sun-tan cream	**dawa ya ngozi**	dawa ya ngozee
sun-tan oil	**mafuta ya ngozi**	mafoota ya ngozee
talcum powder	**podari**	podaree
tissues	**tishu**	teeshoo
toilet paper	**tishu za chooni**	teeshoo za cho-onee
toothbrush	**msuwaki**	msoowakee
toothpaste	**dawa ya meno**	dawa ya meno
towel	**taula**	taoola
tweezers	**twiza [kikoleo]**	tweeza [keekoleo]

For your hair *Kwa nyweleh zako*

colour shampoo	**shampuu ya rangi**	shampoo-oo ya rangee
comb	**kitana**	keetana
curlers	**kals**	kals
dry shampoo	**shampuu**	shampoo-oo
dye	**rangi**	rangee
hairbrush	**brashi la nywele**	brashee la n'weleh
hair gel	**kirimu ya nywele**	keereemoo ya n'weleh
hairgrips	**mafuta ya nywele maalumu**	mafoota ya n'weleh maaloomoo
hair lotion	**mafuta ya nywele**	mafoota ya n'weleh
hairpins	**pini za nywele [chupiyo]**	peenee za n'weleh [choopeeyo]
hair spray	**sprey ya nywele**	sprey ya n'weleh
shampoo	**shampuu**	shampoo-oo
for dry/greasy (oily) hair	**ya nywele kavu/za mafuta**	ya n'weleh kavoo/ za mafoota
tint	**rangi ya nywele**	rangee ya n'wele
wig	**nywele za kubandika**	n'weleh za koobandeeka

For the baby *Kwa watoto*

baby food	**chakula cha watoto**	chakoola cha watoto
bib	**kitambaa cha kulishia mtoto**	keetambaa cha kooleesheeya mtoto
dummy (pacifier)	**mtoto wa sanamu**	mtoto wa sanamoo
feeding bottle	**chupa ya kumnyonyeshea mtoto**	choopa ya koomn'on'eshea mtoto
nappies (diapers)	**winda**	weenda

Clothing *Mavazi*

If you want to buy something specific, prepare yourself in advance. Look at the list of clothing on page 115. Get some idea of the colour, material and size you want. They're all listed on the next few pages.

General *Mazungumzo ya jumla*

I'd like...	**Nataka...**	nataka
I'd like... for a 10-year-old boy/girl.	**Nataka... kwa mtoto wa miaka kumi, wa kiume/kike.**	nataka... kwa mtoto wa meeyaka **koo**mee wa keeoomeh/keekeh
I'd like something like this.	**Ningependa kitu kama hiki.**	neengependa **kee**too kama heekee
I like the one in the window.	**Naipenda ya dir-ishani.**	naeependa ya deereeshanee
How much is that per metre?	**Mita kiasi gani?**	meeta keeyasee ganee

1 centimetre (cm)	= 0.39 in.	1 inch	= 2.54 cm
1 metre (m)	= 39.37 in.	1 foot	= 30.5 cm
10 metres	= 32.81 ft.	1 yard	= 0.91 m.

Colour *Rangi*

I'd like something in...	**Ningependa kitu cha...**	neengependa **kee**too cha
I'd like a darker/lighter shade.	**Nitapenda ilo-koza/ya mwan-gaza.**	neetapenda eelokoza/ya mwangaza
I'd like something to match this.	**Nataka kitu kiende na hiki.**	nataka **kee**too kee-endeh na heekee
I don't like the colour.	**Siipendi rangi hii.**	see-eependee rangee hee-ee

beige	**kahawiya isokoza**	kaha**wee**ya ee**so**koza
black	**nyeusi**	n^ye**oo**see
blue	**bluu**	bloo-oo
brown	**kahawiya/chakleti**	kaha**wee**ya/**chak**letee
fawn	**rangi ya paa**	**ran**gee ya paa
golden	**rangi ya dhahabu**	**ran**gee ya ∂a**ha**boo
green	**kijani**	kee**ja**nee
grey	**kijivujivu**	keejeevoo**jee**voo
khaki	**rangi ya kaki**	**ran**gee ya **ka**kee
mauve	**rangi ya urujuani**	**ran**gee ya ooroo**joo**wanee
orange	**rangi ya machungwa**	**ran**gee ya ma**choo**ngwa
pink	**wardi**	**war**dee
purple	**rangi ya zambarau**	**ran**gee ya zamba**ra**oo
red	**nyekundu**	n^ye**koo**ndoo
scarlet	**nyekundu ilokoza**	n^ye**koo**ndoo ee**lo**koza
silver	**rangi ya fedha**	**ran**gee ya **fe**∂a
turquoise	**rangi ya feruzi**	**ran**gee ya fe**roo**zee
white	**nyeupe**	n^ye**oo**peh
yellow	**manjano**	man**ja**no
light...	**rangi isiyokoza ...**	**ran**gee eesee**yo**koza
dark...	**rangi iliyokoza ...**	**ran**gee eelee**yo**koza

pleni (plenee)	**vyumba vyumba** (vyoomba vyoomba)	**urembo** (oorembo)	**mistari** (meestaree)	**madoadoa** (madowadowa)

Fabric *Kitambaa*

Do you have anything in...?	**Kuna kitu cha...?**	koona keetoo cha...
Is that...?	**Ile ni...?**	eeleh nee...
handmade	**ilotengezwa kwa mkono**	eeloten**ge**zwa kwa m**ko**no
imported	**imetoka nchi za nje**	eemetoka nchee za njeh
made here	**imetengenezwa hapa**	eemetengenezwa hapa
I'd like something thinner.	**Nataka kitu chembamba zaidi.**	nataka keetoo chembamba za**ee**dee
Do you have anything of better quality?	**Unayo ya koliti bora zaidi?**	oonayo ya koleetee bora za**ee**dee

What's it made of?	Imetengenezwa kwa kitu gani?	eemetengenezwa kwa keetoo ganee
baboon skin	kwa ngozi ya nyani	kwa ngozee ya n'yanee
cambric	kwa bafta nyepesi	kwa bafta n'epesee
camel-hair	kwa manyoa ya ngamia	kwa man'yowa ya ngameeya
chiffon	kwa shifoni	kwa sheefonee
corduroy	kwa kodroi	kwa kodroee
cotton	bafta [koton]	bafta [koton]
crepe	kwa kitambaa cha krepe	kwa keetambaa cha krepeh
denim	kwa kitambaa cha denim	kwa keetambaa cha deneem
flannel	kwa kitambaa cha flana	kwa keetambaa cha flana
gabardine	gabadini	gabadeenee
lace	kwa lesi	kwa lesee
leopard skin	kwa ngozi ya chui	kwa ngozee ya chooee
leather	ngozi	ngozee
linen	kwa kitambaa cha linen	kwa keetambaa cha leenen
poplin	kwa poplini	kwa popleenee
satin	kwa satin	kwa sateen
silk	kwa hariri	kwa hareeree
suede	kwa kitambaa cha swedi	kwa keetambaa cha swedee
towelling	kitambaa cha taula	keetambaa cha taoola
velvet	mahmeli	mahmelee
velveteen	kwa mahmeli	kwa mahmelee
velvet monkey skin	kwa mahmeli ya ngozi ya kima	kwa mahmelee ya ngozee ya keema
wool	kwa sufi	kwa soofee

Is it...?	Ni...?	nee
pure cotton/wool	bafta [koton]/sufi safi	bafta [koton]/soofee soofee
synthetic	vitambaa vya kisasa	veetambaa vya keesasa
crease (wrinkle) resistant	hakikunjiki	hakeekoonjeekee
Is it hand washable/ machine washable?	Unweza kufua kwa mkono/kwa mashine?	oonweza koofoowa kwa mkono/kwa masheeneh
Will it shrink?	Itaruka?	eetarooka

Size *Kipimo*

| I take size 38. | **Navaa saizi tha-lathini na nane.** | navaa saeezee thalatheenee na naneh |
| Could you measure me? | **Nipime tafadhali?** | neepeemeh tafaðalee |

Women *Wanawake*

		Dresses/Suits				
American	8	10	12	14	16	18
British	10	12	14	16	18	20
Continental	36	38	40	42	44	46

	Stockings						Shoes			
American	8½	9	9½	10	10½		6	7	8	9
British							4½	5½	6½	7½
Continental	0	1	2	3	4	5	37	38	40	41

Men *Wanaume*

	Suits/overcoats						Shirts			
American British	36	38	40	42	44	46	15	16	17	18
Continental	46	48	50	52	54	56	38	40	42	44

	Shoes									
American British	5	6	7	8	8½	9	9½	10	11
Continental	38	39	40	41	42	43	44	44	45

A good fit? *Mkato wake mzuri?*

Can I try it on?	**Niijaribu?**	nee-eejareeboo
Where's the fitting room?	**Ki wapi chumba cha kujaribia?**	kee wapee choomba cha koojareebeeya
Is there a mirror?	**Kuna kioo?**	koona keeoo
It fits very well.	**Inanifaa [Inakufaa].**	eenaneefaa [eenakoofaa]
It doesn't fit.	**Hainifai [haikufai].**	haeeneefaee [haeekoofaee]
It's too...	**Ni... sana [mno].**	nee... sana [mno]
short/long	**fupi/refu**	foopee/refoo
tight/loose	**inabana/inapwaya**	eenabana/eenapwaya
How long will it take to alter?	**Muda gani itachu-kua kuitengeneza?**	mooda ganee eetachookoowa kooeetengeneza

NUMBERS, see page 147

Clothes and accessories *Nguo na vitu vyenginevyo*

I would like a/an/some...	**Nataka...**	nataka
anorak	**rinkoti**	reenkotee
bathing cap	**kofia ya kuogea [kuogelelea]**	kofeeya ya koowogea [koowogelea]
bathing suit	**nguo ya kuogelea**	ngoowo ya koowogelea
bathrobe	**juba la msalani**	jooba la msalanee
blouse	**blauzi**	blaoozee
bow tie	**botai**	botaee
bra	**sidiria**	seedeereeya
braces	**mikanda**	meekanda
cap	**kofia**	kofeeya
coat	**koti**	kotee
dress	**kanzu [gauni]**	kanzoo [gaoonee]
with long sleeves	**ya mikono mirefu**	ya meekono meerefoo
with short sleeves	**ya mikono mifupi**	ya meekono meefoopee
sleeveless	**isiyokuwa na mikono**	eeseeyokoowa na meekono
evening dress (woman's)	**gauni la usiku [kanzu ya usiku]**	gaoonee la ooseekoo [kanzoo ya ooseekoo]
fez	**tarbushi**	tarbooshee
girdle	**mkanda wa kuzuia tumbo**	mkanda wa koozooeeya toombo
gloves	**glavu**	glavoo
handbag	**mkoba**	mkoba
handkerchief	**kitambaa cha mkono [hanchifu]**	keetambaa cha mkono [hancheefoo]
hat	**kofia**	kofeeya
jacket	**koti**	kotee
jeans	**jins**	jeens
jersey	**sweta**	sweta
kaftan	**kanzu ya kiume [kanzu ya msik-itini]**	kanzoo ya keeoomeh [kanzoo ya mseekeeteenee]
kneesocks	**soksi za mapajani**	soksee za mapajanee
nightdress	**nguo ya kulalia**	ngoowo ya koolaleeya
overalls	**ovaroli**	ovarolee
pair of...	**jozi ya...**	jozee ya
panties	**chupi**	choopee
pants (Am.)	**suruali**	sooroowalee
pullover	**sweta**	sweta
polo (turtle)-neck	**polo nek**	polo nek
round-neck	**la shingo ya duwara**	la sheengo ya doowara
V-neck	**la shingo ya vi**	la sheengo ya vee

pyjamas	**pajama**	pajama
raincoat	**rinkoti**	reenkotee
safari outfit	**safari suti [suti ya safari]**	safaree sootee [sootee ya safaree]
sarong	**saruni**	saroonee
scarf	**skafu [kitambaa cha kichwa]**	skafoo [keetambaa cha keechwa]
shirt	**shati**	shatee
shorts	**kaptura**	kaptoora
skirt	**skati**	skatee
slip	**shumizi [hafu]**	shoomeezee [hafoo]
socks	**soksi**	soksee
stockings	**soksi za kike**	soksee za keekeh
suit (man's)	**suti ya kiume**	sootee ya keeoomeh
suit (woman's)	**suti ya kike**	sootee ya keekeh
sun hat	**kofia ya jua**	kofeeya ya joowa
suspenders	**vishikio vya soksi za kike**	veesheekeeo vya soksee za keekeh
sweater	**sweta**	sweta
sweatshirt	**flana**	flana
swimming trunks	**suruali ya kuogelea**	sorooowalee ya koowogelea
swimsuit	**nguo ya kuogelea ya kike**	ngoowo ya koowogelea ya keekeh
T-shirt	**tishati**	teeshatee
tie	**tai**	taee
tights	**soksi za kike**	soksee za keekeh
tracksuit	**treksuti**	treksoot
trousers	**suruali**	sorooowalee
umbrella	**mwavuli**	mwavoolee
underpants	**chupi**	choopee
undershirt	**flana ya ndani**	flana ya ndanee
vest (Am.)	**flana ya mikono mifupi**	flana ya meekono meefoopee
vest (Br.)	**shumizi**	shoomeezee
waistcoat	**kizibao**	keezeebao

belt	**ukanda**	ookanda
buckle	**bakal**	bakal
button	**kifungo**	keefoongo
collar	**ukosi**	ookosee
pocket	**mfuko**	mfooko
press stud (snap fastener)	**vifungo vya chawa**	veefoongo vya chawa
zip (zipper)	**zipu**	zeepoo

Shoes *Viatu*

I'd like a pair of...	**Nataka jozi moja ya...**	nataka jozee moja ya
boots	**buti**	bootee
hiking boots	**viatu vya mili-mani**	veeyatoo vya meeleemanee
moccasins	**viatu vya ngozi ya paa**	veeyatoo vya ngozee ya paa
plimsolls (sneakers)	**viatu vya raba**	veeyatoo vya raba
sandals	**viatu vya ndara**	veeyatoo vya ndara
shoes	**viatu**	veeyatoo
flat	**fleti**	fletee
with a heel	**vya kisigino**	vya keeseegeeno
with leather soles	**vya soli ya ngozi**	vya solee ya ngozee
with rubber soles	**vya soli ya mpira**	vya solee ya mpeera
slippers	**sapatu**	sapatoo
These are too...	**Hizi ni... sana.**	heezee nee... sana
narrow/wide	**nyembamba/pana**	nᵞembamba/pana
big/small	**kubwa/ndogo**	koobwa/ndogo
Do you have a larger/smaller size?	**Kuna iliyo kubwa zaidi/ndogo zaidi?**	koona eeleeyo koobwa zaeedee/ndogo zaeedee
Do you have the same in black?	**Unayo namna hiyo ya nyeusi?**	oonayo namna heeyo ya nᵞeoosee
cloth	**kitambaa**	keetambaa
leather	**ngozi**	ngozee
rubber	**mpira**	mpeera
suede	**swed**	swed
Is it real leather?	**Ni ya ngozi kweli?**	nee ya ngozee kwelee
I need some shoe polish/shoelaces.	**Nataka rangi ya viatu/nyuzi za viatu.**	nataka rangee ya veeyatoo/nᵞoozee za veeyatoo

Shoes worn out? Here's the key to getting them fixed again:

Can you stitch this?	**Unaweza kunishonea hivi?**	oonaweza kooneeshonea heevee
I want new soles and heels.	**Nataka soli mpya na visigino vipya.**	nataka solee mpya na veeseegeeno veepya
When will they be ready?	**Lini vitakuwa tayari?**	leenee veetakoowa tayaree

COLOURS, see page 113

Electrical appliances *Vyombo vya umeme*

Most major towns in East Africa have an electricity supply, and this is usually 220-volt AC current. However, some smaller towns and villages may have their own generator which may vary in voltage.

A three-pin plug is the one in general use throughout the region. Hotels often provide adaptors for 220 and 110 volts.

What's the voltage?	**Voltage gani umeme?**	"voltage" ganee oomemeh
Do you have a battery for this?	**Unayo betri ya hii?**	oonayo betree ya hee-ee
This is broken. Can you repair it?	**Hii imevunjika. Unaweza kutengeneza?**	hee-ee eemevoonjeeka. oonaweza kootengeneza
Can you show me how it works?	**Unaweza kunionesha vipi ifanyavyo kazi?**	oonaweza kooneeonesha veepee eefan^{y}avyo kazee
I'd like a/an/ some...	**Nataka...**	nataka
adaptor	**edepta**	edepta
amplifier	**bomba la sauti**	bomba la saootee
bulb	**globu**	globoo
CD player	**mashine ya CD**	masheene ya seedee
clock-radio	**saa ya redio**	saa ya redeeo
extension lead (cord)	**waya wa kuongezea**	waya wa koowongezea
hair dryer	**mashine ya kukaushia nywele**	masheeneh ya kookaoosheeya n^{y}weleh
headphones	**hedfons**	hedfons
(travelling) iron	**pasi ndogo [pasi ya kusafiria]**	pasee ndogo [pasee ya koosafeereeya]
lamp	**taa**	taa
plug	**plagi**	plagee
portable...	**... ya mkono**	... ya mkono
radio	**redio**	redeeo
(cassette) recorder	**tepu rikoda**	tepoo reekoda
record player	**rikodi pleya**	reekodee pleya
shaver	**mashine ya kunyolea**	masheeneh ya koon^{y}olea
speakers	**mabomba**	mabomba
(colour) television	**tivi (ya rangi)**	teevee (ya rangee)
transformer	**transfoma**	transfoma

Grocer's *Duka la chakula*

Although the larger towns have supermarkets, it's worth going to the market for your food shopping. There are usually separate sections for fish, meat, fruit and vegetables.

I'd like some bread, please.	**Nipatie mkate, tafadhali.**	neepatee-eh mkateh tafaðalee
What sort of cheese do you have?	**Kuna jibini [chizi] gani?**	koona jeebeenee [cheezee] ganee
A piece of...	**Kipande cha...**	keepandeh cha
that one	**ile [kile]**	eeleh [keeleh]
the one on the shelf	**ya [cha] kwenye shubaka [rafu]**	ya [cha] kwenʸeh shoobaka [rafoo]
I'll have one of those, please.	**Naitaka moja katika hizo, tafadhali.**	naeetaka moja kateeka heezo tafaðalee
May I help myself?	**Nichukue ...? [Nijisaidie ...?]**	neechookooeh [neejeesaeedee-eh]
I'd like...	**Nataka..., tafadhali.**	nataka... tafðalee
a kilo of apples	**kilo moja ya matufaha**	keelo moja ya matoofaha
half a kilo of tomatoes	**nusu kilo ya nyanya [tungule]**	noosoo keelo ya nʸanʸa [toongooleh]
100 grams of butter	**gramu mia za siagi**	gramoo meeya za seeyagee
a litre of milk	**lita moja ya maziwa**	leeta moja ya mazeewa
half a dozen eggs	**nusu dazeni ya mayai**	noosoo dazenee ya mayaee
4 slices of ham	**vipande vinne vya nyama ya nguruwe**	veepandeh veenneh vya nʸama ya ngoorooweh
a packet of tea	**bomba [pakti] moja la majani ya chai**	bomba [paktee] moja la majanee ya chaee
a jar of jam	**mkebe mmoja wa jamu**	mkebeh mmoja wa jamoo
a tin (can) of peaches	**mkebe mmoja wa matunda ya pichi**	mkebeh mmoja wa matoonda ya peechee
a tube of mustard	**tyubu moja ya mastadi**	tyooboo moja ya mastadee
a box of chocolates	**boksi moja la chakleti**	boksee moja la chakletee
a crate of oranges	**sanduku moja la machungwa**	sandookoo moja la machoongwa

FOOD, see also page 63

Household articles *Vitu vya nyumbani*

bottle opener	**kidude cha kufungulia chupa**	keedoodeh cha koofoongooleeya choopa
bucket	**ndoo**	ndoo
can opener	**kidude cha kufungulia mkebe**	keedoodeh cha koofoongooleeya mkebeh
candles	**mishumaa**	meeshoomaa
clothes pegs (pins)	**vibanio vya kuanikia nguo**	veebaneeo vya koowaneekeeya ngoowo
food box	**sanduku la chakula**	sandookoo la chakoola
frying pan	**chuma cha kukaangia**	chooma cha kookaangeeya
matches	**vibiriti**	veebeereetee
paper napkins	**karatasi za kulia**	karatasee za kooleeya
plastic bags	**mifuko ya plastik**	meefooko ya plasteek
saucepan	**sufuria**	soofooreeya
tea towel	**kitambaa cha kufutia vyombo**	keetambaa cha koofooteeya vyombo
vacuum flask	**chupa ya chai**	choopa ya chaee
washing powder	**sabuni ya kufulia**	saboonee ya koofooleeya
washing-up liquid	**sabuni ya kuoshea vyombo**	saboonee ya koowoshea vyombo

Tools *Vifaa [Zana]*

hammer	**nyundo**	n'oondo
nails	**misumari**	meesoomaree
penknife	**kisu cha kukunja**	keesoo cha kookoonja
scissors	**mikasi**	meekasee
screws	**skurubu**	skoorooboo
screwdriver	**bisbis**	beesbees
spanner	**spana**	spana

Crockery *Vyombo vya kulia*

cups	**vikombe**	veekombeh
plates	**sahani**	sahanee
saucers	**visahani vya chai**	veesahanee vya chaee
tumblers	**glasi [bilauli]**	glasee [beelaoolee]

Cutlery (flatware) *Visu*

forks	**uma**	ooma
knives	**visu**	veesoo
spoons	**vijiko**	veejeeko
teaspoons	**vijiko vya chai**	veejeeko vya chaee

Jeweller's—Watchmaker's *Fundi wa saa*

Could I see that, please?	**Nataka kuangalia ile, tafadhali?**	nataka koowangaleeya eeleh tafaðalee
Do you have anything in gold?	**Unacho kitu chochote cha dhahabu?**	oonacho keetoo chochoteh cha ðahaboo
How many carats is this?	**Ni karati ngapi hii?**	nee karatee ngapee hee-ee
Is this real silver?	**Ni fedhal kweli hii?**	nee feðal kwelee hee-ee
Can you repair this watch?	**Unaweza kutengeneza saa hii?**	oonaweza kootengeneza saa hee-ee
I'd like a/an/some …	**Nataka …, tafadhali.**	nataka … tafaðalee
alarm clock	**saa yenye kengele ya kuamsha**	saa yenʸeh kengeleh ya koowamsha
bangle	**bangili**	bangeelee
battery	**betri**	betree
bracelet	**kikuku**	keekookoo
brooch	**beji**	bejee
chain	**mkufu**	mkoofoo
charm	**hirizi**	heereezee
cigarette case	**kijaluba cha sigara**	keejalooba cha seegara
cigarette lighter	**kibiriti cha mafuta/ gesi**	keebeereetee cha mafoota/ gesee
clip	**kibanio [klipu]**	keebaneeo [kleepoo]
clock	**saa**	saa
cross	**msalaba**	msalaba
cuff links	**vifungo vya mikono ya shati**	veefoongo vya meekono ya shatee
cutlery	**visu na vijiko**	veesoo na veejeeko
earrings	**herini**	hereenee
gem	**vyombo vya dhahabu**	vyombo vya ðahaboo
jewel box	**kijaluba cha vyombo vya dhahabu**	keejalooba cha vyombo vya ðahaboo
music box	**kijaluba cha muziki**	keejalooba cha moozeekee
necklace	**kidani**	keedanee
pendant	**lakti**	laktee
pin	**pini**	peenee
pocket watch	**saa ya mfukoni**	sa-a ya mfookonee
powder compact	**kijaluba cha podari**	keejalooba cha podaree

ring	pete	peteh
engagement ring	pete ya uchumba	peteh ya oochoomba
signet ring	pete yenye jina la mtu mwenyewe	peteh yenʸeh jeena la mtoo mwenʸeweh
wedding ring	pete ya harusi	peteh ya haroosee
rosary	tasbihi	tasbeehee
silverware	vyombo vya fedha	vyombo vya feᶞa
tie clip	kibanio cha tai	keebaneeo cha taee
tie pin	pini ya tai	peenee ya taee
watch	saa	saa
automatic	ya automatik	ya aootomateek
digital	ya digital	ya deegeetal
quartz	ya kwatz	ya kwatz
with a second hand	yenye mkono wa nukta	yenʸeh mkono wa nookta
waterproof	isiyoharibika kwa maji	eeseeyohareebeeka kwa majee
watchstrap	ukanda	ookanda ya saa
wristwatch	saa ya mkono	saa ya mkono

amber	ambari	ambaree
amethyst	amethist	ametheest
chromium	krom	krom
copper	shaba	shaba
coral	marjani	marjanee
crystal	jiwe linalongara	jeeweh leenalongara
cut glass	kiyoo kilichokatwa	keeyoo keeleechokatwa
diamond	almasi	almasee
emerald	zumaride	zoomareedeh
gold	dhahabu	ᶞahaboo
gold plate	pande la dhahabu	pandeh la ᶞahaboo
ivory	pembe	pembeh
jade	jiwe la thamani kijani	jeeweh la thamanee keejanee
onyx	kito cha rangi	keeto cha rangee
pearl	lulu	looloo
platinum	madini nyeupe	madeenee nʸeoopeh
ruby	kito chekundu	keeto chekoondoo
sapphire	johari	joharee
silver	fedha	feᶞa
silver plate	pande la fedha	pandeh la feᶞa
stainless steel	chuma cha pua	chooma cha poowa
topaz	yakuti	yakootee
turquoise	feruzi	feroozee

Optician *Mfanya miwani*

I've broken my glasses.	**Miwani yangu imevunjika.**	meewanee yangoo eemevoonjeeka
Can you repair them for me?	**Unaweza kunitengenezea?**	oonaweza kooneetengenezea
When will they be ready?	**Lini itakuwa tayari?**	leenee eetakoowa tayaree
Can you change the lenses?	**Unaweza kunibadilishia viyoo?**	oonaweza kooneebadeeleesheeya veeyoo
I'd like tinted lenses.	**Nataka viyoo vya rangi.**	nataka veeyoo vya rangee
The frame is broken.	**Fremu imevunjika.**	fremoo eemevoonjeeka
I'd like a spectacle case.	**Nataka kifuko cha kutilia miwani, tafadhali.**	nataka keefooko cha kooteeleeya meewanee tafaðalee
I'd like to have my eyesight checked.	**Nataka kupima macho.**	nataka koopeema macho
I'm short-sighted/long-sighted.	**Sioni mbali/sioni karibu.**	seeonee ᵐbalee/seeonee kareeboo
I'd like some contact lenses.	**Nataka vigae vya kubandika machoni.**	nataka veegaeh vya koobandeeka machonee
I've lost one of my contact lenses.	**Nimepoteza vigae cha kubandika machoni.**	neemepoteza veegaeh cha koobandeeka machonee
Could you give me another one?	**Nipatie kingine, tafadhali.**	neepatee-eh keengeeneh tafaðalee
I have hard/soft lenses.	**Nina vigae vinene/vyembamba.**	neena veegaeh veeneneh/vyembamba
Do you have any contact-lens fluid?	**Unayo dawa ya kusafishia vigae vya kubandika machoni?**	oonayo dawa ya koosafeesheeya veegaeh vya koobandeeka machonee
I'd like to buy a pair of sunglasses.	**Nataka kununua miwani ya jua.**	nataka koonoonoowa meewanee ya joowa
May I look in a mirror?	**Niangalie kwenye kiyoo?**	neeyangalee-eh kwenʸeh keeyoo
I'd like to buy a pair of binoculars.	**Nataka kununua darubini.**	nataka koonoonoowa daroobeenee

Photography *Upigaji picha*

You'll need high-speed film for animal shots on safari; well-known brands are often more expensive than at home.

Your equipment will require particular protection; polythene bags are a good means of keeping dust out of cameras and lenses. And be careful to keep your camera out of the sun, whenever possible.

I'd like a(n)... camera.	**Nataka kamera ya...**	nataka kamera ya
automatic	**automatik**	aootomateek
inexpensive	**rahisi**	raheesee
simple	**isiyokuwa na mazonge**	eeseeyokoowa na mazongeh
Can you show me some..., please?	**Unaweza kunionesha...?**	oonaweza kooneeonesha
cine (movie) cameras	**kamera ya kupiga picha za snema**	kamera ya koopeega peecha za snema
video cameras	**kamera ya vidyo**	kamera ya veedyo
I'd like to have some passport photos taken.	**Nataka kupiga picha za paspoti.**	nataka koopeega peecha za paspotee

Film *Filam*

I'd like a film for this camera.	**Nataka filam ya kamera hii.**	nataka feelam ya kamera hee-ee
black and white	**isiyokuwa ya rangi**	eeseeyokoowa ya rangee
colour	**ya rangi**	ya rangee
colour negative	**negativ ya rangi**	negateev ya rangee
colour slide	**slaidi za rangi**	slaeedee za rangee
cartridge	**filam ya katrij**	feelam ya katreej
disc film	**filam ya disk**	feelam ya deesk
roll film	**filam ya roli**	feelam ya rolee
video cassette	**kanda ya vidyo**	kanda ya veedyo
24/36 exposures	**ya picha 24/36**	ya peecha 24/36
this size	**saizi hii**	saeezee hee-ee
this ASA/DIN number	**hii ni nambari ASA/DIN**	hee-ee nee nambaree asa/deen
artificial light type	**ya kutumia ndani na taa**	ya kootoomeeya ndanee na taa
daylight type	**ya kutumia nje na juani**	ya kootoomeeya njeh na joowanee
fast (high-speed)	**ya mara moja**	ya mara moja

NUMBERS, see page 147

Processing *Kusafisha picha*

How much do you charge for processing?	**Bei gani kusafisha picha?**	be-ee ganee koosafeesha peecha
I'd like... prints of each negative.	**Nataka picha... kwa kila negetiv.**	nataka peecha... kwa keela negeteev
with a mat finish	**isiyongara**	eeseeyongara
with a glossy finish	**yenye kungara**	yen^yeh koongara
Will you enlarge this, please?	**Ifanye hii kubwa, tafadhali?**	eefan^yeh hee-ee koobwa tafaðalee
When will the photos be ready?	**Lini picha zitakuwa tayari?**	leenee peecha zeetakoowa tayaree

Accessories and repairs *Vipuli na matengenezo*

I'd like a/an/some...	**Nataka...**	nataka
battery	**betri**	betree
camera case	**mfuko wa kamera**	mfooko wa kamera
(electronic) flash	**taa ya ilektronik**	taa ya eelektroneek
filter	**filta**	feelta
for black and white	**za picha bila rangi**	za peecha beela rangee
for colour	**picha za rangi**	peecha za rangee
lens	**lensi za kamera**	lensee za kamera
telephoto lens	**lensi za aina ya telefoto**	lensee za aeena ya telefoto
wide-angle lens	**lensi za kuanua picha**	lensee za koowanoowa peecha
lens cap	**kifuniko cha lensi**	keefooneeko cha lensee
Can you repair this camera?	**Unaweza kutengeneza kamera hii?**	oonaweza kootengeneza kamera hee-ee
The film is jammed.	**Filam hii imekwama.**	feelam hee-ee eemekwama
There's something wrong with the...	**Mna kilichoharibika...**	mna keeleechohareebeeka
film winder	**kidude cha filam winda**	keedoodeh cha feelam weenda
flash attachment	**kidude cha taa**	keedoodeh cha taa
lens	**lensi**	lensee
light meter	**mita ya jua**	meeta ya joowa
rangefinder	**kiyoo**	keeyoo
shutter	**kidude cha kupigia**	keedoodeh cha koopeegeeya

Tobacconist's *Duka la sigara*

Local brands of cigarettes are inexpensive, as are foreign brands manufactured locally. Imported cigarettes are heavily taxed and therefore sold at a premium price.

Do you have any American/English cigarettes?	**Una sigara za kimarekani/kiige-reza?**	oona seegara za keemarekanee/kee-eegereza
I'd like a carton.	**Nataka katon moja.**	nataka katon moja
Give me a/some..., please.	**Nipatie..., tafad-hali.**	neepatee-eh ... tafaḓalee
candy	**peremende**	peremendeh
chewing gum	**ubani wa kutafuna**	oobanee wa kootafoona
chewing tobacco	**mchuku**	mchookoo
chocolate	**chakleti**	chakletee
cigarette case	**kijaluba cha sigara**	keejalooba cha seegara
cigarette holder	**kidude cha kuvutia sigara**	keedoodeh cha koovooteeya seegara
cigarettes	**sigara**	seegara
clove-flavoured	** za karafuu**	za karafoo-oo
filter-tipped/ without filter	** za filta/bila filta**	za feelta/beela feelta
light/dark tobacco	** tumbaku nyeupe/nyeusi**	toombakoo nʸeoopeh/nʸeoosee
mild/strong	** nyepesi/kali**	nʸepesee/kalee
menthol	** za nanaa**	za nanaa
cigars	**sigaa**	seegaa
lighter	**kibiriti**	keebeereetee
lighter fluid/gas	** kibiriti cha maf-uta/gesi**	keebeereetee cha mafoota/gesee
matches	**kibiriti cha njiti**	keebeereetee cha njeetee
pipe	**mtemba [kiko]**	mtemba [keeko]
pipe cleaners	** waya wa kusaf-ishia mtemba**	waya wa koosafeesheeya mtemba
pipe tobacco	** tumbaku ya mtemba**	toombakoo ya mtemba
postcard	**postkadi**	postkadee
snuff	**tumbaku ya kunusa**	toombakoo ya koonoosa
stamps	**stempu**	stempoo
sweets	**peremende**	peremendeh
wick	**utambi**	ootambee

Miscellaneous *Vitu vingine*

Souvenirs *Vikumbusho*

There are lots of interesting souvenirs you can bring back – particularly popular are the wooden "makonde" carvings. These vary in quality tremendously, so look out for better hand-made carvings, rather than the mass-produced ones. Stone carvings in *kisii* soapstone and wooden pipes can also make attractive gifts or momentos.

On the coast look out for Arab brasswork and Zanzibar chests. For a more unusual souvenir you could bring back some local colourful fabrics, which make good beachwraps, bedspreads or tablecloths.

Another feature of cosmopolitan East Africa is the variety of Indian saris which you can buy. When you do your shopping in the coastal regions you'll certainly come across an Oriental goods store.

Basketwork items, too, are good value. Don't be tempted by any of the animal skins or ivory on offer – all ivory trade and most of the trade in animal skins is illegal – so your goods will be confiscated at customs.

Don't forget, haggling is customary in East African markets and small shops.

chetezo cha udongo	chetezo cha oodongo	earthenware incense burner
kanga	kanga	East African fabrics
kiyondo	keeyondo	Kenyan baskets
kofia ya mkono	kofeeya ya mkono	handmade caps
kombe	kombeh	sea shells
mabegi ya ngozi	mabegee ya ngozee	leather suitcases
makasha	makasha	zanzibar chests
mashanuo	mashanoowo	Swahili combs
mkeka	mkeka	straw mat
mkoba wa ukili	mkoba wa ookeelee	straw basket
tembo wa mti	tembo wa mtee	wooden elephant
viati vya makubadhi	veeyatee vya makoobaðee	handmade leather sandals
vinyago	veen'yago	makonde carvings

Records–Cassettes *Rikordi–Kanda*

I'd like a...	Nataka...	nataka
cassette	kanda	kanda
video cassette	kanda ya vidyo	kanda ya veedyo
compact disc	diski	deeskee
Do you have any records by...?	Unazo rikodi za nyimbo za...?	oonazo reekodee za n'eembo za
Can I listen to this record?	Naweza kusikiliza rikodi hii?	naweza kooseekeeleeza reekodee hee-ee
classical music	muziki ya kizamani	moozeekee ya keezamanee
folk music	muziki wa kitama-duni	moozeekee wa keetamadoonee
folk song	nyimbo za utama-duni	n'eembo za ootamadoonee
instrumental music	muziki bila nyimbo	moozeekee beela n'eembo
jazz	jazi	jazee
light music	muziki wa kubu-rudisha	moozeekee wa koobooroodeesha
orchestral music	tarabu	taraboo
pop music	muziki wa kisasa	moozeekee wa keesasa

Toys *Vitu vya kuchezea*

I'd like a toy/game...	Nataka kitu cha kuchezea/mchezo...	nataka keetoo cha koochezea/mchezo
for a boy	kwa mtoto wa kiume	kwa mtoto wa keeoomeh
for a 5-year-old girl	kwa mtoto wa kike miaka mitano	kwa mtoto wa keekeh meeyaka meetano
(beach) ball	mpira wa kuchezea pwani	mpeera wa koochezea pwanee
bucket and spade (pail and shovel)	ndoo na kidude cha kutekea	ndoo na keedoodeh cha kootekea
building blocks (bricks)	matofali	matofalee
card game	karata	karata
chess set	seti ya chesi	setee ya chesee
doll	mtoto wa sanamu	mtoto wa sanamoo
electronic game	michezo ya kisasa	meechezo ya keesasa
roller skates	rola	rola
snorkel	snorkel	snorkel

Your money: banks—currency

The best place to change money is at a bank or an authorised hotel. The unofficial deals you may be offered in the street should be avoided – they are illegal, and will often leave you with forged notes.

Banks are generally open between 9.00 a.m. and 2.00 p.m. during the week, and sometimes on a Saturday from 9.00 a.m. to 11.00 a.m. The currency exchanges of major airports, however, are open every day round the clock.

Most international credit cards are accepted in the larger towns, though Visa is more common than Access. Traveller's cheques are widely accepted in banks and international hotels.

The basic unit of currency throughout East Africa is the shilling (*shilingi*), which is divided into 100 cents (*senti*). Note that the five cent coin, written -/05, is called the *ndururu*, and in Kenya 10 cents are known as a *peni*. Although the exchange rate of all three shillings is the same, their currencies are not interchangeable.

Visitors to Zanzibar will find that they are required to pay for their services in foreign currency.

Where's the nearest bank?	**Iko wapi benki ya karibu?**	eeko wapee benkee ya kareeboo
Where's the nearest currency exchange office?	**Pako wapi mahali pa karibu pa kuba- dilisha pesa?**	pako wapee mahalee pa kareeboo pa koobadeeleesha pesa

At the bank *Kwenye benki [Katika benki]*

I want to change some dollars/pounds.	**Nataka kubadilisha dala/paun, tafad- hali.**	nataka koobadeeleesha dala/paoon tafaᶁalee

I want to cash a traveller's cheque.	**Nataka kubadilisha hundi za msafiri/ cheki za msafiri.**	nataka koobadeeleesha hoondee za msafeeree/ chekee za msafeeree
What's the exchange rate?	**Kubadilisha pesa ni kiasi gani?**	koobadeeleesha pesa nee keeyasee ganee
How much commission do you charge?	**Malipo yako ni kiasi gani?**	maleepo yako nee keeyasee ganee
Can you cash a personal cheque?	**Unaweza kuniba-dilishia hundi [cheki] ya binafsi?**	oonaweza kooneebadeeleesheeya hoondee [chekee] ya beenafsee
Can you fax my bank in London?	**Unaweza kunitu-mia feksi benki yetu London?**	oonaweza kooneetoomeeya feksee benkee yetoo london
I have a/an/some...	**Nina...**	neena
credit card	**kadi ya benki**	kadee ya benkee
Eurocheques	**kadi inayotumika benki za Ulaya**	kadee eenayotoomeeka benkee za oolaya
letter of credit	**barua ya benki**	baroowa ya benkee
I'm expecting some money from New York. Has it arrived?	**Nategemea pesa kutoka New York, zishafika?**	nategemea pesa kootoka new york zeeshafeeka
Please give me notes (bills) and some small change.	**Tafadhali nipatie noti na chenji.**	tafaðalee neepatee-eh notee na chenjee
Give me... large notes and the rest in small notes.	**Nipatie... noti kubwa na nyingine noti ndogo, tafad-hali.**	neepatee-eh... notee koobwa na nᵞeengeeneh notee ndogo tafaðalee

Deposits–Withdrawals *Kuweka–Kutoa*

I want to...	**Nataka kufun-gua...**	nataka koofoongoowa
open an account	**akaunti**	akaoontee
withdraw... shillings	**Kutoa shilingi...**	kootowa sheeleengee
Where should I sign?	**Nitie sahihi wapi?**	neetee-eh saheehee wapee
I'd like to pay this into my account.	**Nataka kutia pesa katika akaunti yangu.**	nataka kooteeya pesa kateeka akaoontee yangoo

NUMBERS, see page 147

Business terms *Shuruti za kibiashara*

My name is...	Jina langu ni...	**jee**na langoo nee
Here's my card.	Hii ni kadi yangu.	hee-ee nee **ka**dee yangoo
I have an appointment with...	Nina miadi na...	**nee**na **mee**yadee na
Can you give me an estimate of the cost?	Unakisia itafika kiasi gani?	oonakee**see**ya eetafeeka **kee**yasee ganee
What's the rate of inflation?	Bei zimeongezeka kwa kiasi gani?	**be**-ee zeemeongezeka kwa **kee**yasee ganee
Can you provide me with a(n)...?	Nipatie... tafadhali? [Unaweza kunipatia...?]	neepatee-eh ... tafaðalee [oona**we**za kooneepa**tee**ya]
interpreter	mtu wa kufasiri/ mkalimani	mtoo wa koofa**see**ree/ mkalee**ma**nee
personal computer	kompyuta yangu mwenyewe [binafsi]	kom**pyoo**ta **ya**ngoo mwen^yeweh [beenafsee]
secretary	seketeri	seke**te**ree
Where can I make photocopies?	Wapi nitaweza kupigafotokopi [kutoa chapa]?	**wa**pee neeta**we**za koopeegafotokopee [koo**to**wa **cha**pa]

amount	idadi	ee**da**dee
balance	baki	**ba**kee
capital	rasilmali	raseel**ma**lee
cheque	hundi [cheki]	**hoon**dee [**che**kee]
contract	mkataba	mka**ta**ba
discount	punguzo la bei	poon**goo**zo la **be**-ee
expenses	matumizi	matoo**mee**zee
interest	riba	**ree**ba
investment	kitega uchumi	kee**te**ga oo**choo**mee
invoice	ankara [invoisi]	an**ka**ra [eenvoo**ee**see]
loss	hasara	ha**sa**ra
mortgage	mkopo wa kununulia nyumba	mkopo wa koonoo-**noo**leeya n^**yoom**ba
payment	malipo	ma**lee**po
percentage	asilimia	aseelee**mee**ya
profit	faida	**fa**eeda
purchase	kununua	koonoo**noo**wa
sale	kuuza [mauzo]	koo-**oo**za [ma**oo**zo]
share	hisa [sheya]	**hee**sa [**she**ya]
transfer	kuhamisha	koohamee**sha**
value	thamani	tha**ma**nee

At the post office

Post offices are indicated by the sign PTT (Post, Telephone and Telegraph) and postboxes are painted red. You can also often buy stamps at hotels and shops selling postcards.

Opening hours are usually from 8.00 a.m. until noon or 1.00 p.m., reopening at 2.00 p.m. until 4.30 p.m. or 5.00 p.m. On Saturdays they normally close for the day at noon.

Where's the nearest post office?	**Posta ya karibu iko wapi?**	posta ya kareeboo **ee**ko wapee
What time does the post office open/ close?	**Posta hufunguliwa/ hufungwa saa ngapi?**	posta hoofoongoo**lee**wa/ hoofoongwa saa **nga**pee
A stamp for this letter/postcard, please.	**Nipatie stempu ya barua/postkadi hii, tafadhali.**	neepatee-eh **stem**poo ya baroowa/postkadee hee-ee tafaðalee
A...-shilling stamp, please.	**Ya shilingi..., tafadhali.**	ya sheeleengee... tafaðalee
What's the postage for a letter to London?	**Stempu ya London bei gani?**	stempoo ya london be-ee ganee
What's the postage for a postcard to Los Angeles?	**Stempu ya Los Angeles bei gani?**	stempoo ya los angelees be-ee ganee
Where's the letter box (mailbox)?	**Liko wapi sanduku la kupostia barua?**	leeko wapee sandookoo la kooposteeya baroowa
I want to send this parcel.	**Nataka kupeleka mzigo huu.**	nataka koopeleka mzeego hoo-oo
I'd like to send this (by)...	**Nataka kupeleka... kwa.**	nataka koopeleka... kwa
airmail	**ndege**	ndegeh
express (special delivery)	**haraka**	haraka
registered mail	**rejesta**	rejesta

At which counter can I cash an international money order?	**Kaunta ipi naweza kubadilisha manioda za nchi za nje?**	kaoonta eepee naweza koobadeeleesha maneeoda za nchee za njeh
Where's the poste restante (general delivery)?	**Iko wapi sehemu ya barua zinazongojewa na wenyewe [poste restante]?**	eeko wapee sehemoo ya baroowa zeenazongojewa na wen'eweh [posteh restanteh]
Is there any post (mail) for me? My name is...	**Kuna baruwa zangu? Jina langu ni...**	koona baroowa zangoo. jeena langoo nee

STEMPU	STAMPS
MIZIGO	PARCELS
MANIODA	MONEY ORDERS

Telegrams–Telexes–Faxes *Simu za upepo [barua]–Teleksi–Feksi*

Faxes can often be sent from your hotel. There are also facilities at most main post offices. Telexes are widely used and can be sent from any post office. Telgrams can be sent by telephone through the operator.

I'd like to send a telegram/fax.	**Nataka kupeleka simu/feksi.**	nataka koopeleka seemoo/feksee
May I have a form, please?	**Nipatie fomu tafadhali?**	neepatee-eh fomoo tafaдalee
How much is it per word?	**Kiasi gani kila neno?**	keeyasee ganee keela neno
How much will this (tele)fax cost?	**Nitalipa kiasi gani kwa feksi hii?**	neetaleepa keeyasee ganee kwa feksee hee-ee

134

Telephoning *Kupiga simu*

The telephone service in East Africa is a joint one, covering Kenya, Tanzania and Uganda. Numbers in any of these countries can be dialled using the correct area code. Local and international calls are usually quite dependable, but some long-distance calls can prove more difficult to make.

Phone boxes are painted red, and can be found in most towns and at major post offices. They are usually coin operated and take 2-shilling pieces. You can also make calls from hotels, but these can be considerably more expensive. Calls within East Africa are cheaper after 6 p.m.

International calls can be made from the main post office. You normally pay in advance for a call, and get a refund if you fail to connect. It is possible to dial international calls direct, using a phone card which you can get from the post office or from news-stands. International calls are cheaper after 10.00 p.m.

Where's the telephone?	**Iko wapi simu?**	eeko wapee **see**moo
I'd like a telephone token.	**Nataka kadi ya kupigia simu.**	nataka kadee ya koopeegeeya **see**moo
Where's the nearest telephone booth?	**Simu ya karibu iko wapi?**	**see**moo ya kareeboo eeko wapee
May I use your phone?	**Naweza kutumia simu yako tafad-hali?**	naweza kootoomeeya **see**moo yako tafaẟalee
Do you have a telephone directory for Nairobi?	**Unacho kitabu cha simu cha Nairobi?**	oonacho keetaboo cha **see**moo cha naeerobee
I'd like to call... in England.	**Nataka kupiga simu... Uingereza.**	nataka koopeega **see**moo... ooweenge**re**za
What's the area code for Arusha?	**Namba ya kodi ya Arusha ni ngapi?**	namba ya kodee ya aroosha nee **nga**pee
How do I get the international operator?	**Vipi nitampata opereta wa simu za nchi za nje?**	veepee neetampata opereta wa **see**moo za nchee za njeh

Operator *Mzee/Mama*

The appropriate term of address is *bwana* to a man and *bibi* to a woman.

NUMBERS, see page 147

I'd like Kampala 234 567.	**Nipatie Kampala namba 234 567, tafadhali.**	neepatee-eh kampala namba 234 567 tafaðalee
Can you help me get this number?	**Nisaidie kuipata namba hii, tafadhali?**	neesaeedee-eh kooweepata namba hee-ee tafaðalee
I'd like to place a personal (person-to-person) call.	**Hasa nataka kumpigia simu mtu huyu.**	hasa nataka koompeegeeya seemoo mtoo hooyoo
I'd like to reverse the charges (call collect).	**Nataka gharama za simu zilipwe na atayepokea huko.**	nataka RHarama za seemoo zeeleepweh na atayepokea hooko

Speaking *Ni mimi [Miye]*

Hello. This is...	**Halo, ni mimi...**	halo nee meemee
I'd like to speak to...	**Nataka kusema na... tafadhali.**	nataka koosema na... tafaðalee
Extension...	**Ekstenshan [Simu ya ndani]...**	ekstenshan [seemoo ya ndanee]
Speak louder/more slowly, please.	**Sema kwa sauti/ pole pole, tafadhali.**	sema kwa saootee/poleh poleh tafaðalee

Swahili telephone alphabet

A	**Ali**	alee	N	**Nakuru**	nakooroo
B	**Banda**	banda	O	**Ona**	ona
C	**Chakechake**	chakechakeh	P	**Punda**	poonda
D	**Dodoma**	dodoma	Q	**Kyela**	kyela
E	**Entebe**	entebeh	R	**Rangi**	rangee
F	**Fumba**	foomba	S	**Simu**	seemoo
G	**Gogo**	gogo	T	**Tatu**	tatoo
H	**Homa**	homa	U	**Uganda**	ooganda
I	**Imba**	eemba	V	**Vitu**	veetoo
J	**Jambo**	jambo	W	**Wali**	walee
K	**Kenya**	kenʸa	X	**Eksrei**	eksre-ee
L	**Lala**	lala	Y	**Yai**	yaee
M	**Mama**	mama	Z	**Zanzibar**	zanzeebar

TELEPHONING

Bad luck *Bahati mbaya.*

Would you try again later, please?	**Jaribu baadaye, tafadhali?**	jareeboo baadayeh tafaðalee
Operator, you gave me the wrong number.	**Mzee [Mama], umenipa namba siyo.**	mzeeh [mama] oomeneepa namba seeyo
Operator, we were cut off.	**Mama [Mzee], simu imekatika.**	mama [mze-eh] seemoo eemekateeka

Not there *Hayupo*

When will he/she be back?	**Wakati gani [Lini] atarudi?**	wakatee ganee [leenee] ataroodee
Will you tell him/her I called? My name is...	**Mwambie kwamba nimepiga simu, tafadhali. Jina langu...**	mwambee-eh kwamba neemepeega seemoo tafaðalee. jeena langoo
Would you ask him/her to call me?	**Mwambie anipigie simu, tafadhali?**	mwambee-eh aneepeegee-eh seemoo tafaðalee
Would you take a message, please?	**Mpe maagizo, tafadhali?**	mpeh maageezo tafaðalee

Charges *Malipo [Gharama]*

What was the cost of that call?	**Yalikuwa kiasi gani malipo ya simu?**	yaleekoowa keeyasee ganee maleepo ya seemoo
I want to pay for the call.	**Nataka kulipia simu.**	nataka kooleepeeya seemoo

Kuna simu yako.	There's a telephone call for you.
Unapiga namba gani?	What number are you calling?
Simu inaongea sasa.	The line's engaged.
Hakuna majibu. [Inaita tu.]	There's no answer.
Umepiga namba siyo.	You've got the wrong number.
Simu mbovu [Imeharibika].	The phone is out of order.
Subiri kidogo.	Just a moment.
Subiri, tafadhali.	Hold on, please.
Ametoka kidogo. [Hayupo.]	He's/She's out at the moment.

Kupiga simu

Doctor

You should take out special travel insurance to cover yourself in case of accident or illness. Other precautions required before travelling are vaccinations for typhoid and hepatitis A. Cholera and yellow fever inoculations are also advisable, and you should check that your tetanus and polio boosters are up to date. Malaria is a problem throughout the region, and the taking of a course of anti-malaria tablets prior to your visit is recommended. In mosquito-infested areas it is a good idea to sleep under a net and to use an insect repellent.

One important precaution to take during your stay is avoid drinking the tap water. It can contain anything from parasites to dysentery and typhoid bacilli.

Another serious problem throughout the region is that of AIDS, so do take all necessary precautions. Many travellers nowadays take with them a medical kit of their own, complete with clean needles and syringes, in case medical treatment is needed.

Can you get me a doctor?	**Nipatie daktari tafadhali?**	neepatee-eh daktaree tafaðalee
I need a doctor, quickly.	**Nahitaji daktari, haraka [halan].**	naheetajee daktaree haraka [halan]
Where can I find a doctor who speaks English?	**Wapi naweza kupata daktari anayesema Kizungu [Kiingereza]?**	wapee naweza koopata daktaree anayesema keezoongoo [kee-eengereza]
Where's the surgery (doctor's office)?	**Zahanati/Klinik iko wapi?**	zahanatee/kleeneek eeko wapee
What are the surgery (office) hours?	**Zahanati hufunguliwa saa ngapi?**	zahanatee hoofoongoo-leewa saa ngapee
Could the doctor come to see me here?	**Daktari ataweza kuja kuniangalia hapa?**	daktaree ataweza kooja kooneeyangaleeya hapa
What time can the doctor come?	**Wakati gani daktari ataweza kuja?**	wakatee ganee daktaree ataweza kooja
Can I have an appointment... ?	**Naweza kuja...?**	naweza kooja
as soon as possible	**sasa hivi/haraka iwezekanavyo**	sasa heevee/haraka eewezekanavyo

CHEMIST'S, see page 108

Parts of the body *Sehemu za mwili*

appendix	**chango**	chango
arm	**mkono**	mkono
back	**mgongo**	mgongo
bladder	**kibofu cha mkojo**	keebofoo cha mkojo
bone	**mfupa**	mfoopa
bowel	**matumbo**	matoombo
breast	**ziwa/matiti**	zeewa/mateetee
chest	**kifua**	keefooa
ear	**sikio**	seekeeo
eye(s)	**jicho (plur. macho)**	jeecho (macho)
face	**uso**	ooso
finger	**kidole**	keedoleh
foot	**mguu**	mgoo-oo
genitals	**sehemu za siri**	sehemoo za seeree
hand	**mkono**	mkono
head	**kichwa**	keechwa
heart	**moyo**	moyo
jaw	**taya**	taya
joint	**kiungo**	keeoongo
kidney	**figo**	feego
knee	**goti/futi**	gotee/footee
leg	**mguu**	mgoo-oo
ligament	**kano**	kano
lip	**mdomo**	mdomo
liver	**ini**	eenee
lung	**pafu**	pafoo
mouth	**kinywa**	keen^ywa
muscle	**msuli**	msoolee
neck	**shingo**	sheengo
nerve	**mshipa**	msheepa
nose	**pua**	poowa
rib	**mbavu**	ᵐbavoo
shoulder	**bega**	bega
skin	**ngozi**	ngozee
spine	**uti**	ootee
stomach	**tumbo**	toombo
tendon	**ugwe**	oogweh
thigh	**paja**	paja
throat	**koo/roho**	koo/roho
thumb	**kidole gumba cha mkono**	keedoleh goomba cha mkono
toe	**kidole gumba cha mguu**	keedoleh goomba cha mgoo-oo
tongue	**ulimi**	ooleemee
tonsils	**tonsil/mafindo**	tonseel/mafeendo
vein	**mshipa wa damu**	msheepa wa damoo

Accident—Injury *Ajali–Kuumia*

There's been an accident.	**Kumetokea ajali.**	koometokea ajalee
My child has had a fall.	**Mtoto wangu ameanguka [kaanguka].**	mtoto wangoo ameangooka [kaangooka]
He/She has hurt his/her head.	**Ameumia kichwa.**	ameoomeeya keechwa
He's/She's unconscious.	**Amezimia/amepoteza fahamu.**	amezeemeeya/amepoteza fahamoo
He's/She's bleeding heavily.	**Anatoka damu nyingi.**	anatoka damoo nᵞeengee
He's/She's injured.	**Ameumia vibaya.**	ameoomeeya veebaya
His/Her arm is broken.	**Mkono wake umevunjika.**	mkono wakeh oomevoonjeeka
His/Her ankle is swollen.	**Kifundo cha mguu wake kimevimba.**	keefoondo cha mgoo-oo wakeh keemeveemba
I've been stung.	**Nimeumwa [Nimetafunwa] na mdudu.**	neemeoomwa [neemetafoonwa] na mdoodoo
I've got something in my eye.	**Nimeingia kitu jichoni**	neeme-eengeeya keetoo jeechonee
I've got a/an ...	**Nimepata/Nina ...**	neemepata/neena
blister	**lengelenge**	lengelengeh
boil	**jipu**	jeepoo
bruise	**mchubuko**	mchoobooko
burn	**kuungua moto**	koo-oongoowa moto
cut	**jeraha**	jeraha
graze	**mkwaruzo**	mkwaroozo
insect bite	**kuumwa na mdudu**	koo-oomwa na mdoodoo
lump	**donge**	dongeh
rash	**mwasho/harara**	mwasho/harara
sting	**msumari wa mdudu**	msoomaree wa mdoodoo
swelling	**uvimbe**	ooveembeh
wound	**kidonda**	keedonda
Could you have a look at it?	**Unaweza kuniangalia?/Niangalie tafadhali?**	oonaweza kooneeyangaleeya/neeyangalee-eh tafaδalee
I can't move my ...	**Siwezi kunyanyuka ...**	seewezee koonᵞanᵞooka
It hurts.	**Inauma.**	eenaooma

Wapi panauma?	Where does it hurt?
Unapata maumivu ya namna gani?	What kind of pain is it?
madogo/makali/ya kupwitapwita	dull/sharp/throbbing
mfululizo/yanakuja na kuondoka	constant/on and off
Ime...	It's...
imevunjika/imeteteereka	broken/sprained
imeteguka/imeachana	dislocated/torn
Nataka upigwe ekserei.	I'd like you to have an X-ray.
Lazima tukutie gamba.	We'll have to put it in plaster.
Imetunga usaha.	It's infected.
Umewahi kudungwa [kupigwa] sindano ya tetenas?	Have you been vaccinated against tetanus?
Nitakupatia dawa za kupunguza maumivu.	I'll give you a painkiller.

Illness *Magonjwa/Maradhi*

I'm not feeling well.	**Sjisikii vizuri.**	sjeeseekee-ee veezooree
I'm ill.	**Naumwa.**	naoomwa
I feel...	**Nasikia...**	naseekeeya
dizzy	**kizunguzungu/ kisunzi**	keezoongoozoongoo/ keesoonzee
nauseous	**kichefuchefu**	keechefoochefoo
shivery	**baridi/kutetemeka**	bareedee/kootetemeka
I have a temperature (fever).	**Nina homa.**	neena homa
My temperature is 38 degrees.	**Nimepata homa kali.**	neemepata homa kalee
I've been vomiting.	**Nikitapika**	neekeetapeeka
I'm constipated/ I've got diarrhoea.	**Sipati choo/Naharisha.**	seepatee choo/nahareesha
My... hurt(s).	**Naumwa na...**	naoomwa na
I've got (a/an)...	**Nimepata.../ Nina...**	neemepata/neena

asthma	pumu	poomoo
backache	maumivu ya mgongo	maoomeevoo ya mgongo
cold	mafua [baridi]	mafoowa [bareedee]
cough	kikohozi	keekohozee
cramps	musuli hupandana	moosoolee hoopandana
earache	maumivu ya sikio	maoomeevoo ya seekeeo
hay fever	kamasi [hijabu]	kamasee [heejaboo]
headache	maumivu ya kichwa	maoomeevoo ya keechwa
indigestion	kiungulia	keeoongooleeya
nosebleed	kutoka damu puani	kootoka damoo poowanee
palpitations	moyo unapiga kwa kasi	moyo oonapeega kwa kasee
rheumatism	baridi yabisi	bareedee yabeesee
sore throat	maumivu ya koo	maoomeevoo ya koo
stiff neck	shingo imekaza	sheengo eemekaza
stomach ache	maumivu ya tumbo	maoomeevoo ya toombo
sunstroke	kuzimia kwa joto	koozeemeeya kwa joto
I have difficulties breathing.	napata tabu kuvuta pumzi	napata taboo koovoota poomzee
I have chest pains.	Nina maumivu ya kifua.	neena maoomeevoo ya keefoowa
I had a heart attack... years ago.	Nilipata ugonjwa wa... zamani.	neeleepata oogonjwa wa... zamanee
My blood pressure is too high/too low.	Presha yangu imepanda/imeshuka.	presha yangoo eemepanda/eemeshooka
I'm allergic to...	... hunidhuru/huniletea matatizo.	hoonee∂ooroo/ hooneeletea matateezo
I'm diabetic.	Nina kisukari/ ugonjwa wa sukari.	neena keesookaree/ oogonjwa wa sookaree

Women's section *Sehemu ya wanawake*

I have period pains.	Nina tumbo la zingizi.	neena toombo la zeengeezee
I have a vaginal infection.	Natoka uchafu sehemu za siri.	natoka oochafoo sehemoo za seeree
I'm on the pill.	Natumia dawa za kuzuwia uzazi.	natoomeeya dawa za koozooweeya oozazee
I haven't had a period for 2 months.	Sikupata siku zangu kwa miezi miwili.	seekoopata seekoo zangoo kwa mee-ezee meeweelee
I'm (3 months) pregnant.	Nina mimba ya miezi mitatu.	neena meemba ya mee-ezee meetatoo

Kwa muda gani unajisikia hali hii?	How long have you been feeling like this?
Hii ni mara ya kwanza kuwa hali hii?	Is this the first time you've had this?
Nitakupima homa/presha.	I'll take your temperature/blood pressure.
Tafadhali vua nguo (mpaka kiunoni).	Please undress (down to the waist).
Tafadhali lala hapa.	Please lie down over here.
Fungua mdomo.	Open your mouth.
Vuta pumzi kwa nguvu.	Breathe deeply.
Kohowa, tafadhali.	Cough, please.
Wapi panauma?	Where does it hurt?
Umepata...	You've got (a/an)...
ependiks	appendicitis
kichocho	bilharzia
kipindupindu	cholera
ugonjwa wa kibofu cha mkojo	cystitis
homa ya mafua	flu
umedhurika na chakula kibaya	food poisoning
ugonjwa wa matumbo	gastritis
homa ya manjano	hepatitis
mchomo wa...	inflammation of...
homa ya manjano	jaundice
homa ya malaria	malaria
surua	measles
homa ya mapafu	pneumonia
magonjwa ya zinaa	venereal disease
Inaambukiza.	It's contagious.
Inadhuru.	It's an allergy.
Utadungwa [utapigwa] sindano.	I'll give you an injection.
Nataka kupima damu yako/choo chako/mkojo wako.	I want a specimen of your blood/stools/urine.
Lazima upumzike kitandani kwa siku...	You must stay in bed for... days.
Nataka uangaliwe na daktari maalumu wa magojwa haya.	I want you to see a specialist.
Nataka uende hospitali ukapimwe kila kitu.	I want you to go to the hospital for a general check-up.

Prescription—Treatment *Cheti cha dawa–Matibabu*

This is my usual medicine.	**Hizi ndizo nitumiazo kwa kawaida.**	heezee ndeezo neetoomeeyazo kwa kawaeeda
Can you give me a prescription for this?	**Niandike cheti cha/kwa dawa hizi, tafadhali?**	neeyandeekee-eh chetee cha/kwa dawa heezee tafaðalee
Can you prescribe a/an/some...?	**Unaweza kuniandikia...?**	oonaweza kooneeyandeekeeya
antidepressant	**dawa za kuondoa wasi wasi**	dawa za koowondowa wasee wasee
malaria tablets	**dawa za malaria**	dawa za malareeya
sleeping pills	**dawa za kupata usingizi**	dawa za koopata ooseengeezee
tranquillizer	**dawa za kutuliza hali**	dawa za kootooleeza halee
I'm allergic to penicillin.	**Zinanidhuru baadhi ya dawa za penisilin.**	zeenaneeðooroo baaðee ya dawa za peneeseeleen
I don't want anything too strong.	**Sitaki dawa iliyo kali sana.**	seetakee dawa eeleeyo kalee sana
How many times a day should I take it?	**Nitumie kutwa mara ngapi?**	neetoomee-eh kootwa mara ngapee
Is that needle sterilized?	**Sindano imechemshwa/i safi?**	seendano eemechemshwa/ee safee

Unapata matibabu gani?	What treatment are you having?
Unatumia dawa gani?	What medicine are you taking?
Sindano au dawa ya kumeza?	By injection or orally?
Kunywa... dawa hii vijiko vidogo...	Take... teaspoons of this medicine.
Meza kidonge kimoja.	Take one pill with a glass of water.
kila saa...	every... hours
mara... kwa siku	... times a day
kabla/baada ya kula	before/after each meal
asubuhi/usiku	in the morning/at night
kama unapata maumivu	if there is any pain
kwa siku...	for... days

CHEMIST'S, see page 108

Fee *Malipo*

How much do I owe you?	**Nilipe kiasi gani?**	neeleepeh keeyasee ganee
May I have a receipt for my health insurance?	**Nipatie risiti kwaa-jili ya bima yangu, tafadhali?**	neepatee-eh reeseetee kwa-ajeelee ya beema yangoo tafaðalee
Can I have a medical certificate?	**Nipatie barua kue-leza ugonjwa wangu, tafadhali?**	neepatee-eh baroowa kooweleza oogonjwa wangoo tafaðalee
Would you fill in this health insurance form, please?	**Tafadhali jaza fomu hii ya bima?**	tafaðalee jaza fomoo hee-ee ya beema

Hospital *Hospitali*

Please notify my family.	**Tafadhali wajulishe familia yangu.**	tafaðalee wajooleesheh fameeleeya yangoo
What are the visiting hours?	**Saa gani za kuzuru wagonjwa?**	saa ganee za koozooroo wagonjwa
When can I get up?	**Naweza kutoka kitandani lini?**	naweza kootoka keetandanee leenee
When will the doctor come?	**Lini daktari ata-kuja?**	leenee daktaree atakooja
I'm in pain.	**Nina maumivu.**	neéna maoomeevoo
I can't eat/sleep.	**Siwezi kula/kulala.**	seewezee koola/koolala
Where is the bell?	**Iko wapi kengele?**	eeko wapee kengeleh

nurse	**nesi/muuguzi**	nesee/moo-oogoozee
patient	**mgonjwa**	mgonjwa
anaesthetic	**nusukaputi**	noosookapootee
blood transfusion	**kusaidiwa damu**	koosaeedeewa damoo
injection	**sindano**	seendano
operation	**operesheni/ kupasuliwa**	opereshenee/ koopasooleewa
bed	**kitanda**	keetanda
bedpan	**bed peni**	bed penee
thermometer	**kipima homa**	keepeema homa

Dentist *Daktari wa meno*

If you're travelling in remote areas, you may well have to rely on the local doctor for dental treatment.

Can you recommend a good dentist?	**Nielekeze daktari wa meno atayefaa, tafadhali?**	nee-elekezeh daktaree wa meno atayefaa tafaðalee
Can I make an (urgent) appointment to see Dr...?	**Naweza kumwona daktari... kwa haraka?**	naweza koomwona daktaree... kwa haraka
Couldn't you make it earlier?	**Unaweza kuja mapema?**	oonaweza kooja mapema
I have a broken tooth.	**Nina jino limevun-jika.**	neena jeeno leemevoonjeeka
I have toothache.	**Naumwa na jino.**	naoomwa na jeeno
I have an abscess.	**Nina jipu.**	neena jeepoo
This tooth hurts.	**Linauma jino hili.**	leenaooma jeeno heelee
at the top	**la juu**	la joo-oo
at the bottom	**la chini**	la cheenee
at the front	**la mbele**	la ᵐbeleh
at the back	**la nyuma**	la nʸooma
Can you fix it temporarily?	**Unaweza kuliziba kwa muda?**	oonaweza kooleezeeba kwa mooda
I don't want it pulled out.	**Sitaki lingolewe.**	seetakee leengoleweh
Could you give me an anaesthetic?	**Nipatie dawa ya ganzi?**	neepatee-eh dawa ya ganzee
I've lost a filling.	**Risasi imetoka kwenye jino.**	reesasee eemetoka kwenʸeh jeeno
My gums...	**Ufizi wangu...**	oofeezee wangoo
are very sore	**umevimba sana**	oomeveemba sana
are bleeding	**unatoka damu**	oonatoka damoo
I've broken my dentures.	**Meno yangu ya kubandika yame-vunjika.**	meno yangoo ya koobandeeka yamevoonjeeka
Can you repair my dentures?	**Unaweza kuni-tengenezea meno yangu?**	oonaweza kooneetengenezea meno yangoo
When will they be ready?	**Lini yatakuwa tayari?**	leenee yatakoowa tayaree

Reference section

Where do you come from? *Unatoka wapi [nchi gani]?*

Africa	**Afrika**	afreeka
Asia	**Eshia**	esheeya
Europe	**Ulaya**	oolaya
North America	**Marekani**	marekanee
South America	**Marekani ya kusini**	marekanee ya kooseenee
Algeria	**Algiria**	algeereeya
Australia	**Australia**	aoostraleeya
Belgium	**Belgiji/Ubelgiji**	belgeejee/oobelgeejee
Burundi	**Burundi**	booroondee
Canada	**Kanada**	kanada
Denmark	**Denmak**	denmak
Egypt	**Misri**	meesree
England	**Uingereza**	ooweengereza
Ethiopia	**Ithopia**	eethopeeya
France	**Ufaransa**	oofaransa
Germany	**Ujarumani**	oojaroomanee
Great Britain	**Uingereza**	ooweengereza
India	**India**	eendeeya
Ireland	**Ailend**	aeelend
Italy	**Italia/Italii**	eetaleeya/eetalee-ee
Japan	**Japani**	japanee
Kenya	**Kenya**	kenʸa
Malawi	**Malawi**	malawee
Morocco	**Moroko**	moroko
Mozambique	**Msumbiji**	msoombeejee
Netherlands	**Uholanzi**	ooholanzee
New Zealand	**Nyuzilend**	nʸoozeelend
Russia	**Urusi**	ooroosee
Rwanda	**Rwanda**	rwanda
Scotland	**Skotlend**	skotlend
South Africa	**Afrika kusini**	afreeka kooseenee
Spain	**Spen**	spen
Sudan	**Sudan**	soodan
Sweden	**Swiden**	sweeden
Switzerland	**Uswisi**	oosweesee
Tanzania	**Tanzania**	tanzaneeya
Tunisia	**Tunisia**	tooneeseeya
Uganda	**Uganda**	ooganda
United States	**Marekani**	marekanee
Wales	**Welz**	welz
Zaire	**Zaire**	zaeereh
Zambia	**Zambia**	zambeeya
Zanzibar	**Unguja na Pemba**	oongooja na pemba

Numbers *Nambari*

0	**sufuri/ziro**	soo**foo**ree/**zee**ro
1	**moja**	**mo**ja
2	**mbili**	ᵐbeelee
3	**tatu**	**ta**too
4	**nne**	nneh
5	**tano**	**ta**no
6	**sita**	**see**ta
7	**saba**	**sa**ba
8	**nane**	**na**neh
9	**tisa [kenda]**	**tee**sa [**ken**da]
10	**kumi**	**koo**mee
11	**kumi na moja**	**koo**mee na **mo**ja
12	**kumi na mbili**	**koo**mee na ᵐbeelee
13	**kumi na tatu**	**koo**mee na **ta**too
14	**kumi na nne**	**koo**mee na nneh
15	**kumi na tano**	**koo**mee na **ta**no
16	**kumi na sita**	**koo**mee na **see**ta
17	**kumi na saba**	**koo**mee na **sa**ba
18	**kumi na nane**	**koo**mee na **na**neh
19	**kumi na tisa**	**koo**mee na **tee**sa
20	**ishirini**	eeshee**ree**nee
21	**ishirini na moja**	eeshee**ree**nee na **mo**ja
22	**ishirini na mbili**	eeshee**ree**nee na ᵐbeelee
23	**ishirini na tatu**	eeshee**ree**nee na **ta**too
24	**ishirini na nne**	eeshee**ree**nee na nneh
25	**ishirini na tano**	eeshee**ree**nee na **ta**no
26	**ishirini na sita**	eeshee**ree**nee na **see**ta
27	**ishirini na saba**	eeshee**ree**nee na **sa**ba
28	**ishirini na nane**	eeshee**ree**nee na **na**neh
29	**ishirini na tisa**	eeshee**ree**nee na **tee**sa
30	**thalathini**	thala**thee**nee
31	**thalathini na moja**	thala**thee**nee na **mo**ja
32	**thalathini na mbili**	thala**thee**nee na ᵐbeelee
33	**thalathini na tatu**	thala**thee**nee na **ta**too
40	**arbaini [arobaini]**	arba**ee**nee [aroba**ee**nee]
41	**arbaini na moja**	arba**ee**nee na **mo**ja
42	**arbaini na mbili**	arba**ee**nee na ᵐbeelee
43	**arbaini na tatu**	arba**ee**nee na **ta**too
50	**hamsini**	ham**see**nee
51	**hamsini na moja**	ham**see**nee na **mo**ja
52	**hamsini na mbili**	ham**see**nee na ᵐbeelee
53	**hamsini na tatu**	ham**see**nee na **ta**too
60	**sitini**	see**tee**nee
61	**sitini na moja**	see**tee**nee na **mo**ja
62	**sitini na mbili**	see**tee**nee na ᵐbeelee
63	**sitini na tatu**	see**tee**nee na **ta**too

70	**sabiini**	sabee-eenee
71	**sabiini na moja**	sabee-eenee na moja
72	**sabiini na mbili**	sabee-eenee na ᵐbeelee
73	**sabiini na tatu**	sabee-eenee na tatoo
80	**thamanini**	thamaneenee
81	**thamanini na moja**	thamaneenee na moja
82	**thamanini na mbili**	thamaneenee na ᵐbeelee
83	**thamanini na tatu**	thamaneenee na tatoo
90	**tisiini**	teesee-eenee
91	**tisiini na moja**	teesee-eenee na moja
92	**tisiini na mbili**	teesee-eenee na ᵐbeelee
93	**tisiini na tatu**	teesee-eenee na tatoo
100	**mia**	meeya
101	**mia na moja**	meeya na moja
102	**mia na mbili**	meeya na ᵐbeelee
110	**mia na kumi**	meeya na koomee
120	**mia na ishirini**	meeya na eesheereenee
130	**mia na thalathini**	meeya na thalatheenee
140	**mia na arbaini**	meeya na arbaeenee
150	**mia na hamsini**	meeya na hamseenee
160	**mia na sitini**	meeya na seeteenee
170	**mia na sabiini**	meeya na sabee-eenee
180	**mia na thamanini**	meeya na thamaneenee
190	**mia na tisiini**	meeya na teesee-eenee
200	**mia mbili**	meeya ᵐbeelee
300	**mia tatu**	meeya tatoo
400	**mia nne**	meeya nneh
500	**mia tano**	meeya tano
600	**mia sita**	meeya seeta
700	**mia saba**	meeya saba
800	**mia nane**	meeya naneh
900	**mia tisa**	meeya teesa
1000	**elfu moja**	elfoo moja
1100	**elfu moja na mia moja**	elfoo moja na meeya moja
1200	**elfu moja na mia mbili**	elfoo moja na meeya ᵐbeelee
2000	**elfu mbili**	elfoo ᵐbeelee
5000	**elfu tano**	elfoo tano
10,000	**elfu kumi**	elfoo koomee
50,000	**elfu hamsini**	elfoo hamseenee
100,000	**laki moja**	lakee moja
1,000,000	**milioni moja**	meeleeeonee moja
1,000,000,000	**milioni elfu**	meeleeeonee elfoo

first	kwanza	kwanza
second	pili	peelee
third	tatu	tatoo
fourth	nne	nneh
fifth	tano	tano
sixth	sita	seeta
seventh	saba	saba
eighth	nane	naneh
ninth	tisa	teesa
tenth	kumi	koomee
once/twice	mara moja/mara mbili	mara moja/mara ᵐbeelee
three times	mara tatu	mara tatoo
a half	nusu	noosoo
half a...	nusu	noosoo
half of...	nusu ya...	noosoo ya
half (adj.)	unusu	oonoosoo
a quarter/one third	robo/thuluthi	robo/thooloothee
a pair of	pea/jozi ya...	pea/jozee ya
a dozen	dazeni	dazenee
one per cent	asilimia moja	aseeleemeeya moja
3.4%	asilimia 3.4	aseeleemeeya 3.4

Date and time *Tarehe na saa [wakati]*

1981	mwaka thamanini na moja	mwaka thamaneenee na moja
1995	mwaka tisiini na tano	mwaka teesee-eenee na tano
2009	mwaka elfu mbili na tisa	mwaka elfoo ᵐbeelee na teesa

Year and age *Mwaka na miaka [umri]*

year	mwaka	mwaka
leap year	mwaka mdogo	mwaka mdogo
decade	mwongo	mwongo
century	karne	karneh
this year	mwaka huu	mwaka hoo-oo
last year	mwaka jana [mwaka ulopita]	mwaka jana [mwaka oolopeeta]
each year	kila mwaka	keela mwaka
2 years ago	miaka miwili iliopita	meeyaka meeweelee eeleeopeeta
in one year	katika mwaka mmoja	kateeka mwaka mmoja
in the eighties	mnamo miaka ya thamanini	mnamo meeyaka ya thamaneenee

in the 20th century	**katika karne ya ishirini**	kateeka karneh ya eesheereenee
How old are you?	**Una miaka min-gapi? [Una umri gani?]**	oona meeyaka meengapee [oona oomree ganee]
I'm 30 years old.	**Mimi miaka tha-lathini.**	meemee meeyaka thalatheenee
He/She was born in 1960.	**Alizaliwa mwaka sitini.**	aleezaleewa mwaka seeteenee

Months *Miezi*

Months may be called either by names that will be familiar to English speakers, or by the Swahili for "first month", "second month", and so on.

January	**Januari/Mwezi wa kwanza**	janoowaree/mwezee wa kwanza
February	**Febuari/Mwezi wa pili**	feboowaree/mwezee wa peelee
March	**Machi/Mwezi wa tatu**	machee/mwezee wa tatoo
April	**Aprili/Mwezi wa nne**	apreelee/mwezee wa nneh
May	**Mei/Mwezi wa tano**	me-ee/mwezee wa tano
June	**Juni/Mwezi wa sita**	joonee/mwezee wa seeta
July	**Julai/Mwezi wa saba**	joolaee/mwezee wa saba
August	**Agosti/Mwezi wa nane**	agostee/mwezee wa naneh
September	**Septemba/Mwezi wa tisa**	septemba/mwezee wa teesa
October	**Oktoba/Mwezi wa kumi**	oktoba/mwezee wa koomee
November	**Novemba/Mwezi wa kumi na moja**	novemba/mwezee wa koomee na moja
December	**Disemba/Mwezi wa kumi na mbili**	deesemba/mwezee wa koomee na ᵐbeelee
in September	**katika Septemba**	kateeka septemba
since October	**tangu Oktoba**	tangoo oktoba
the beginning of January	**mwanzo wa Januari**	mwanzo wa janoowaree
the middle of February	**katikati ya Febuari**	kateekatee ya feboowaree
the end of March	**mwisho wa Machi**	mweesho wa machee

Days and date *Siku na tarehe*

What day is it today?	**Tarehe gani leo?**	tareheh ganee leo
	[Mwezi ngapi leo?]	[mwezee ngapee leo]
Sunday	**Jumapili**	joomapeelee
Monday	**Jumatatu**	joomatatoo
Tuesday	**Jumanne**	joomanneh [joomaaneh]
	[Jumaane]	
Wednesday	**Jumatano**	joomatano
Thursday	**Alhamisi**	alhameesee
Friday	**Ijumaa**	eejoomaa
Saturday	**Jumamosi**	joomamosee
It's...	**Ni...**	nee
July 1	**Julai mosi**	joolaee mosee
March 10	**Machi kumi**	machee koomee
in the morning	**asubuhi**	asooboohee
during the day	**mchana**	mchana
in the afternoon	**mchana**	mchana
in the evening	**jioni**	jeeonee
at night	**usiku**	ooseekoo
the day before yesterday	**juzi**	joozee
yesterday	**jana**	jana
today	**leo**	leo
tomorrow	**kesho**	kesho
the day after tomorrow	**kesho kutwa**	kesho kootwa
the day before	**siku kabla**	seekoo kabla
the next day	**siku inayofuatia**	seekoo eenayofoowateeya
two days ago	**siku mbili zilizopita**	seekoo ᵐbeelee zeeleezopeeta
in three days' time	**baada ya siku tatu**	baada ya seekoo tatoo
last week	**wiki ilopita/juma lililopita**	weekee eelopeeta/jooma leeleelopeeta
next week	**wiki ijayo/juma lijalo**	weekee eejayo/jooma leejalo
for two weeks	**kwa wiki mbili**	kwa weekee ᵐbeelee
birthday	**sikukuu ya kuzaliwa**	seekookoo-oo ya koozaleewa
day off	**siku ya kupumzika**	seekoo ya koopoomzeeka
holiday	**mapumziko**	mapoomzeeko
holidays/vacation	**likizo/safari**	leekeezo/safaree
week	**wiki**	weekee
weekend	**mwisho wa wiki [juma]/wikendi**	mweesho wa weekee [jooma]/weekendee
working day	**siku ya kazi**	seekoo ya kazee

Public holidays *Sikukuu*

The following public holidays and festivals observed in Kenya, Tanzania and Uganda:

1 Jan	**Mwaka mpya**	New Year's Day
1 May	**Kwanza ya mei**	May Day
25/26 December	**Krismas**	Christmas
Variable dates:	**Ijumaa Kuu**	Good Friday
	Jumatatu pasaka	Easter Monday
	Eid-ul-Fitr	(at the end of Ramadan)

Holidays also observed in each country are:

Kenya		
1 June	**Madaraka Day**	(celebrating Kenyan self-government)
10 Oct	**Moi Day**	(anniversary of his inauguration)
20 Oct	**Kenyatta Day**	(anniversary of his imprisonment)
12 Dec	**Jamhuri Day**	(celebrating independence)
Tanzania		
12 Jan	**Zanzibar Revolution Day**	
5 Mar	**CCM Day**	(the ruling party)
26 Apr	**Union Day**	
7 Dec	**Independence/ Republic Day**	
Variable dates:	**Eid-ul-Adha**	(end of pilgrimage to Mecca)
	Maulid Day	(Birthday of Prophet Mohammad)
Uganda		
26 Jan	**Liberation Day**	
8 Mar	**Women's Day**	
3 June	**Martyrs' Day**	
9 June	**National Heroes' Day**	
9 Oct	**Independence Day**	
Variable date:	**Eid-ul-Adha**	(end of pilgrimage to Mecca)

Greetings and wishes *Maamkizi na kutakiana kheri [heri]*

Merry Christmas!	**Heri za krismas!**	heree za kreesmas
Happy New Year!	**Heri ya mwaka mpya!**	heree ya mwaka mpya
Happy Easter!	**Heri ya pasaka!**	heree ya pasaka
Happy birthday!	**Hepi bathade!**	hepee bathadeh
Best wishes!	**Nakutakia heri**	nakootakeeya heree
Congratulations!	**Hongera! [Nakupongeza!]**	hongera [nakoopongeza]
Good luck/All the best!	**Nakutakia kila la heri!**	nakootakeeya keela la heree
Have a good trip!	**Safari njema!**	safaree njema
Have a good holiday!	**Safiri salama!**	safeeree salama
Best regards from...	**... anakusalimu**	anakoosaleemoo
My regards to...	**Nisalimie...**	neesaleemee-eh

What time is it? *Saa ngapi?*

Time is counted in two 12-hour cycles in East Africa. The daytime cycle (*asubuhi*) begins at sunrise – 6 a.m. – and ends with sunset. The night-time cycle (*jioni*) then stretches from approximately 6 p.m. to dawn. Thus 8 a.m. (*saa mbili*) is literally "two hours" of the morning cycle.

Excuse me. Can you tell me the time?	**Samahani, saa ngapi eh?**	samahanee saa ngapee eh
It's...	**Ni...**	nee
five past one	**saa saba na dakika tano**	saa saba na dakeeka tano
ten past two	**saa nane na dakika kumi**	saa naneh na dakeeka koomee
a quarter past three	**saa tisa na robo**	saa teesa na robo
twenty past four	**saa kumi na dakika ishirini**	saa koomee na dakeeka eesheereenee
twenty-five past five	**saa kumi na moja na dakika ishirini na tano**	saa koomee na moja na dakeeka eesheereenee na tano
half past six	**saa kumi na mbili na nusu**	saa koomee na ᵐbeelee na noosoo
twenty-five to seven	**saa moja kasoro dakika ishirini na tano**	saa moja kasoro dakeeka eesheereenee na tano

twenty to eight	**saa mbili kasoro dakika ishirini**	saa ᵐbeelee kasoro dakeeka eesheereenee
a quarter to nine	**saa tatu kasorobo**	saa tatoo kasorobo
ten to ten	**saa nne kasoro dakika kumi**	saa nneh kasoro dakeeka koomee
five to eleven	**saa tano kasoro dakika kumi na moja**	saa tano kasoro dakeeka koomee na moja
twelve o'clock (noon/midnight)	**saa sita mchana/usiku**	saa seeta mchana/ooseekoo
in the morning	**asubuhi**	asooboohee
in the afternoon	**mchana**	mchana
in the evening	**jioni**	jeeonee
The train leaves at ...	**Treni inaondoka ...**	trenee eenaondoka
13.04 (1.04 p.m.)	**saa saba na dakika nne mchana**	saa saba na dakeeka nneh mchana
0.40 (0.40 a.m.)	**saa sita na dakika arbaini usiku**	saa seeta na dakeeka arbaeenee ooseekoo
in five minutes	**baada ya dakika tano**	baada ya dakeeka tano
in a quarter of an hour	**baada ya robo saa**	baada ya robo saa
half an hour ago	**nusu saa ilopita**	noosoo saa eelopeeta
about two hours	**baada ya saa mbili**	baada ya saa ᵐbeelee
more than 10 minutes	**zaidi ya dakika kumi**	zaeedee ya dakeeka koomee
less than 30 seconds	**haifiki sekunde thalathini**	haeefeekee sekoondeh thalatheenee
The clock is fast/slow.	**Saa inakwenda mbio/pole pole.**	saa eenakwenda ᵐbeeo/poleh poleh

Common abbreviations *Ufupisho wa maneno*

Bi.	bibi	madam
Br.	barabara	street
Bw.	bwana	mister/sir
Dk.	daktari	doctor
ji.	jina	noun
JKT	jeshi la kujenga taifa	national service
ki.	kitendo	verb
k.m.	kwa mfano	for example/e.g.
MK.	mwenyekiti	chairman
na.	nambari	number
Nd.	ndugu	comrade
n.k.	na kadhalika	etc.
S.L.P.	sanduku la posta	P.O. Box
taz.	tazama	look, refer to

Signs and notices *Ilani*

Baridi	Cold
Chini	Down
Haifanyi kazi	Out of order
... hairuhusiwi	... forbidden
Hakuna kazi	No vacancies
Hatari (mauti)	Danger (of death)
Inakodishwa [Inapangishwa]	To let
Ina mtu/Mtu ameekesha	Reserved
Inauzwa	For sale
Ingia bila hodi	Enter without knocking
Ishauzwa	Sold out
Joto/Moto	Hot
Juu	Up
Kuingia	Entrance
Kuingia bila malipo [bure]	Free admittance
Kuna mtu ndani [Inatumika]	Occupied
Kutoka	Exit
Lifti	Lift
Maelezo	Information
Mafuriko	Flood
Maji haya hayafai kwa kunywa	Non-drinkable water
Mbwa mkali	Beware of the dog
Mlango wa dharura	Emergency exit
Njia ya mtu yake mwenyewe	Private road
Njia ya waendeshaji baskeli	Path for cyclists
Pole/pole Taratibu	Caution
Rangi haijakauka	Wet paint
Seli	Sale
Si ruhusa kuingia	No admittance
Sukuma	Push
Tafadhali piga kengele [hodi]	Please ring
Tafadhali subiri	Please wait
Tupu/Haina mtu	Vacant
Usichafue	No littering
Usiguse	Do not touch
Usinisumbue	Do not disturb
Usivute sigara	No smoking
Usizibe njia/mlango	Do not block entrance
Vuta	Pull
Wanaume	Gentlemen
Wanawake	Ladies
Wapitao watashtakiwa	Trespassers will be prosecuted
Wazi	Open
Ya kukodi [Inakodishwa]	For hire

Emergency *Dharura*

Call the police	**Mwite polisi**	mweeteh poleesee
Consulate	**Ubalozi**	oobalozee
DANGER	**HATARI**	hataree
Embassy	**Ubalozi**	oobalozee
FIRE	**MOTO**	moto
Gas	**Gesi**	gesee
Get a doctor	**Daktari**	daktaree
Go away	**Nenda [Kwenda] huko**	nenda/kwenda hooko
HELP	**MSAADA [KUSAIDIA]**	msa-ada [koosaeedeeya]
Get help quickly	**Saidia haraka**	saeedeeya haraka
I'm ill	**Naumwa**	naoomwa
I'm lost	**Nimepotea**	neemepotea
Leave me alone	**Usinisumbue/ Niache**	ooseeneesoombooweh/ neeyacheh
LOOK OUT	**ANGALIA/TAZAMA**	angaleeya/tazama
Poison	**Sumu**	soomoo
POLICE	**POLISI**	poleesee
Stop that man/ woman	**Msimamishe bwana/bibi yule**	mseemameesheh bwana/ beebee yooleh
STOP THIEF	**MKAMATE MWIZI**	mkamateh mweezee

Emergency telephone numbers *Namba za dharura*

Police, Fire, Ambulance 999

Lost property—Theft *Vitu vilivyopotea–Wizi*

Where's the ...?	**... iko wapi?**	eeko wapee
lost property (lost and found) office	**ofisi ya vitu vilivyopotea**	ofeesee ya veetoo veeleevyopotea
police station	**kituo cha polisi**	keetoowo cha poleesee
I want to report a theft.	**Nataka kuripoti wizi.**	nataka kooreepotee weezee
My ... has been stolen.	**... yangu imeibiwa**	yangoo eeme-eebeewa
I've lost my ...	**Nimepoteza ...**	neemepoteza
handbag	**mkoba/mfuko**	mkoba/mfooko
passport	**paspoti**	paspotee
wallet	**kikoba cha pesa**	keekoba cha pesa

CAR ACCIDENTS, see page 78

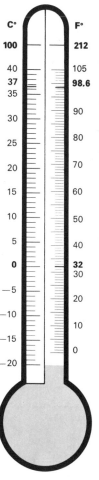

Conversion tables

Centimetres and inches

To change centimetres into inches, multiply by .39.

To change inches into centimetres, multiply by 2.54.

	in.	feet	yards
1 mm	0.039	0.003	0.001
1 cm	0.39	0.03	0.01
1 dm	3.94	0.32	0.10
1 m	39.40	3.28	1.09

	mm	cm	m
1 in.	25.4	2.54	0.025
1 ft.	304.8	30.48	0.304
1 yd.	914.4	91.44	0.914

(32 metres = 35 yards)

Temperature

To convert Centigrade into degrees Fahrenheit, multiply Centigrade by 1.8 and add 32.

To convert degrees Fahrenheit into Centigrade, subtract 32 from Fahrenheit and divide by 1.8.

Kilometres into miles

1 kilometre (km.) = 0.62 miles

km.	10	20	30	40	50	60	70	80	90	100	110	120	130
miles	6	12	19	25	31	37	44	50	56	62	68	75	81

Miles into kilometres

1 mile = 1.609 kilometres (km.)

miles	10	20	30	40	50	60	70	80	90	100
km.	16	32	48	64	80	97	113	129	145	161

Fluid measures

1 litre (l.) = 0.88 imp. quart or 1.06 U.S. quart
1 imp. quart = 1.14 l.   1 U.S. quart = 0.95 l.
1 imp. gallon = 4.55 l.   1 U.S. gallon = 3.8 l.

litres	5	10	15	20	25	30	35	40	45	50
imp. gal.	1.1	2.2	3.3	4.4	5.5	6.6	7.7	8.8	9.9	11.0
U.S. gal.	1.3	2.6	3.9	5.2	6.5	7.8	9.1	10.4	11.7	13.0

Weights and measures

1 kilogram or kilo (kg.) = 1000 grams (g.)

100 g. = 3.5 oz.	½ kg. = 1.1 lb.
200 g. = 7.0 oz.	1 kg. = 2.2 lb.
1 oz. =	28.35 g.
1 lb. =	453.60 g.

Swahili grammar

The grammar of Swahili is relatively easy. The structure is quite simple: verbs, nouns, adjectives and adverbs often all come from the same basic root. The most important feature of Swahili grammar is the prefix, which is added to the root to form different words.

Prefixes are used not only to indicate the singular and plural of nouns and the tenses of verbs, and to form adjectives, adverbs, and pronoun objects, but many other things as well.

Nouns

Nouns in Swahili aren't preceded by definite or indefinite articles (a, an, the). The meaning is understood from the context.

Nouns in Swahili don't have a gender but they belong to classes; each class consists of nouns of a certain type (e.g. abstract concepts, living things, human beings). There are eight such classes. In each class the nouns take a different sort of prefix. For example, the word **kitu** (thing) belongs to the **ki**-class, while the word **mtu** (man) belongs to the **m**-class. If you really want to learn Swahili well, it's always best to learn the word and the class it belongs to together.

Here's a basic list showing the eight classes of nouns. Note that the prefixes shown are subject to numerous exceptions especially when they precede words starting with a vowel.

Class of nouns	Sing. prefix	Plural prefix	Examples	
1. Human beings	**m-** or **mw-**	**wa-** or **w-**	**mtoto** **watoto**	child children
2. a) Inanimate objects b) plants	**m-** or **mw-** or **mu-**	**mi-**	**mti** **miti**	tree trees
3. Miscellaneous	**n-** (often dropped)	**n-** (often dropped)	**nyumba**	house/ houses
4. Inanimate objects	**ki-** or **ch-**	**vi-** or **vy-**	**kiko** **viko**	pipe pipes
5. Miscellaneous	–	**ma-**	**ua** **maua**	flower flowers
6. Words without a plural, abstract concepts, names of countries, etc.	**u-**	–	**(-refu** **urefu**	long) length
7. One word only: **mahali**	in agreements: **pa-**	in agreements: **pa-**	**mahali** **pazuri**	a nice place
8. Verbs used as nouns	**ku-**	–	**kuandika**	to write, writing

Adjectives

The basic rule is that the class prefix of the noun is also added to the adjective that modifies it.

The adjective always follows the noun it modifies. It agrees in class and number with the noun except in the case of adjectives derived from Arabic which are all invariable.

Example: **kitu** thing
  -dogo small
  kitu kidogo a small thing

Even if the prefix of the noun has been dropped (as is the case in the **n**-class), the adjective will still take the prefix. However, here again, the prefix rule is quite complicated and there are many exceptions.

Numerals are considered as adjectives so they also take the class prefix, except for numbers six, seven, nine and decimal numbers.

Example:	**kitabu**	the book
vitabu	the books
-tano	five
vitabu vitano	five books

Adverbs

Most adverbs have one single form which doesn't change and doesn't take a prefix. Some examples:

nyuma	behind
ndani	inside
nje	outside
karibu	nearby
sasa	now

But adverbs can also be formed from adjectives and nouns:

-zuri	nice
vizuri	nicely
askari	soldier
kiaskari	like a soldier

Verbs

The verb has to agree with the subject noun by taking the same prefix. When the subject of a verb isn't a noun, but what we call a personal pronoun, Swahili verbs again take a prefix. Here they are:

Singular		Plural	
I	**ni-**	we	**tu-**
you	**u-**	you	**m-**
he, she	**a-**	they	**wa-**

The tenses are also indicated by prefixes. They're inserted between the subject prefix and the root of the verb. These prefixes denoting the tenses are: **-na-** for the present tense, **-li-** for the past tense, and **-ta-** for the future tense.

Examples:

ni | na | soma	I'm reading
ni | ta | soma	I shall read
a | li | soma	he read
wa | na | soma	they're reading
wa | ta | soma	they'll read
tu | li | soma	we read

Kisu kimoja kitatosha. One knife will do.

The **-na-** tense is basically a continuous present. There's another present tense which takes the prefix **-a-** and has no particular sense of time attached to it.

Prefixes are also used to indicate the direct object of the verb. They're the same as the subject prefixes and are often used even if the object noun itself is also expressed in the sentence. For example: **milikisoma** (I read it). When referring to persons, the object prefixes are:

Singular		Plural	
I	-ni-	us	-tu-
you	-ku-	you	-wa-
him, her	-m-	them	-wa-

In order to ask a question in Swahili, the word order of the sentence doesn't change. Questions are understood from the intonation.

In the present tense the verb *to be* is dropped, and only the personal prefix is used.

Examples: **U imara.** You're strong.
Yu tayari. He's ready.

The verb *to have* is expressed in the present tense by the pronoun followed by **-na**.

nina	I've	**tuna**	we've
una	you've	**mna**	you've
ana	he/she has	**wana**	they've

The negative form in this tense again uses the suffix **-na** with a negative pronoun:

sina	I haven't	**hatuna**	we haven't
huna	you haven't	**hamnayo**	you haven't
hana	he/she hasn't	**hawana**	they haven't

Demonstratives

Demonstratives, whether they're used as adjectives (this/that house) or as pronouns (this/that is good), are rendered by means of **hi-/ha-/hu-**, etc. (this, these), or **-le** (that, those). The form varies according to the class.

Here's the table of demonstratives:

Class:	1	2	3	4	5	6	7	8
this these	**huyu** **hawa**	**huu** **hii**	**hii** **hizi**	**hiki** **hivi**	**hili** **haya**	**huu** **hizi**	**hapa** –	**huku** –
that those	**yule** **wale**	**ule** **ile**	**ile** **zile**	**kile** **vile**	**lile** **yale**	**ule** **zile**	**pale** –	**kule** –

For example:

mtu huyu	this man
watu hawa	these men
kitu kile	that thing
vitu vile	those things

DICTIONARY

Kamusi

Dictionary
and alphabetical index

English–Swahili

Note: not all alternatives listed in brackets [ ] appear in all the relevant cross-referenced phrases.

A

abbreviation ufupisho wa maneno 154
above juu 15, 63
abscess jipu 145
accept, to kubali 63
accessories vitu vyenginevyo 115, 125
accident ajali 79, 139
account akaunti [hesabu] 130
ache maumivu 141
adaptor edepta 118
address anwani 21, 31, 77, 79, 102
address book kitabu cha anwani 104
adhesive tape gundi 104
admission kiingilio 82, 90
Africa Afrika 146
after baadaye 15, 77
after-shave lotion dawa ya kunyolea 109
afternoon, in the mchana 151, 153
again tena 96
age umri 149, 150
ago zilizopita 149, 151
air bed kitanda 106
air conditioning eyakandishan [kiyoyozi] 23, 28
air mattress godoro la pumzi 106
airmail ndege 133
airplane ndege 65
airport uwanja wa ndege 21, 66
aisle seat kiti cha ujiani 65
alarm clock saa ya kuamsha 121
alcohol pombe 37, 59
Algeria Algiria 146
all yote 103
allergic inayodhuru 141, 143
almonds lozi 55
also pia, vilevile 15
alter, to (garment) badilisha 114

amazing inashangaza 84
amber ambari 122
ambulance ambalesi 79
American za/la kimerikani 105, 126; (person) Mmarekani 93
amount idadi [kiasi] 131
amplifier bomba la sauti 118
anaesthetic nusukaputi 144, 145
analgesic dawa ya kupunguza maumivu 108
and na 15
animal mnyama 85
ankle kifundo cha mguu 139
anorak rinkoti 115
another nyengine 123
answer jibu 136
antelope pofu 86
antibiotic dawa za antibayotik 143
antidepressant dawa za kuondoa wasi wasi 143
antique shop duka la vitu vya kizamani 98
antiques vitu vya kizamani 83
antiseptic cream malhamu ya kupunguza maumivu 108
appendicitis ependiks 142
appendix chango 138
apple matufaha [maepul] 55, 119
appliance vyombo 118
appointment miadi 131, 137, 145
apricot aprikoti 55
April Aprili, Mwezi wa nne 150
aquarium tangi la kuweka samaki 81
archaeology magofu [athari za kale] 83
architect mchoraji ramani za majengo 83
area code kodi ya simu 134
arm mkono 138, 139

around *(approximately)* kama [kiasi] 31
arrival kuwasili [kufika] 16
arrive, to fika 66, 68, 130
art sanaa 83
art gallery jumba la sanaa [ukumbi wa sanaa] 81, 98
artificial siya asili 124
artificial light mwangaza wa taa 124
artist msanii 83
ashtray eshtrei 36
Asia Eshia 146
ask for, to taka 25; omba 61
aspirin aspirini 108
asthma pumu 141
astringent maji ya kusafishia uso 109
at kwa, kwenye 15
aubergine biringani 51
August Agosti, Mwezi wa nane 150
aunt *(paternal)* shangazi 93; *(maternal)* mama mdogo 93
Australia Australia 146
automatic automatik 20, 122, 124
avocado peya 55
awful mbaya 84, 94

B

baboon nyani 86
baboon skin ngozi ya nyani 113
baby mtoto mchanga 110
baby food chakula cha watoto wachanga 110
babysitter mtu wa kuangalia mtoto 27
back mgongo 138
back, to be/to get rudi 21, 80, 136
backache maumivu ya mgongo 141
backpack shanta [mfuko wa safari] 106
bacon nyama ya nguruwe 39, 47
bad mbaya 14, 95
bag mkoba, shanta 18; *(shopping)* mfuko 103
baggage cart vigari vya kuchukulia mizigo 18, 71
baggage check kupima mizigo 71
baggage locker kabati la kuweka mizigo 71
baggage *(luggage)* mizigo 18, 26, 31, 71
baked iliyookwa 45, 47

baker's muuza mikate 98
balance *(finance)* baki 131
balcony roshani 23
ball-point pen kalamu [peni] 104
banana ndizi 55
banana fritters vitumbua vya ndizi 57
bandage bendeji 108
Bandaid® plasta 108
bangle bangili 121
bangs mchano wa nywele 30
bank *(finance)* benki 98, 129
banknote noti 130
bar baa 67
barber's kinyozi 30, 98
basketball mpira wa mikono 90
bath bafu 23, 25, 27
bath salts chumvi ya kutia kwenye maji ya kuogea 109
bath towel taulo la kuogea 27
bathing cap kofia ya kuogea [kuogelelea] 115
bathing suit nguo ya kuogelea 115
bathrobe juba la msalani 115
bathroom bafu 28
battery betri 76, 78, 119, 121, 125
beach pwani 91
bean haragwe 39
beard ndevu 31
beauty salon duka la urembo wa kike 98
bed kitanda 23, 24, 29, 142, 144
bed and breakfast kulala na chakula cha asubuhi 24
bedpan dishi la kwendea haja 144
beef nyama ya ngombe 47
beer biya 58, 64
before *(time)* kabla [saa] 15
begin, to anza 87
beginning mwanzo 151
behind nyuma ya 15, 77
beige kahawiya isokoza 112
Belgium Belgiji, Ubelgiji 146
bell *(electric)* kengele 144
below chini ya 15
belt ukanda 116
berth kitanda 69, 70, 71
better bora zaidi 14, 25
between baina ya 15
bicycle baskeli 74
big kubwa 14, 101
bilharzia kichocho 142

bill hesabu [bili] 28, 31, 63, 102
bill *(banknote)* noti 130
billion *(Am.)* milioni elfu 148
binoculars darubini 123
bird ndege 85
birth kuzaliwa 25
birthday bathade [sikukuu ya kuzaliwa] 153
biscuit *(Br.)* biskuti 64
bitter chungu chungu 61
black nyeusi 112
black and white *(film)* filamu isiyo ya rangi 124, 125
black coffee kahawa bila maziwa 41, 61
bladder kibofu cha mkojo 138
blanket blangeti 27
bleed, to toka damu 139, 145
blind *(window shade)* pazia 29
blister lengelenge 139
blocked imeziba 29
blood damu 142
blood pressure peresha 141, 142
blood transfusion kusaidiwa damu 144
blouse blauzi 115
blow-dry bloo drai 30
blue buluu 112
blusher rangi ya mashavu 109
boar nguruwe dume 49, 86
boat meli 74
body mwili 138
boil jipu 139
boiled egg yai la kuchemsha 39
bone mfupa 138
book kitabu 12, 104
booking office ofisi ya kuekesha tikiti 19, 67
bookshop duka la vitabu 98, 104
boot buti 117
born, to be zaliwa 150
botany mambo ya mimea 83
bottle chupa 17, 59, 60
bottle-opener cha kufungulia chupa 120
bottom chini 145
bow tie botai 115
bowel matumbo 138
box boksi 119
boxing ndondi 90
boy mtoto wa kiume 128

boyfriend rafiki [mwanamme] 93
bra sidiria 115
bracelet kikuku 121
braces *(suspenders)* mikanda ya suruali 115
brake fluid mafuta ya breki 76
brakes breki 79
bread mkate 37, 41, 64
break down, to haribikiwa 78
break, to vunjika 29
breakdown kuharibika 78
breakdown van gari la kukokota 79
breakfast chakula cha asubuhi 24, 27, 34, 39
breast ziwa, matiti 138
breathe, to vuta pumzi 141, 142
bridge daraja 85
bring, to leta 13, 59
broken imevunjika 118, 123, 139, 140, 145
brooch beji 121
brother kaka 93
brown kahawiya 112
bruise mchubuko 139
brush brashi 110
bucket ndoo 120, 128
buckle bakali 116
buffalo nyati 86
build, to jenga 83
building jengo [jumba] 81, 83
building blocks/bricks matofali 128
bulb *(light)* globu 29, 76, 119
burn kuungua 139
burn out, to *(bulb)* ungua [kwisha] 29
bus basi 18, 19, 66, 72, 80
bus stop kituo cha basi 73
bushbaby kombo 86
business biashara 131
business class daraja ya pili 65
business district madukani [sehemu ya biashara] 81
busy kushughulika 96
but lakini 15
butane gas gesi ya butane 32, 106
butcher's duka la nyama [muuza nyama] 98
butter siagi 37, 41, 64
button kifungo 116
buy, to nunua 82, 100, 104, 123

C

cabbage kabeji 51
cabin *(ship)* kebin [chumba] 74
cable car gari ya kebul 75
café mkahawa 33
cake keki 37, 64
calculator kalkuleta 105
calendar kalenda 104
call, to *(give name)* ita 11
call, to *(phone)* piga simu 134, 136
call, to *(summon)* ita 79, 156
cambric bafta nyepesi 113
camel-hair manyoa ya ngamia 113
camera kamera 124, 125
camera case mfuko wa kamera 125
camera shop duka la kamera 98
camp site kambi 32
camp, to piga kambi 32
campbed kitanda cha kambini 106
camping kupiga kambi 32
camping equipment vifaa vya kambini 106
can opener cha kufungulia mkebe 120
can *(be able to)* weza 12, 13
can *(container)* mkebe 119
Canada Kanada 146
cancel, to kensel [kuvunja] 66
candle mishumaa 120
candy peremende 126
cap kofia 115
capital *(finance)* rasilimali [mtaji] 131
car kari 19, 20, 32, 75
car hire kukodi gari [gari za kukodi] 20
car mechanic fundi wa gari 78
car park mahali pa kuegesha gari 78
car racing mbio za magari 90
car rental kukodi gari [gari za kukodi] 20
carafe jagi 59
carat karati 121
caravan karavani 32
carbon paper karatasi ya kukopia 104
carburettor karbureta 79
card karata 94, 131
card game karata 128
carrot karoti 51
cart vigari vya mizigo 18
carton (of cigarettes) boksi (la sigara) 17; katon 126
cartridge *(camera)* filam ya katriji 124

case kijaluba 121; fuko 125
cash desk sehemu ya malipo 103
cash, to badili 130, 133
cashew nuts korosho 55
cassava mhogo 51
cassette tepu [kanda] 118, 127
cassette recorder tepu rikoda 118
castle kasri 81
catalogue katalogi 82
cathedral kanisa kuu 81
Catholic mkatoliki 84
cauliflower kaulifulawa 51
caution hadhari 155
cave pango 81
celery seleri 51
cemetery kiunga cha kuzikia [makaburini] 81
centre katikati 21
century karne 149
ceramics vigae vya kila aina 83
certificate cheti 144
chain *(jewellery)* mkufu 121
chair kiti 106
change *(money)* chenji 63, 78
change, to badilisha 62, 66, 68, 72, 76, 123
change, to *(money)* badilisha (pesa) 18, 129
charcoal mkaa [makaa] 106
charm *(trinket)* hirizi 121
cheap rahisi 14, 24, 25, 101
check *(Am.)* hundi [cheki] 76, 130, 131; *(restaurant)* 63
check-up *(medical)* kuangaliwa afya 142
check, to pima 123; angalia 76
check in, to *(airport)* fika uwanja wa ndege 66
check out, to *(hotel)* ondoka 31
check, to *(luggage)* andikisha 71
checkered makunguru 112
cheers! tunywe! [afya!] 59
cheese jibini [chizi] 64
cheetah duma 86
chemist's muuza dawa [duka la dawa] 98, 107
cheque hundi [cheki] 130, 131
chess dama 93
chess set seti ya dama 128
chest kifua 138, 141
chewing gum ubani wa kutafuna 126

chewing tobacco mshuku 126
chicken kuku 49
child mtoto 82, 93, 139
chilli pepper pilipili kalia 54
chips chipsi 64
chocolate chakleti 64, 119, 126
chocolate (hot) chokleti ya kunywa 41, 61
chocolate bar chakleti 64
Christmas Krismas 152, 153
chromium krom 122
church kanisa 81, 85
cigar sigireti 126
cigarette sigara 17, 126
cigarette case kijaluba cha sigara 121, 126
cigarette holder cha kuvutia sigara 126
cigarette lighter kibiriti cha gesi 121, 126
cine camera kamera ya kupiga picha za senema 124
cinema sinema 87, 96
city centre mjini 81
classical ya kizamani 128
clean safi 63
clean, to safisha 29, 76
cleansing cream kirimu ya kusafishia ngozi 109
cliff mlima mdogo 85
clip kibanio [klipu] 121
cloakroom msalani 87
clock saa 121
clock-radio saa ya redio 118
close, to funga 11, 82, 107, 132
cloth kitambaa 117
clothes nguo 29, 115
clothing nguo 111
cloud mawingu 94
clove karafuu 54
coach (bus) basi 72
coat koti 115
coconut nazi 55
cod mkizi 44
coffee kahawa 41, 62, 64
coin sarafu 83
cold baridi 14, 25, 94, 155
cold (illness) mafua 107, 140
cold season siku za baridi 150
collar ukosi 116
colour rangi 103, 112, 124, 125

colour rinse kutia rangi ya muda tu 30
colour shampoo shampuu ya rangi 110
colour slide slaidi za rangi 124
colourfast haitoki rangi [haichujuki] 113
comb kitana 110
come, to kuja 35, 93, 95, 137, 144
comedy mchezo wa kuchekesha 87
commission (fee) malipo [ada] 130
common (frequent) inatumika sana 154
compact disc diski 127
compartment (train) behewa 70
compass dira 106
complaint malalamiko 61
computer kompyuta 131
concert muziki 88
concert hall jumba la muziki 81, 88
condom makondom 108
conference room chumba cha mkutano 23
confirm, to hakikisha [thibitisha] 66
confirmation thibitisho [ithbati] 23
congratulation hongera [nakupongeza] 153
connection (transport) kupata chombo kuendelea na safari 65
constipation kutopata choo [kabdhi] 140
contact lens vigae 123
contagious magonjwa ya kuambukizwa 142
contraceptive dawa ya kuzuia uzazi 108
contract mkataba 131
control forodha 16
cookie biskuti 64
cool box sanduku la kuhifadhi chakula cha baridi 106
copper shaba 122
coral marjani 122
corduroy kodroi 113
corn plaster palasta ya ndunda 108
corn (Am.) mahindi 51
corner kona 21, 77; (room) pembe 36
cost bei 131, 136
cost, to gharimu 11
cot kitanda cha mtoto 24
cotton bafta [koton] 113
cotton wool pamba 108

cough kikohozi 107, 141
cough drops dawa ya kifua 108
cough, to kohowa 142
counter kaunta 133
country nchi 93
countryside shamba 85
court house mahakama [korti] 81
cousin jamaa 93
cover charge malipo ya mwanzo 63
crab kaa 44
cramp musuli hupandana 141
crawfish (crawfish) aina ya kamba 44
crayon penseli za rangi 104
cream maziwa mtindi 62
cream (toiletry) kirimu 109
crease resistant hakikunjiki 113
credit mkopo 130
credit card kadi ya benki 20, 31, 63, 102, 130
crockery vyomba vya kulia 120
crocodile mamba 86
cross msalaba 121
crossing (maritime) kuvuka 74
crossroads njia panda 77
cruise safari ya meli 74
crystal jiwe linalongara 122
cucumber tango 51
cuff link vifungo vya mikono ya shati 121
cuisine mapishi 35
cup kikombe 36, 143
curler kals 110
currency fedha 129
currency exchange office ofisi ya kubadilisha [kuvunja pesa] 18, 67, 129
curry mchuzi 54
curtain mapazia 28
customs forodha 16, 102
cut off, to (interrupt) katika 135
cut (wound) jeraha [kidonda] 139
cut, to (with scissors) kata 31
cutlery visu na vijiko 120, 121
cutlet katlesi 47
cycling kuendesha baskeli 90
cystitis ugonjwa wa kibofu cha mkojo 142 ▾

D
dance dansa 88

dance, to cheza dansa 88; dansi 89
dancing kudansi 96
danger hatari 156
dark nyeusi 25, 101, 111, 112
date (day) tarehe 25, 151; (appointment) tarehe 95
date (fruit) tende 56
daughter mtoto 93
day siku 20, 24, 32, 80, 94, 151
day off siku ya kupumzika 151
daylight mchana 124
decade mwongo 149
decaffeinated kahawa isiyokuwa kali 41, 61
December Disemba, Mwezi wa kumi na mbili 150
decision uamuzi 25, 102
deck chair kiti cha kukunja 91
deck (ship) deki 74
declare, to (customs) onesha vitu vya ushuru 17
degree (temperature) homa 140
delay kuchelewa 69
delicious -zuri sana 63
deliver, to peleka [tuma] 102
delivery kupokea 102
denim kitambaa cha denim 113
Denmark Denmak 146
dentist daktari wa meno 98, 145
denture meno ya kubandika 145
deodorant mafuta ya kukata jasho 109
department store duka kubwa [supa maket] 98
departure kuondoka 66
deposit (down payment) rubuni 20
dessert vitamu tamu 37, 57
diabetic mgonjwa wa kisukari 37, 141
dialling code kodi ya simu 134
diamond almasi 122
diaper winda 110
diarrhoea kuharisha 140
dictionary kamusi 104
diesel mafuta ya dizeli 76
diet dayat 38
difficult ngumu 14
difficulty ngumu 28
digital ya digital 122
dine, to kula 95
dining room chumba cha kulia 28
dinner chakula cha usiku 27, 34, 95
direct moja kwa moja 65

direct, to elekeza [onesha] 13
direction kwendea 76
directory *(phone)* kitabu cha simu 134
disabled walemavu, vilema 82
discotheque disko 89, 96
discount punguza bei 131
disease ugonjwa 142
disinfectant dawa ya wadudu 108
dislocated teguka 140
display case sanduku la vitu viuzwayyo 100
dissatisfied kutoridhika 103
disturb, to sumbua 155
dizzy kuzunguzungu, kisunzi 140
doctor daktari 79, 137, 144, 145
doctor's office kwa daktari 137
dog mbwa 155
doll mtoto wa sanamu 128
dollar dala 18, 102, 129
donkey punda 75
double bed kitanda cha watu wawili 23
double room chumba cha watu wawili 19, 23
down chini 15
downtown mitaani 81
dozen dazeni 149
drawing paper karatsi za kuchorea 104
drawing pins pini za kupachikia 104
dress kanzu [gauni] 115
drink kinywaji 58, 61
drink, to kunywa 36
drinking water maji ya kunywa 32
drip, to vuja 29
drive, to endesha 76
driving licence (driver's license) leseni ya gari 20, 79
drop *(liquid)* dawa ya maji 108
drugstore duka la dawa 98, 107
dry kavu 110
dry cleaner's dobi 29, 98
duck bata 49, 86
dummy *(baby's)* wtoto wa sanamu 110
during wakati wa [kipindi cha] 15
duty-free shop duka lisilotoza ushuru 19
duty *(customs)* ushuru 17
dye rangi 30, 110

E

each kila 149
ear sikio 138
ear drops dawa ya masikio 108
earache maumivu ya sikio 141
early mapema 14, 31
earring herini 121
east masharika 77
Easter pasaka 152, 153
easy rahisi [nyepesi] 14
eat, to kula 36, 144
eel mkunga 44
egg mayai 40, 42
eggplant biringani 51
Egypt Misri 146
eight nane 147
eighteen kumi na nane 147
eighth nane 149
eighty thamanini 148
electric(al) umeme 118
electrical appliance vyombo vya umeme 118
electricity umeme 32
electronic ya umeme 128
elephant tembo [ndovu] 86
elevator lifti 28, 100
eleven kumi na moja 147
embarkation point mahali pa kupandia 74
embassy ubalozi 156
emerald zumaride 122
emergency dharura 156
emergency exit mlango wa dharura [mlango wa kutumia wakati wa hatari] 28, 99
empty kutupu 14
end mwisho 151
engaged *(phone)* inatumika 136
engagement ring pete ya uchumba 122
engine *(car)* injini 79
England Uingereza 134, 146
English kiigereza 126; *(person)* Mwingereza 94
English *(language)* Kizungu [Kiingereza] 16, 80, 82, 104
enjoyable inafurahisha 31
enlarge, to fanya kubwa 125
enough kutosha 14, 68
entrance kuingia 67, 99, 155
entrance fee kiingilio 82

envelope bahasha za barua 104
equipment vifaa 91, 106
eraser raba 105
estimate *(cost)* inafika shilingi ngapi 79
Ethiopia Ithopia 146
Europe Ulaya 146
evening jioni 95, 96
evening dress *(woman's)* gauni la usiku [kanzu ya usiku] 115
evening, in jioni 151, 153
every kila 143
exchange rate kiasi gani kubadilisha pesa 19, 130
exchange, to badilisha 103
excuse, to omba samahani 11
exercise book daftari [kitabu cha kuandikia] 105
exhaust pipe egsozi paipu 79
exhibition maonyesho 81
exit kutoka 67, 99, 155
expect, to tegemea 130
expenses matumizi 131
expensive ghali [gali] 14, 19, 24, 101
express haraka 133
expression maneno [msemo] 10
expressway bara bara kuu 76
extension cord/lead waya wa kuongezea 118
extension *(phone)* ekstenshan [simu ya ndani] 135
extra zaidi 27
eye jicho 138, 139
eye drops dawa ya macho 108
eyebrow pencil wanja wa nyusi 109
eyes macho 138
eyesight nuru 123

F
fabric *(cloth)* kitambaa 112
face uso 138
face powder podari ya uso 109
factory kiwanda 81
fair maonyesho 81
fall, to anguka 139
family familia [ukoo] [jamaa] 93, 144
fan belt fenibelti 76
far mbali 14, 100
fare *(ticket)* nauli 68, 72
farm shamba 85

fast haraka 124
fat *(meat)* mafuta 37
father baba 93
faucet bomba [mfareji] 28
fax feksi 133
fax, to tuma [peleka] feksi 130
February Februari, Mwezi wa pili 150
feeding bottle chupa ya kumnyonyesha mtoto 110
feel, to *(physical state)* sikia 140, 142
ferry feri [pantoni] 74
fever homa 140
few chache 14
fez tarbushi 115
field konde 85
fifteen kumi na tano 147
fifth tano 149
fifty hamsini 147
fig tini 56
file *(tool)* tupa ya makucha 109
fill in, to jaza 26, 144
filling station kituo cha petroli [stesheni ya petroli] 75
filling *(tooth)* risasi ya jino 145
film filam 87, 124, 125
film winder filam wainda 125
filter filta 125
filter-tipped za kuchuja 126
find, to kuta 11, 100
fine arts sanaa za kila aina 83
fine *(OK)* nzuri [salama] 10, 92
finger kidole 138
fire moto 156
first kwanza 68, 72, 149
first-aid kit kisanduku cha huduma ya kwanza 108
first class klasi [daraja] ya kwanza 69
first name jina lako wewe mwenyewe 25
fish samaki 44
fishing kuvua 90
fishing tackle mshipi wa kuvulia 106
fishmonger's duka la samaki [muuza samaki] 98
fit, to faa 114
fitting room chumba cha kujaribia nguo 114
five tano 147
fix, to tengeneza 145
fizzy drink *(soda)* soda 61
flamingo korongo 86

flannel kitambaa cha flana 113
flash attachment *(photography)* kidude cha taa 125
flashlight taa 106
flat tyre tairi limeoboka 79
flat *(shoe)* viatu visivyokuwa na kisigino 117
flea market soko la mitumba 81
flight flaiti 65
floor ghorofa [sakafu] 27
floor show michezo 89
florist's duka la mauwa [muuza mauwa] 98
flour unga 37
flower mauwa 85
flu mafua na homa 142
fluid dawa (ya ...) 123
folding chair kiti cha kukunja 106
folding table meza ya kukunja 106
folk music muziki wa kitamaduni 128
follow, to fuata 77
food chakula 37, 62
food box sanduku la chakula 120
food poisoning kudurika kwa chakula 142
foot mguu 138
foot cream kirimu ya miguu 109
football futboli [kandanda] 90
footpath njia ya miguu 85
for kwa 15
forbidden hairuhusiwi 155
forest msitu 85
forget, to sahau 63
fork uma 36, 61, 120
form *(document)* fomu 26, 133, 144
fortnight wiki mbili 151
fortress ngome 81
forty arbaini [arobaini] 147
foundation cream vipodozi 109
fountain chemchem 81
fountain pen peni ya wino 105
four nne 147
fourteen kumi na nne 147
fourth nne 149
frame *(glasses)* fremu ya miwani 123
France Ufaransa 146
free *(vacant)* hamna mtu 14, 70; *(no charge)* bila malipo [bure] 82, 155
fresh freshi 62
Friday ljumaa 151
fried iliyokaangwa 45, 47

fried egg mayai ya kukaanga 40
friend rafiki 95
fringe nywele zilioteremka kipajini 30
from kutoka 15
front mbele 76
frost umande 94
fruit matunda 55
fruit juice maji ya matunda *[jus]* 40, 61
frying pan chuma cha kukaangia 120
full imejaa 14
full board malazi pamoja na chakula 24
full insurance bima kamili 20
furniture vyomba vya nyumba [fenecha] 83

G

gallery ukumbi wa sanaa 81, 98
game michezo 128
game *(food)* nyama ya kuwinda 49
garage garaji 26
garden bustani 85
gardens bustani 81
gas gesi 156
gasoline petroli 76, 78
gastritis maumivu ya matumbo 142
gauze pamba 108
gazelle swala 86
gear giya 76
gecko mjusi 86
gem vyomo vya dhahabu 121
general kwa jumla 27, 100, 137
general delivery kupeleka kwa kawaida 133
genitals sehemu za siri 138
gentleman wanaume 155
genuine halisi 117, 121
geology sayansi ya mawe udongo na ardhi 83
Germany Ujarumani 146
get off, to teremka 73
get past, to pita 70
get to, to fika 19, 76
get up, to inuka 144
get, to *(fetch)* kupata 137
get, to *(find)* pata 11, 19, 21, 32, 90, 134
gift zawadi 17
giraffe twiga 86
girdle mkanda wa kuzuia tumbo 115

girl mtoto wa kike 128
girlfriend rafiki yangu 93
give, to pa 13, 63, 123, 126, 135
glass *(drinking)* gilasi [bilauli] 36, 60
glasses miwani 123
gloomy imejiinamia 84
glove glavu 115
glue gundi 105
go away! nenda [kwenda] huko 156
go back, to rudi 77
go out, to enda toka 96
go, to kwenda 72, 77, 96
goat mbuzi 49
gold dhahabu 121, 122
gold plated dhahabu ilochovywa 122
golden rangi ya dhahabu 112
golf gofu 90
golf course uwanja wa gofu 90
good nzuri 14, 86, 101
good afternoon habari ya mchana 10
good evening habari za jioni 10
good morning habari ya [za] asubuhi 10
good night lala salama [usiku mwema] [ala msiki] 10
good-bye kwaheri 10
goose bata 49
gram gramu 119
grammar sarufi 159
grammar book kitabu cha sarufi 105
grape zabibu mbichi 55
grapefruit balungi 55
grapefruit juice maji ya balungi 40, 60
gray kijivijivu 112
graze mkwaruzo 139
greasy ya mafuta 110
Great Britain Uingereza 146
great *(excellent)* nzuri kabisa 95
green kijani 112
greengrocer's duka la mboga [muuza mboga] 98
greeting hujambo [habari] 10; maamkizi 153
grey kijivijivu 112
grilled iliyochomwa 45, 47
grocer's duka la chakula 98, 119
groundsheet turubali 106
group vikundi 82
guava mapera 55
guesthouse nyumba ya wageni 19, 22
guide kiongozi 80

guidebook kitabu cha uwongozi 82, 104, 105
guinea fowl kanga 49
gum *(teeth)* ufizi 145

H
hair nywele 30, 110
hair dryer mashine ya kukaushia nywele 118
hair gel mafuta ya kuseti nywele 30
hair lotion mafuta ya nywele 110
hair spray sprey ya nywele 110
hairbrush brashi la nywele 110
haircut mkato wa nywele 30
hairdresser mtengenezaji nywele 30
hairgrip mafuta ya nywele maalumu 110
hairpin pini za nywele [chupiyo] 110
half nusu 149
half an hour nusu saa 153
half price nusu bei 69
hall porter mbebaji mizigo 26
hall *(large room)* jumba 81, 88
ham paja la nguruwe 47
hammer nyundo 120
hand mkono 138
hand cream kirimu ya miguu 109
handbag mkoba 115, 156
handicrafts vitu vilivyotengenezwa kwa mkono 83
handkerchief kitambaa cha mkono 115
handmade ilotengezwa kwa mkono 112
handwashable inafulika kwa mkono 113
hanger vitundikia nguo 27
harbour bandari, gati 74, 81
hard ngumu 123
hard-boiled egg mayai la kuchemsha gumu 40
hardware store duka la vitu vya ujenzi 98
hare sungura wa pori 49
hartebeest kongoni 49, 86
hat kofia 115
have to, to *(must)* lazima 17, 68, 69, 77, 95
hay fever kamasi 107, 141
he a- 161
head kichwa 138, 139

head waiter mwandikiaji mkuu 62
headache maumivu ya kichwa 141
headphones hedfons 118
health food shop duka la vyakula vya siha 98
health insurance company kampuni ya bima 144
health insurance form fomu ya bima 144
heart moyo 138
heart attack maumvimu ya moyo 141
heating mtambo wa joto 29
heavy nzito 14, 101, 139
heel kisigino 117
helicopter helikopta 75
hello vipi [mambo!] 10; (tel.) halo 135
help msaada 156
help saidia 156
help, to saidia 13, 71, 100, 134
help, to (oneself) jisaidia 119
hepatitis homa ya manjano 142
her -m- 162
herb tea mchai mchai 60
here hapa 13
hi! vipi [mambo!] 10
high kali 141; haik 91
hill bonde [kilima] 85
him -m- 162
hippopotamus kiboko 86
hire ya kukodi 20, 74
history historia 83
hitchhike, to kuomba usafiri [lifti] 74
hold on! (phone) subiri 136
hole tundu 29
holiday likizo, mapumziko 151
holidays likizo 151
home nyumbani 96
home town mji unaotoka 25
honey asali 41
honey badger nyerege 86
hope, to tumaini 96
horse racing mashindano ya farasi 90
horseback riding kupanda farasi 75, 90
hospital hospitali 99, 142, 144
hot (warm) joto [moto] 14, 25, 94
hot water maji ya moto 24, 28
hot-water bottle mfuko wa maji ya moto 27
hotel hoteli 19, 21, 22, 26, 80, 102
hotel directory/guide orodha ya hoteli 19

hotel reservation uwekeshaji [uwandikishaji] wa hoteli 19
hour saa 80, 143, 153
house nyumba 83, 85
household article vitu vya nyumbani 120
how vipi 11
how far umbali gani 11, 76, 85
how long (time) muda gani 11, 24, 115
how many ngapi 11
how much (price) bei gani [shilingi ngapi] 11; kiasi gani 24, 85, 133
hundred mia 148
hungry, to be njaa, kuwa na 13, 36
hunting kuwinda 90
hurry, to be in a kuwa na haraka 21
hurt (to be) kuumia 139
hurt, to umiza 139; sakit 140, 142, 145
husband mume [bwana] 93
hydrofoil meli ya haidrofoili 74
hyena fisi 86

I
I ni- 161
ice barafu 94
ice cream skirimu 57
ice cube barafu 27
ice pack kifuko cha barafu 106
iced tea chai baridi 61
if kama [ikiwa] 143
ill kuumwa [mgonjwa] 140
illness magonjwa, maradhi 140
impala swala 49, 86
important muhimu 13
imported imetoka nchi za nje 112
impressive inavutia 84
in ndani 15
include, to pamoja na, inakuwa 24
included pamoja na 20, 63
India India 146
indigestion kiungulia 141
inexpensive rahisi 35, 124
infected kuambukizwa 140
infection magonjwa ya kuambikizwa 141
inflammation kutunga 142
inflation maisha kuwa ghali 131
inflation rate vile maisha yalivyo ghali 131

influenza mafua na homa 142
information maelezo 67, 155
injection sindano 142, 144
injure, to kuumiza 139
injured kuumia 139
injury jeraha 139
ink wino 105
inquiry uliza hapa [maulizo] 68
insect bite kuumwa na mdudu 107, 139
insect repellent dawa ya kujikinga na vidudu 108
insect spray dawa ya wadudu 106
inside ndani ya 15
instead of badala ya 38
insurance bima 20, 144
insurance company kampuni ya bima 79
interest (finance) riba 131
interested, to be penda 96
interesting inapendeza 84
international kila nchi 133, 134
interpreter mkalimani 131
intersection njia panda 77
introduce, to julishana 92
introduction (social) kujulishana 92
investment kitega uchumi 131
invitation mwaliko 95
invite, to alika 95
invoice ankara 131
iodine aidini 108
Ireland Ailend 146
iron (for laundry) pasi 118
iron, to piga pasi 29
ironmonger's duka la vyombo vya chumba 99
Italy Italia, Itali 146
ivory pembe 122

J

jackal mbweha 86
jacket koti 115
jade jiwe la thamani la kijani 122
jam (preserves) jamu 41
jam, to nasa 29, 125
January Januari, Mwezi wa kwanza 150
Japan Japani 146
jar (container) mkebe 119
jaundice homa ya manjanoo 142

jaw taya 138
jazz muziki wa jazi 128
jeans jins 115
jersey sweta 115
jewel box kijaluba cha vyombo vya dhahabu 121
jeweller's sonara 99
joint kiungo 138
journey safari 72
juice maji ya matuda [jus] 37, 60
July Julai, Mwezi wa saba 150
June Juni, Mwezi wa sita 150
jungle pori 85
just (only) tu 37, 100

K

kaftan kanzu ya kiume [kanzu ya msikitini] 115
kerosene mafuta ya taa 106
key ufunguo 27
kidney figo 138
kilo(gram) kilo 119
kilometre kilomita 20, 79
kind (type) aina ya 85
knee goti, futi 138
kneesocks soksi za magotini 115
knife kisu 37, 120
know, to jua 16, 24, 96, 114
kudu tandala 49, 86

L

lace lesi [hal maria] 113
lady wanawake 155
lake ziwa 81, 85, 90
lamb (meat) nyama ya kondoo mchanga 47
lamp taa 28, 106, 118
large kubwa 20, 101, 130
last ya mwisho 14, 68, 73, 149; ilopita 151
late chelewa 14
later baadaye 135
laugh, to cheka 95
launderette mahalipa kufulia 99
laundry service huduma za dobi 23
laundry (clothes) nguo 29
laundry (place) kwa dobi 29, 99
laxative haluli [masahala] 108

lead *(metal)* chuma 76
leap year mwaka mdogo 149
leather ngozi 113, 117
leave, to ondoka 31, 68, 95
leave, to *(deposit)* weka kwenye dhamana 26
leave, to *(leave behind)* ondoka 20, 71
leek liki 51
left kushoto 21, 77
left-luggage office ofisi ya kuweka mizigo 67
leg mguu 138
lemon ndimu 37, 41, 55, 60
lemonade soda ya ndimu 61
lens *(glasses)* vioyo 123; *(contact)* vigae 123; *(camera)* lensi 125
lentils adesi 51
leopard chui 86
less kasoro 14
let, to *(hire out)* kodi 155
letter barua 132
letter box sanduku la barua 132
letter of credit barua ya benki 130
library maktaba 81, 99
licence *(driver's)* leseni 20
lie down, to lala 142
life belt laif belti 74
life boat laif boti 74
lift *(elevator)* lifti 28, 100
light taa 28, 124
light meter mita ya taa 125
light *(colour)* ya mwangaza 101; muda 112
light *(weight)* nyepesi 14, 57, 101
lighter kibiriti 126
lighter fluid/gas kibiriti cha mafuta/gesi 126
lightning umeme 94
like kama 111
like, to penda, taka 13, 20, 23, 61, 103, 122
like, to *(please)* penda 25, 93, 102
linen *(cloth)* kitambaa cha linen 113
lion simba 86
lioness simba jike 86
lip mdomo 138
lipsalve kirimu ya mdomo 109
lipstick rangi ya mdomo 109
listen, to sikiliza 128
litre lita 76, 119

little *(a little)* kidogo 14
live, to ishi [kaa] 83
liver ini 138
lizard kenge 86
lobster kamba 44
lobster kamba wakubwa 45
long refu 115
long-sighted aonaye mbali 123
look for, to tafuta 13
look out! angalia, tazama 156
look, to angalia [tazama] 100, 123, 139
loose *(clothes)* inapwaya 114
lose, to poteza 123, 156
loss hasara 131
lost and found office/lost property office ofisi ya mizigo iliyopotea/iliyoonekana 67, 156
lost, to be potea 13
lot *(a lot)* nyingi 14
loud *(voice)* toa sauti 135
lovely nzuri 94
low chini 141
lower chini 69, 70
luggage mizigo 18, 21, 26, 31, 71
luggage locker makabati ya mizigo 71
luggage trolley vigari vya kuchukulia mizigo 18, 71
lump *(bump)* donge 139
lunch chakula cha mchana 27, 34, 95
lung pafu 138

M

macaroni makoronya 54
machine washable inafulika kwa mashine 113
mackerel kibuwa 44
magazine magazeti 105
maid mfanyakazi wa kike 26
mail barua 28, 133
mail, to *(post)* tia posta 28
mailbox sanduku la barua 132
main kuu 100
make-up remover vya kufutia vipodozi 109
make up, to *(prepare)* tutandikia 29, 71
malaria homa ya malaria 142
malaria tablets dawa za malaria 143
Malawi Malawi 146
mall madukani 99
mallet nyundo 106

man wanaume 114
manager mkuu wa hoteli [meneja] 26
mango embe 55
manicure kutengeneza makucha ya mikono 30
many nyingi 14
March Machi, Mwezi wa tatu 150
market soko 81, 99
marmalade mamiledi 41
married ameoa [men]; ameolewa [women] 94
mask maski 127
mat(t) *(finish)* isiyongara 125
match *(matchstick)* kibiriti cha njiti 106, 126
matinée senema ya mchana 87
mattress godoro 106
May Mei, Mwezi wa tano 150
may *(can)* weza 12
me -ni- 162
meal chakula 24, 34, 143
mean, to maanisha 11, 26
means usafiri 74
measles surua 142
measure, to pima 113
meat nyama 37, 46, 47, 61
meatball kababu 47
mechanic fundi wa gari 79
medical certificate cheti cha daktari 144
medicine dawa 83; *(drug)* 143
medium-sized ya kiasi 20
medium *(meat)* ya kuiva kiasi 47
meet, to kutana 96
mend, to *(clothes)* tengeneza 29
menu orodha ya chakula 36, 39, 40
message maagizo [ujumbe] 136
metre mita 111
middle kati 69, 150
midnight saa sita usiku 154
milk maziwa 41, 61, 64
millet mtama 51
milliard mamilioni elfu 148
million milioni 148
mineral water maji ya chupa 60
minute dakika 21, 69, 153
mirror kiyoo 114, 123
miscellaneous vitu vingine 127
Miss Bibi 10
mistake kosa 31, 63, 102

moccasin viatu vya ngozi ya paa 117
moisturizing cream kirimu ya kurutubisha ngozi 109
moment ngoja kidogo 12, 136
Monday Jumatatu 151
money pesa [fedha] 18, 130
money order manioda 133
mongoose nguchiro 86
monkey nyani 86
month mwezi 16, 150
monument ukumbusho 81
moon mwezi 94
moped kipikipiki 75
more zaidi 14
morning, in the asubuhi 143, 151, 153
Morocco Moroko 146
mortgage mkopo wa kununulia nyumba 131
mosque msikiti 84
mosquito net chandarua 106
mother mama 93
motorbike pikipiki 75
motorboat mataboti 91
motorway njia kuu 76
mountain mlima 85
mountain range milimani 85
mountaineering kupanda milima 90
moustache masharubu 31
mouth kinywa 138, 142
mouthwash dawa ya kusukutua 108
movie filam 87
movie camera kamera ya kupiga picha za senema 124
movies sinema 87, 96
Mozambique Msumbiji 146
Mr. Bwana [Mzee] 10
Mrs. Bibi [Mama] 10
much nyingi, mengi 14
mug vikombe vikubwa 120
muscle musuli 138
museum makumbusho 81
mushroom uyoga 51
music muziki [ngoma] 83, 128
musical mchezo wenye nyimbo 87
must *(have to)* lazima 142
mustard mastadi 54
mutton nyama ya kondoo 47

N

nail brush brashi ya kucha 109

nail clippers cha kukatia kucha 109
nail file cha kuchongea kucha 109
nail polish rangi ya kucha 109
nail scissors mkasi wa kukatia makucha 109
nail *(human)* kucha 109
name jina 23, 26, 79, 92, 131, 136
napkin kitambaa cha kulia 36, 105, 120
nappy winda 110
narrow nyembamba 117
nationality uraiya 25, 93
natural history historia ya viumbe wa kale 83
nature reserve hifadhi ya mazingira 85
nausea kichefu chefu 140
near karibu 14, 15
nearby karibu na 78
nearest ya karibu 75, 78, 98
neat *(drink)* kavu 60
neck shingoni 30, 138
necklace kidani 121
need, to hitaji 29, 90
needle sindano 27
needle *(medical)* sindano 143
negative negativ 124, 125
nerve mshipa 138
Netherlands Uholanzi 146
never hapana kabisa [katu] 15
new mpya 14
New Year mwaka mpya 153
New Zealand Nyuzilend 146
newspaper gazeti 104, 105
newsstand mahali pa kununua magazeti [muuza magazeti] 19, 67, 99, 104
next nyengine 14, 65, 68, 73, 77; ijayo 151
next to karibu na 15, 77
night usiku 155, 156
night cream kirimu ya kujipaka unapolala 109
night, at usiku 151
nightclub vilabu, klabu 89
nightdress/-gown nguo ya kulalia 115
nine tisa [kenda] 147
nineteen kumi na tisa 147
ninety tisiini 148
ninth tisa 149
no a-a [hapana] 10
noisy kelele 25
non smoker kwa wasiovuta sigara 36

none hamna, hakuna 15
noon saa sita mchana [adhuhuri] 30, 153
north kaskazini 77
North America Marekani 146
nose pua 138
nose drops dawa ya pua 108
nosebleed kutoka damu puani 141
not si 15
note paper karatasi ya kuandikia 105
note *(banknote)* noti 130
notebook kijidaftari [kijitabu] 105
nothing si kitu 15, 17
notice *(sign)* ilani 155
notify, to julisha 144
November Novemba, Mwezi wa kumi na moja 150
now sasa 15
number nambari 26, 66, 135, 136, 147
nurse nesi, muuguzi 144

O

o'clock saa 154
oasis kijiji [kijito] kati ya jangwa 85
occupation *(profession)* kazi 25
occupied kuna mtu 14, 155
October Oktoba, Mwezi wa kumi 150
octopus pweza 46
office ofisi 19, 67, 80, 99, 132, 133, 156
oil mafuta 37
oily *(greasy)* ya mafuta 110
old ya zamani 14
on juu ya 15
on foot kwa miguu 76
on request kuomba 73
on time kwa wakati 68
once mara moja 149
one moja 147
one-way ticket kwenda tu 65, 69
one-way *(traffic)* kupita tu 77
onion vitunguu 51
only tu 15, 25, 80, 87
open fungua 14, 82
open, to fungua 11, 17, 82, 107, 130, 132, 142
opera tarabu 88
operation operesheni, kupasuliwa 144
operator *(man)* mzee, *(woman)* mama 134
opposite mbele na 77

optician mpima miwani 99, 123
or au [ama] 15
orange chungwa 55, 64
orange juice maji ya machungwa 40, 60
orange (colour) rangi ya machungwa 112
orangeade soda ya machungwa 60
orchestra kikundi cha muziki 88
order, to (goods, meal) agiza 62, 102
ornithology sayansi ya ndege 83
ostrich mbuni 86
other nyengine 74, 101
out of order haifanyi kazi 155
outlet (electric) plagi 27
outside nje 15, 36
oval ya mviringo 101
overalls ovaroli 115
overdone (meat) imepikwa sana 61
overheat, to (engine) injini inafoka 78
owe, to daiwa 144
oyster chaza 44

P

pacifier (baby's) mtoto wa sanamu 110
pail ndoo 128
pain maumivu 140, 141, 144
painkiller dawa za kupunguza maumivu 140, 144
paint rangi 155
paint, to chora 83
paintbox kisanduku cha rangi 105
painter mchoraji 83
painting picha za kuchora 83
pair jozi 116, 117
pajamas panjama 116
palace jumba la mfalme 81
palpitations moyo unapiga kwa kasi 141
pancake mkate wa maji 64
panties chupi 115
pantomime mchezo wa watoto 87
pants (trousers) suruali 115
papaya papai 56
paper karatasi 105
paper back kitabu cha gamba laini 105
paper napkin karatasi za kulia 120
paperclip vibanio vya karatasi 105

paraffin (fuel) mafuta ya taa 106
parcel mzigo 133
pardon, I beg your samahani 10
parents wazazi 93
park bustani ya kupunga upepo 81
park, to egesha 78
parking kuegesha gari 78
parking lot (car park) mahali pa kuegesha gari 78
parliament building bunge [bungeni] 81
part sehemu 138
party (social gathering) karamu [pati] 95
passport pas poti 16, 17, 25, 26, 156
passport photo picha za paspoti 124
pasta pasta 53
paste (glue) gundi 105
pastry shop duka la keki 99
patch, to (clothes) tia kiraka 29
path njia 85
patient mgonjwa 144
patterned ya nakshi 112
paw paw papai 56
pay, to lipa 17, 31, 63, 102, 136
payment malipo 102, 131
pea mbaazi 51
peak kilele 85
peanut njugu nyasa 55
pearl lulu 122
peg (tent) vishikio vya hema 106
pen kalamu [peni] 105
pencil penseli 105
pencil sharpener cha kuchongea penseli 105
pendant lakti 121
penicillin penisilin 143
penknife kisu cha kukunja 120
pensioner wazee 82
people watu 93
pepper pilipili manga 37, 41, 54
per cent asilimia 149
per day kwa siku 82
per hour kwa saa 78, 90
per person kwa mtu mmoja 32
per week kwa wiki 24
percentage asilimia 131
perch (fish) peshi 45
perfume mafuta mazuri 109
perhaps labda 15
period pains zingizi 141

period *(monthly)* siku za mwezi 141
permit *(fishing)* kibali [ruhusa] 90
person mtu mmoja 32
personal binafsi 17, 130
personal call/person-to-person call
   simu ya mtu maalumu 135
personal cheque cheki ya binafsi 130
personal computer kompyuta ya
   binafsi 131
petrol petroli 76, 78
pharmacy duka la dawa 107
pheasant kuku mwitu 49
photo picha 124, 125
photocopy fotokopi 131
photographer mpiga picha 99
photography upigaji picha 124
phrase kifungu cha maneno 12
pick up, to *(person)* mchukua 80
picnic mandari 64
pill vidonge 143
pillow mto wa kulalia 27
pin pini 121
pineapple nanasi 55
pink waridi 112
pipe mtemba [kiko] 126
pipe cleaner waya wa kusafishia
   mtemba 126
pipe tobacco tumbaku ya mtemba 126
place mahali 25, 77
place of birth mahali pa kuzaliwa 25
plain *(pattern)* pleni 112
plane ndege 65
planetarium pleniterium 81
plantain ndizi za mkono wa tembo 56
plantation shamba 85
plaster palasta 140
plastic plastik 120
plastic bag mifuko ya plastik 120
plate sahani 36, 61, 120
platform *(station)* jukwaa, pletfom 67,
   69
platinum madini nyeupe 122
play *(theatre)* mchezo 87
play, to cheza 87, 88, 94
playground uwanja wa kuchezea/
   michezo 32
playing card karata 105, 128
please tafadhali [kwa hisani yako] 10
plimsolls viatu vya raba 117
plug *(electric)* plagi 29, 118
pneumonia homa ya mapafu 142

poached aliyechemshwa 45
pocket mfuko 116
pocket calculator kalkuleta ndogo 105
pocket watch saa ya mfukoni 121
point of interest *(sight)* sehemu za
   kupendeza 80
point, to onesha 12
poison sumu 108, 156
poisoning kudhurika 142
pole *(tent)* boriti 106
police polisi 79, 156
police station kituo cha polisi 99, 156
polka dots madoadoa 112
pond kidimbwi 85
poplin poplini 113
porcupine nungunungu 86
pork nyama ya nguruwe 47
port bandari 74
portable pasi ndogo 118
porter wachukuzi 18, 71; *(hailing)*
   mzee, bwana 18
possible, as soon as haraka
   iwezekanavyo 137
post office posta 99, 132
post *(mail)* barua 28, 133
post, to tia posta 28
postage stempu 132
postage stamp stempu 28, 126, 132,
   133
postcard *(picture)* postkadi 105, 126,
   132
poste restante Poste restante 133
potato viazi ulaya 51
pottery ufinyanzi 83
poultry kuku 49
pound pauni 18, 102, 129
powder podari 109
powder compact kijaluba cha podari
   121
prawn kamba wadogo 45
pregnant mwenywe mimba 141
premium *(gasoline)* petroli bora 76
prescribe, to andikiwa dawa 143
prescription cheti 107, 143
presidential palace Ikulu [jumba la
   rais] 81
press stud vifungo vya chawa 116
pressure pumzi 76, 141
pretty nzuri 84
price bei 24
print *(photo)* picha 125

private binafsi 24, 81, 91, 155
processing *(photo)* kusafisha picha 125
profit faida 131
programme ratiba 87
pronounce, to tamka 12
pronunciation matamshi 6
propelling pencil penseli maalumu 105
Protestant Mprotestanti 84
provide, to toa 131
public holiday sikukuu ya taifa 152
pull, to vuta 155
pull, to *(tooth)* ngoa 145
pullover sweta 115
pump pampu, bomba 106
pumpkin boga 51
purchase kununua 131
pure safi 113
purple rangi ya zambarau 112
push, to sukuma 155
pyjamas panjama 116
python chatu 86

Q

quality hali yake 103, 112
quantity wingi 14
quarter robo 149
quarter of an hour robo saa 154
quartz kwatz 122
question suala 11
quick(ly) upesi [haraka] 14, 79, 137, 156
quiet kimya 23, 25

R

rabbit sungura 49
race course/track uwanja wa resi za gari 90
racket *(sport)* reketi 90
radiator *(car)* rediyeta 79
radio redio 24, 28, 118
radish aina ya kiazi cha figili 51
railway station stesheni ya reli/treni 19, 21, 67
rain mvua 94
rain, to nyesha 94
raincoat rinkoti 116
rainy season siku za mvua 150

rangefinder kiyoo 125
rare *(meat)* iliyoiva kidogo 47
rash mwasho, harara 139
rate *(inflation)* vile maisha yalivyo ghali 131
rate *(of exchange)* kiasi gani kubadilisha pesa 19, 130
rate *(price)* bei 20
razor wembe [kijembe] 109
razor blades vijembe 109
read, to soma 40
reading lamp taa ya kusomea 27
ready tayari 29, 123, 125, 145
rear nyuma 69, 76
receipt risiti [stakbadhi] 103
reception mapokezi 23
receptionist mpokezi 26
recommend, to pendekeza 35, 80, 87, 137, 145
record player rikodi pleya 118
record *(disc)* rikordi 128
recorder rikoda 118
rectangular ya pembe nne 101
red nyekundu 105, 112
red *(wine)* (mvinyo/divai) nyeupe 59
reduction kupunguza bei 24, 82
refill *(pen)* kalamu ya kujalizia 105
refund rejeshewa pesa 103
regards salamu 153
register, to *(luggage)* andikisha 71
registered mail rejesta 133
registration kuandikisha 25
registration form fomu (ya kujiandikisha) 26
regular *(petrol/gasoline)* petroli ya kawaida 76
religion dini 84
religious service ibada 84
rent, to kodi 19, 20, 74, 90, 91, 118
rental ya kukodi 20, 74
repair matengenezo 125
repair, to tengeneza 119, 121, 123, 125, 145; mereparasi 118
repeat, to sema tena [rudia] 11
report, to *(a theft)* ripoti 156
request maombi 73
required inatakiwa 88
requirement mahitaji 27
reservation uwekeshaji 19, 69
reservations office ofisi ya kuekesha tikiti za safari 68

reserve, to ekeshea 19, 23, 36, 69, 87
reserved ina mtu, mtu ameekesha 155
rest mapumziko 130
restaurant mkahawa, hoteli 19, 32, 33, 36, 68
return ticket kwenda na kurudi 65, 69
return, to *(come back)* rudi 21, 80
return, to *(give back)* rudisha 103
rheumatism baridi yabisi 141
rhinoceros kifaru 86
rib mbavu 138
rice wali 51
right *(correct)* sawa 14
right *(direction)* kulia 21, 77
ring *(jewellery)* pete 122
ring, to *(door bell)* piga kengele 155
river mto 85, 90
river trip safari ya kutembea mtoni 74
road barabara 76, 77, 85
road assistance msaada barabarani 78
road map ramani ya barabara 105
road sign alama za bara bara 79
roll andazi 41, 64
roll film roli ya filamu 124
room chumba 19, 23, 24, 25, 27, 28
room number namba ya chumba 26
room service huduma za vyumbani 24
room *(space)* nafasi 32
rope kamba 106
rouge rangi ya mashavu 109
round ya duwara 101
round-neck shingo ya duwara 115
round-trip ticket kwenda na kurudi 65, 69
round *(golf)* raundi 90
rowing boat ngarawa 91
rubber mattress godoro 106
rubber *(eraser)* raba 105
rubber *(material)* mpira 117
ruby kito chekundu 122
rucksack shanta 106
ruin magofu 81
ruler *(for measuring)* rula 105
Russia Urusi 146
Rwanda Rwanda 146

S
safari safari 86
safe sefu 26
safe *(free from danger)* hakuna hatari

91; salama 85
safety pin pini ya winda 109
saffron zafarani 54
sailing boat mashua 91
salad saladi 39, 43
sale seli 100, 131
salt chumvi 37, 41, 64
salty yenye chumvi 61
sandal viatu vya ndara 117
sapphire cha samawati 122
sardine dagaa 44
satin satin 113
Saturday Jumamosi 151
sauce mchuzi 51
saucepan sufuria 120
saucer visahani vya chai 120
sausage sosej 47
scarf skafu/kitambaa cha kichwa 116
scarlet nyekundu ilokoza 112
scenery mandhari 93
scissors mkasi 120
scooter skuta 75
Scotland Skotlend 146
scrambled eggs mayai ya kuvuruga 41
screwdriver bisibisi 106, 120
sculptor mchongaji masanamu [vinyago] 83
sculpture kuchonga vinyago, sanamu 83
sea bahari 85, 91
season majira 150
seasoning viungo 37
seat kiti 65, 69, 70, 87
second pili 149; sekunde 153
second-hand shop duka la mitumba 99
second class klasi [daraja] ya pili 69
second hand *(watch)* mkono wa nukta ya saa 122
secretary seketeri 131
section sehemu 104
see, to ona 25, 26, 87, 90, 121
sell, to uza 100
send, to peleka 102, 133
sentence sentensi [mtungo] 12
separately peke yake 63
September Septemba, Mwezi wa tisa 150
serval cat mondo 86
service huduma 24, 100

service *(church)* sala 84
serviette kitambaa cha kulia 36
set menu menu maalumu 36
set *(hair)* kuchana nywele 30
setting lotion mafuta ya kuseti nywele 30
seven saba 147
seventeen kumi na saba 147
seventh saba 149
seventy sabiini 148
shampoo shampuu 30, 110
shampoo and set kuosha na kuchana 30
shape shepu 103
share *(finance)* hisa [sheya] 131
sharp *(pain)* maumivu makali 140
shave nyoa 31
shaver mashini ya kunyolea 27, 118
shaving brush brashi ya kunyolea 110
shaving cream kirimu ya kunyolea 110
she a- 161
shelf shubaka 119
shilling shilingi 21, 101, 130, 132
ship meli 74
shirt shati 116
shivery baridi, kutetemeka 140
shoe viatu 117
shoe polish rangi ya viatu 117
shoe shop duka la viatu 99
shoelace nyuzi za viatu 117
shop duka 98
shop window dirisha la duka 100, 111
shopping kwenda madukani 97
shopping area madukani 81, 100
shopping centre madukani 99
shopping facilities maduka 32
short fupi 30, 115
short-sighted aonaye karibu 123
shorts kaptura/suruali kipande 116
shoulder bega 138
shovel kipauro 128
show mchezo 87, 89
show, to onesha 13, 100, 101, 103, 119, 124
shower shawa 23, 32
shrink, to ruka 113
shut funga 14
shutter *(camera)* kidude cha kupigia picha 125
shutter *(window)* mbao za dirisha 29
sick *(ill)* mgonjwa, kuumwa 140

side pembeni 31
sideboards/-burns ndevu za pembeni 31
sightseeing kuona mji 80
sightseeing tour safari ya kwenda kuona mji 80
sign *(notice)* alama 77; ilani 155
sign, to tia saini, sahihi 26, 130
signature sahihi [saini] 26
signet ring pete yenye jina la mtu mwenyewe 122
silk hariri 113
silver fedha 121, 122; *(colour)* rangi ya fedha 112
silver plate pande la fedha 122
silverware vyombo vya fedha 122
simple rahisi 124
since tangu 15, 150
sing, to imba 88
single cabin kebin ya mtu mmoja [chumba cha mtu mmoja] 74
single room chumba cha mtu mmoja 19, 23
single *(ticket)* kwenda tu 65, 69
single *(unmarried)* mjane 94
sister dada 93
sit down, to kaa 95
six sita 147
sixteen kumi na sita 147
sixth sita 149
sixty sitini 147
size *(clothes, shoes)* kipimo 113, 117, 124
skin ngozi 138
skin-diving kuzamia mbizi 91
skin-diving equipment vifaa vya kuzamia mbizi 91, 106
skirt skati 116
sky mbingu 94
sleep, to lala 144
sleeping bag mfarishi 106
sleeping car behewa la kulala 69, 70
sleeping pill dawa za usingizi 108, 143
sleeve mikono 115, 142
sleeveless haina mikono 115
slice vipande 119
slide *(photo)* slaidi 124
slip *(underwear)* shumizi [hafu] 116
slipper sapatu 117
slow(ly) pole pole [taratibu] 11, 14, 135
small ndogo 14, 20, 25, 101, 117, 130

smoked aliyekaushwa 45
smoker wavutao sigara 70
snack vitafunio 64
snack bar mahali wanauza vitafunio [vyakula vidogo vidogo] 68
snake nyoka 86
snap fastener vifungo vya chawa 116
snuff tumbaku ya kunusa 126
soap sabuni 27, 109
soccer futboli [kandanda] 90
sock soksi 116
socket *(electric)* plagi 27
soda soda 61, 64
soft laini 123
soft-boiled egg mayai la kuchemsha laini 39
soft drink soda 64
sold out zimekwisha 87
sole *(shoe)* soli 117
some baadhi 14
something kitu 30, 57, 107, 111, 112, 125, 139
somewhere mahali 87
son mtoto wa kiume 93
song nyimbo 128
soon sasa hivi, upesi 15
sore throat maumivu ya koo 141
sore *(painful)* inauma 145
sorry samahani 16, 88, 103; pole 10
sort *(kind)* aina 119
soup supu 42
south kusini 77
South Africa Afrika kusini 146
South America Marekani ya kusini 146
souvenir vikumbusho 127
souvenir shop duka la kitalii 99
spade jembe dogo 128
Spain Speni 146
spare tyre tairi speya 76
spark(ing) plugs plagi ya spaki 76
speak, to sema 11, 12, 16, 135
speaker *(loudspeaker)* kikuza sauti 118
special maalumu 20
special delivery haraka 133
specialist daktari wa magonjwa maalumu 142
specimen *(medical)* sampuli (ya ...) 142
spectacle case kifuko cha kutilia miwani 123
spell, to andika neno kwa neno 12

spend, to tumia 101
spinach mchicha 51
spine uti wa mgongo 138
sponge spanji 110
spoon kijiko 36, 61, 120
sport michezo 89
sporting goods shop duka la vitu vya michezo 99
sprained teterea 140
spring *(water)* chemchem 85
square pembe nne 101
squid ngisi 44
stadium uwanja wa michezo [stediyum] 82
staff *(personnel)* wafanyakazi 26
stain doa 29
stainless steel chombo kisoingia kutu 122
stamp *(postage)* stempu 28, 126, 132, 133
star nyota 94
start, to anza 80, 89
station *(railway)* stesheni 19, 21, 67, 70
stationer's muuza kalamu na karatasi 99, 104
statue sanamu 82
stay kaa 31, 92
stay, to kaa 16, 24, 26, 142
steak steki 47
steal, to iba 156
steamed ailyepikwa 45
steamer stima 74
steinbok tondoro 86
sterilized zilizochemshwa, zilizosafishwa 143
stewed mchuzi 47
stiff neck shingo imekaza 141
sting msumari wa mdudu 139
sting, to umwa na mdudu 139
stitch, to shoona 30, 117
stock exchange soko la fedha 82
stocking soksi za kike 116
stomach tumbo 138
stomach ache maumivu ya tumbo 141
stools choo 142
stop thief! mkamate mwizi 156
stop *(bus)* kituo 73
stop! simama 156
stop, to simama 21, 69, 70, 72
store *(shop)* duka 98

straight ahead moja kwa moja 21, 77
strange ya ajabu 84
strawberry fursadi 55
street mtaa 25, 77
street map ramani ya mitaa 19, 105
string kamba 105
striped mistari 112
student wanafunzi 82, 94
study, to soma 93
sturdy pana 101
Sudan Sudan 146
suede swedi 113, 117
sugar sukari 37, 64
suit (man's) suti ya kiume 116
suit (woman's) suti ya kike 116
suitcase sanduku [begi] 18
sun jua 94
sun-tan cream dawa ya ngozi 110
sun-tan oil mafuta ya ngozi 110
sunburn kuunguzwa na jua kali 107
Sunday Jumapili 151
sunglasses miwani ya jua 123
sunshade (beach) mwavuli 91
sunstroke kuzimia kwa joto 141
super (petrol/gasoline) petroli ya
daraja ya kwanza 76
superb ya hali ya juu 84
supermarket supamaket 99
suppository vidonge vya kutia nyuma
108
surgery (consulting room) zahanati
137
suspenders (Am.) vishikio vya soksi za
kike 116
Swahili Kiswahili 11, 95, 113
sweater sweta 116
sweatshirt flana 116
Sweden Swiden 146
sweet tamu 62
sweet shop duka la peremende 99
sweet (confectionery) peremende 126
sweetener sukari 36
swelling uvimbe 139
swim, to ogelea 90
swimming kuogelea 90, 91
swimming pool bwawa la kuogelea
32, 90
swimming trunks suruali ya kuogelea
116
swimsuit nguo ya kuogelea 116
switch (electric) swichi 29

switchboard operator opereta
[mfanyakazi wa simu] 26
Switzerland Uswisi 146
swollen imevimba 139
synthetic vitambaa vya kisasa 113

T

T-shirt tishati 116
table meza 36, 106
tablet (medical) vidonge [tembe] 108
tailor's mshoni 99
take away, to chukua 63, 102
take off, to (plane) ondoka 65
take to, to peleka 21, 67
take, to chukua 18, 102
talcum powder podari mwili 110
tampon pedi za wanawake 108
Tanzania Tanzania 146
tap (water) bomba [mfereji] 28
taxi teksi 19, 21, 31, 67
taxi rank/stand mahali pa teksi 21
tea chai 41, 61, 64
teaspoon vijiko vya chai 120
telegram simu za upepo [barua] 133
telegraph office ofisi ya simu 99
telephone simu 28, 78, 79, 134
telephone booth kibanda cha simu
134
telephone call simu 136
telephone directory kitabu cha simu
134
telephone number namba ya simu
135, 136, 156
telephone token kadi ya kupigia simu
134
telephone, to (call) piga simu 134
telephoto lens lenzi za aina ya telefoto
125
television televisheni 24, 28, 118
telex teleksi 133
tell, to ambia 13, 73, 76, 136, 153
temperature ujoto 91; homa 140, 142
temporary kwa muda 145
ten kumi 147
tendon ugwe 138
tennis kucheza tenis 90
tennis court uwanja wa kuchezea tenis
90
tennis racket ubao wa kuchezea tenis
90

tent hema 32, 106
tent peg vishikio vya hema 106
tent pole boriti za hema 106
tenth kumi 149
terrace baranzani 36
terrifying inatisha [inaogopesha] 84
tetanus pepo punda 140
than kuliko 14
thank you asante [nashukuru] 10, 96
that ile 11; itu 100
theatre thiyeta 87
theft wizi 156
them -wa- 162
then halafu, kisha, tena 15
there pale 14
thermometer kipima homa 108, 144
these hizi 163
they wa- 161
thief mwizi 156
thigh paja 138
thin nyembamba 112
think, to (believe) fikiri 31, 63, 94
third tatu 149
thirsty, to be kuwa na kiu 13, 36
thirteen kumi na tatu 147
thirty thalathini 147
this hii 11, 100, 162
thousand elfu 148
thread uzi 27
three tatu 147
throat koo, roho 138, 141
throat lozenge dawa za koo 108
throbbing kupwitapwita 140
through katika 15
thumb kidole gumba cha mkono 138
thunder radi 94
thunderstorm dharuba 94
Thursday Alhamisi 151
ticket tikti 65, 69, 87, 89
ticket office ofisi ya tikti 68
tie tai 116
tie clip kibanio cha tai 122
tie pin pini ya tai 122
tight (close-fitting) inabana 114
tights soksi za kike 116
time (occasion) mara 142, 143, 149
time-table (trains) saa za [ratiba ya] safari 69
tin (container) mkebe 119
tint rangi ya nywele 110

tinted miwa ya rangi 123
tire (tyre) tairi 76
tired, to be choka 13
tissue (handkerchief) tishu 110
to kwa [mpaka] 15
toast tosti 41
tobacco tumbaku 126
tobacconist's duka la sigara [muuza sigara] 99, 126
today leo 29, 151
toe kidole gumba cha mguu 138
toilet paper tishu za chooni 110
toiletry vitu vya urembo na usafi wa muwili 110
toilets choo [vyoo] 24, 28, 32, 37, 68; msalani 68
tomato nyanya 51
tomato juice maji ya nyanya 61
tomb kaburi 82
tomorrow kesho 29, 96, 151
tongue ulimi 138
tonic water maji ya tonik 61
tonight leo usiku 29, 86, 87, 96
tonsils tonsil, mafindo 138
too vilevile 14
too (also) pia, vilevile 15
tools vifaa [zana] 120
tooth jino 145
toothache kuumwa jino 145
toothbrush msuwaki 110, 118
toothpaste dawa ya meno 110
top juu 30
torch (flashlight) tochi 106
torn achana 140
tortoise kobe 86
touch, to gusa 155
tough (meat) ngumu 61
tourist office ofisi ya watalii 80
tow truck gari la kukokota 79
towards kuendea, kuelekea 15
towel taulo 27, 110
tower mnara 82
town mji 19, 76, 89
town centre mjini 21, 72, 76
town hall ofisi ya baraza la mji 82
toy vitu vya kuchezea 128
toy shop duka la vitu vya kuchezea 99
track njia 85
tracksuit treksut 116
traffic light taa za usalama barabarani

77
trailer karavani 32
train treni 66, 68, 69, 70
tranquillizer dawa za kutuliza hali 108, 143
transfer *(finance)* kuhamisha fedha 131
transformer transfoma 118
translate, to fasiri 12
transport, means of usafiri 74
travel agency wakala wa usafiri 99
travel guide kitabu cha maelezo ya safari 105
travel sickness mkunguru wa safari 107
traveller's cheque cheki za safari 18, 63, 102, 130
travelling bag mkoba, shanta 18
treatment matibabu 143
tree mti 85
trim, to *(a beard)* tengeneza 30
trip safari 72, 153
trolley vigari 18, 71
trousers suruali 116
trout papa 45
try on, to jaribu 114
tube *(container)* tyubu 119
Tuesday Jumanne, Jumaane 151
tumbler glasi [bilauli] 120
tuna jodari 45
Tunisia Tunisia 146
tunny sumbururu 45
turn, to *(change direction)* nenda 21, 77
turnip aina ya kiazi 51
turquoise feruzi 122
turquoise *(colour)* rangi ya feruzi 112
turtle kasa 86
turtleneck poloneki 115
tweezers twiza [kikoleo] 110
twelve kumi na mbili 147
twenty ishirini 147
twice mara mbili 149
twin beds vitanda viwili 23
two mbili 147
typewriter Taipu 27
tyre tairi 76

U
Uganda Uganda 146

ugly mbaya 14, 84
umbrella mwavuli wa pwani 116; *(beach)* mwavuli 91
uncle *(paternal)* mjomba 93; *(maternal)* baba mdogo 93
unconscious hana fahamu 139
under chini ya 15
underdone *(meat)* iliyoiva kidogo 47
underpants chupi 116
undershirt flana ya ndani 116
understand, to fahamu [elewa] 12, 16
undress, to vua 142
United States Marekani 146
university chuo kikuu 82
unleaded petroli isiyo na lead 76
until mpaka [hadi] 15
up juu 15
upper juu 69
upset stomach maumivu ya tumbo 107
upstairs juu 15
urgent haraka 13
urine mkojo wako 142
us -tu- 162
useful inafaa 15

V
vacancy nafasi 23
vacant hamna mtu 14, 155
vacation likizo, safari 151
vaccinated, to be chanjwa 140
vacuum flask chupa ya chai 120
vaginal infection kuambikizwa maradhai ya sehemu za siri 141
value thamani 131
value-added tax pamoja na kodi ya mauzo 24
veal nyama ya ndama 47
vegetable mboga 51
vegetable store duka la mboga 99
vegetarian *(food)* wasiokula nyama 36
vein mshipa 138
velvet mahmeli 113
venereal disease magonjwa ya zinaa 142
vermicelli tambi 54
very sana 15
vest shumizi 116
vest *(Am.)* flana ya mikono mifupi 116
veterinarian daktari wa wanyama 99

video camera kamera ya vidyo 124

view *(panorama)* mandhari 23, 25

village kijij 76, 85

vinegar siki 37, 54

visa viza 16

visiting hours saa za kutembelea wagonjwa 144

vitamin pill vidonge vya kutia nguvu 108

volcano jabali la volkeno 85

volleyball kucheza voliboli 90

voltage voltage 118

vomit, to tapika 140

W

waist kiuno 142

waistcoat kizibao 116

wait, to ngoja 21

waiter mhudumu wa mkahawani 26, 37

waiting room chumba cha kungojea [chumba cha kusubiri] 68

waitress msaidizi wa mkahawa [mwandikiaji] 26

wake, to amsha 27, 71

Wales Welz 146

walk, to tembea [kwenda] kwa miguu 74, 85

wall ukuta 85

wallet kikoba cha pesa 156

want, to taka 13, 101, 102

warthog ngiri [nguruwe mwitu] 86

wash, to fua 29, 113

washable inafulika 113

washbasin beseni 28

washing powder sabuni ya kufulia 120

washing-up liquid sabuni ya kuoshea vyombo 120

watch saa 121, 122

watchmaker's fundi wa saa 99, 121

watchstrap ukanda wa saa 122

water maji 24, 29, 32, 41, 60, 76

water-skis wota-skis 91

water flask chupa ya maji 106

waterbuck kuku 49, 86

waterfall mporomoko wa maji 85

watermelon tikiti 56

waterproof isiyoharibika kwa maji 122

way njia 76

we tu- 161

weather hali ya hewa 94

wedding ring pete ya harusi 122

Wednesday Jumatano 151

week wiki [juma] 16, 20, 25, 80, 92, 151

well uzima 10, 140

well-done *(meat)* iliyoiva sawa sawa 47

west magharibi 77

what nini 11

wheel gurudumu 79

when lini 11

where wapi 11

where from unatoka wapi [nchi gani] 93, 146

which gani [ipi] 11

whisky wiski 17, 60

white nyeupe 112

who nani 11

why kwa nini 11

wick utambi 126

wide pana 117

wide-angle lens leni za pana 125

wife mke [bibi] 93

wig nywele za kubandika 110

wild boar nguruwe dume 49

wild cat paka mwitu 86

wildebeest nyumbu 86

wind upepo 94

window dirisha 29, 35, 65, 69

window *(shop)* kuangalia vitu madukani 100, 111

windscreen/shield windiskrini [kiyoo] 76

windsurfer windsafa 91

wine mvinyo, divai 59

wine merchant's muuza mvinyo [pombe] 99

wiper *(car)* waipa 76

wish kutakia kheri [heri] 153

with na 15

withdraw, to *(from account)* toa pesa 131

withdrawal kutoa 130

without bila 15

woman wanawake 114

wood mbao 85

wool sufi 113

word neno 12, 15, 133

work, to inafanya kazi 118

working day siku ya kazi 151

Faharasa